El Mall

# El Mall

THE SPATIAL AND CLASS POLITICS OF
SHOPPING MALLS IN LATIN AMERICA

Arlene Dávila

UNIVERSITY OF CALIFORNIA PRESS

University of California Press, one of the most distinguished university presses in the United States, enriches lives around the world by advancing scholarship in the humanities, social sciences, and natural sciences. Its activities are supported by the UC Press Foundation and by philanthropic contributions from individuals and institutions. For more information, visit www.ucpress.edu.

University of California Press
Oakland, California

Library of Congress Cataloging-in-Publication Data

Dávila, Arlene M., 1965– author.
   El mall : the spatial and class politics of shopping malls in Latin America / Arlene Dávila.
      pages   cm
   Alternative form of title: El mall
   Includes bibliographical references and index.
   ISBN 978-0-520-28684-9 (cloth : alk. paper) — ISBN 978-0-520-28685-6 (pbk. : alk. paper) — ISBN 978-0-520-96192-0 (ebook)
      1. Shopping malls—Latin America.    2. Social classes—Latin America.
   I. Title.    II. Title: El mall.
   HF5430.6.L29D38 2016    2016
   381′.1—dc23                                        2015035144

Manufactured in the United States of America

25   24   23   22   21   20   19   18   17   16
10   9   8   7   6   5   4   3   2   1

In keeping with a commitment to support environmentally responsible and sustainable printing practices, UC Press has printed this book on Natures Natural, a fiber that contains 30% post-consumer waste and meets the minimum requirements of ANSI/NISO Z39.48-1992 (R 1997) *(Permanence of Paper)*.

# CONTENTS

*Illustrations follow page 92*

# PREFACE AND ACKNOWLEDGMENTS

I must have been five or six years old when my mom first took my siblings and me to Bayamón Shopping Center in Puerto Rico. It was an open strip mall with shiny new stores like Thom McAnn, Sears, and Belk Lindsey, and I was so impressed by the experience that I named a doll "Belklinsi." This was decades before the highways had shrunk the island, so it would take hours of travel to reach the mall in my father's farm truck that barely fit three, much less an entire family. The trip was long, hot, and uncomfortable, especially dressed in our Sunday best, outfits my mom made us wear to go back-to-school shopping.

This was 1970s Puerto Rico, when it was the boom in consumer culture that most directly carried a familiar colonial message: whatever came from the United States was better, the stores, the products, everything. As a child encountering *el mall,* a new space of consumerism, I looked at my family and my background and felt we were unmodern and lacking. The mall was bright, clean, and modern—everything we were not. It would take years of unlearning to recognize how the seductive realm of consumer culture was central to U.S. cultural hegemony in Puerto Rico.

Decades later, after years of exploring issues of consumption and global culture, I recognized my own family story in the many new shopping mall consumers I met in Bogotá, Mexico City, Lima, and elsewhere in Latin America. In every place I visited, people told me that shopping malls were "modern, clean, and safe," what Latin American middle and upwardly mobile classes most seek in their cities. The same mantra is the impetus for the current boom in mega-mall construction throughout cities in Latin America.

Of course, contemporary shopping malls are far from the modest strip malls of my youth. "It's like a giant spaceship," is the way Oscar, the store clerk who gave me a tour of Titan Shopping Mall in Bogotá, Colombia, explained it. He was referring to the enclosed, curvilinear architecture and futuristic feel of the mall, which gave the impression that a massive spaceship had landed from nowhere, an alien structure with little relationship to the surrounding neighborhood. He could also have referred to the surreal time-space experience that visiting the shopping mall conveys. Stepping into the mall meant entering "the Bogotá that worked," he told me. His words echoed the commercial jargon I heard from shopping mall managers throughout Latin America who enthusiastically described their malls as privately run mini-cities and models of how cities and citizenship should work.

I quickly came to see that the explosive growth of shopping malls in Latin America presents a set of complex and expanding issues. Critics of mall expansion in the region express concern that shopping malls will produce new generations of passive consumers or zombies à la *Dawn of the Dead* (1978). Others fear that malls act as machines that spread an insipid globalizing "postmodern" culture. But I see something far more complex overtaking new consumers and transforming cities and urban landscapes throughout the region. I see dynamics that my previous work in Puerto Rico—a well-known laboratory for every social policy and strategy of accumulation ever invented across the Americas—makes it impossible for me not to take note of and explore.

This book documents the epic rise of shopping malls in urban Latin America. While shopping malls have been linked to the spread of U.S. consumer culture, my work points to how shopping mall culture in Latin America is not simply a derivative form of U.S. or any other consumer culture. Shopping malls in Latin America undoubtedly propel North American and "global" consumer culture and values throughout the region, not unlike what I experienced in Puerto Rico. However, their rise also coincides with a growing regional boosterism whereby shopping malls anchor significant debates about modernity, democracy, and the very future of Latin American societies. Shopping malls are also key engines of urban growth, transforming Latin American cities and launching new processes of urbanization across the region. Further, they are spearheading new types of class differentiation in Latin America. To ignore the rise of malls in Latin America or to dismiss them solely as containers of North American culture is to risk overlooking vital dynamics of class and social inequality exactly when these issues are becoming more salient and pervasive throughout the region.

This book was made possible by summer research grants from New York University's Center for Latin American and Caribbean Studies, an NYU Provostial Research Challenge Fund grant, and a research fellowship from the Wenner-Gren Anthropological Foundation.

It was also made possible by the help I received from numerous friends, collaborators and colleagues. First, I am indebted to Jorge Lizán, who headed the International Council of Shopping Centers (ICSC) Latin America and who first put the idea of writing a book about shopping malls in Latin America in my mind. Our visions about the industry differ, as I learned in our numerous conversations, but I trust that he and other professionals in the industry recognize that I have written these pages with enormous respect. Special thanks are also due to Juana Suárez, who generously shared important contacts and commented on sections of this work. Diego Quintero accompanied me on scores of shopping trips in Bogotá and always had great insights to share. Orizon Perdomo was a wonderful roommate and city guide, and Oriana Prieto opened my eyes to dance culture and offered insightful feedback on some of the chapters. Many retail and shopping mall professionals in Bogotá offered generous assistance to this project, but I owe special thanks to Agustín Villamarín for sharing his vast local experience on the local retail scene; to Camilo Herrera for doing the same in the field of consumer research, to Carlos Hernán Betancourt Sanclemente and Acecolombia (Colombia's Shopping Mall Association) for their help with logistics in Colombia, and to Maria Bird Picó, journalist-writer extraordinaire, for pointing me to numerous sources and contacts.

Thanks are also due to my academic colleagues, Maria José Alvarez Rivadulla, Thomas Ordoñez, Marisol de la Cadena, Jeff Maskovsky, Omar Rincón, Carlos Martín Carbonell-Higuera, Sergio Alvarez Guarín, and Sandra Modragón who provided support throughout the development of the project. I am also indebted to Teo Ballve for sharing important sources and contacts in Bogotá, to Liliana De Simone for sharing her expertise on shopping malls in Chile and commenting on sections of this work, and Félix Manuel Burgos for his assistance with idioms and the politics of language. Charles Hale, Patricia Zavella, Elizabeth Chin and Junot Diaz were constant cheerleaders, especially Junot, who sent me scores of news articles on shopping malls to remind me of my work's currency and relevance exactly when I needed it most. Conversations with Jennifer Lyn Ayres, Thuy Linh Tu, and Johana Londoño contributed to my thinking on and discussion of the power of fast-fashion. Annabel Rivera provided valuable research assistance on the topic of fashion and styling. Natalia Duarte was the best field research assistant I could have imagined and helped facilitate research logistics with expediency and humor. Finally, Molly Rogers, Katherine Smith, and Stephanie Meadowcroft provided valuable assistance with the project's budget and the organization of visual materials.

This work was enriched by the feedback from students and participants in City University of New York's Urban Futures seminar, from a discussion panel on the topic "Cities of the Americas" at Princeton University, and from a keynote presentation at the inaugural launch of UC Santa Cruz's new PhD program in Latin American and Latino Studies. I also thank James Rodriguez and the graduate students in my Culture and Consumption seminar for graciously hearing me talk about shopping malls throughout the course, especially Marcel Salas for her feedback.

Tomás Ariztía, Steven Gregory, and Tom Angotti were excellent reviewers, and I thank them for their insightful feedback and enthusiasm for this project. At UC Press, Naomi Schneider and Kate Marshall believed in this project from the start and provided invaluable encouragement and help. Finally, I thank Gladys Alvarez and Sandra Modragón for becoming my Bogotá family and Marcela and Gloria Clavijo, my longtime Colombian family in New York, for their friendship and continuous support.

As always, my hope is that these pages serve others and encourage readers, students, and researchers to explore this subject further. Most important, I hope visitors to shopping malls everywhere begin to see them differently and find in them clues, not only about the larger political economic dynamics of globalization, but also about their own society's most intimate expressions of class and social inequality.

# On Shopping Malls and the "New Middle Classes"

All over the world, shopping malls are becoming key landmarks in most contemporary cities, including those in some of the poorest nations. Just in Latin America, according to the International Council of Shopping Centers (ICSC), 326 new malls were constructed in the span of five years, adding to the hundreds already built throughout the region, and a new annual Latin American regional conference is devoted exclusively to promoting their growth.[1] Related to this development is growing interest in the advent of the newest and most coveted sector in contemporary Latin American societies: the middle class. Touted as emergent and vibrant, this sector has become the primary driver for new neoliberal policies and developments, including the unprecedented boom in the construction of new shopping malls.

This book explores this attention to Latin America's "new middle classes" alongside the growth in shopping mall construction in order to expose key linkages between neoliberal urban development and consumption. I ask, what are the local, regional, and global forces behind these developments, what accounts for all these new malls, and who are the new consumers who seem to be contributing to their growth? In particular, I consider urban planning and the political economy of the shopping mall industry as generative spaces in which to explore neoliberalization processes and their multiple material effects. *El Mall* makes these visible by looking at the spatial transformations shopping malls are spearheading throughout Latin America but also, and most significantly, by examining how they are affecting people's livelihoods and everyday social imaginaries of identity and class.

Of course, shopping malls—like all major developments in infrastructure—always involve real estate speculation and the reevaluation of land and should be appropriately considered as key engines of neoliberal urban growth across the Americas. Interestingly, shopping malls have seldom been analyzed in this manner.[2] Instead, when not dismissed and overlooked as mundane spaces of consumption, the tendency is to analyze shopping malls as dreamy spaces for identity creation and imagery. A key trend has been a focus on how they create and interpellate people as consumers/citizens while helping to impart modernity across the globe. Retail professionals and lay observers, for their part, have viewed shopping and retail as the primary activities that create and establish value within malls, veiling the enormous investments in land and infrastructure and the material implications of shopping malls as mega developments in and of themselves.

Foremost, we tend to dismiss shopping malls in the developing world as homogenous and derivative of the United States and the rest of the "developed" world, or as institutions producing a totalizing and globalizing "postmodern" culture, rather than as differentiated spaces that intersect, draw from, and feed into the particular conditions of their host societies and users.[3] This is so even when important comparative research on shopping malls in the developing world suggests that they share more commonalities with malls in other developing contexts than they do with malls in the United States (Stillerman et al. 2013).[4] In contrast to the United States and Europe, shopping malls in the developing world were established beginning in the 1980s as part of neoliberal free market policies. And in contrast to the United States, they were and are more likely to share space and intersect with different types of informal economies and commerce, and they are more often located in urban areas that are accessible via public transportation. Finally, often associated with globalization itself, shopping malls are implicated in debates surrounding the effects of modernity and globalization on the fate of national cultural identities (Dávila-Santiago 2005; Ortiz-Negrón 2013; Sarlo 1994; Stillerman 2015; Stillerman et al. 2013).[5] Still, we have barely begun to analyze these developments and remain unaware of their implications in particular contexts. We know very little about what it means for people throughout the developing world to access these shiny new spaces of consumption, or what stakes are involved when global chains like Zara and Forever 21 become the new standards of fashion and taste, or even what class and spatial politics may be unleashed by the advent of the mega malls at the core of most Latin American cities.

*El Mall* addresses these questions by examining shopping malls as revealing spaces that help materialize the latest incarnations of contemporary neoliberal capitalism as they play out on both the level of political economy and that of people's everyday imaginaries. In addition, I trouble constructions of "middle-class" consumers and the boosterism around global middle classes as discourses that help sustain these types of mega developments, beyond the actual needs of emerging classes and consumers. In particular, I show how retailers and shopping mall developers are turning to the developing world as a fertile ground for opportunities, which may have more to do with the large numbers and concentration of new consumers than with their economic well-being or purchasing power. Another draw for retailers and developers is the opportunity to establish infrastructural footprints in densely populated urban areas, which are the most profitable areas according to industry standards and which are already saturated in the United States and Europe. In this process we see the spread and importation of a model of retail and consumption that has already proven unsustainable in the United States and many parts of Europe, as evident in the rise of "death malls" and in the continued salience of Internet shopping over brick-and-mortar sales.[6] As I show, shopping malls have acquired new life in many cities across Latin America, even if their future is uncertain, which may have little to do with their level of efficiency and sustainability or the quality of products and jobs they circulate and foster. I suggest that this model of consumption is best understood in relation to the speculative processes it unleashes around land and space and especially in terms of its marketing of flashy, modern, organized spaces for leisure and consumption anchored in the illusion of accessibility to a middle-class world. In this way, the growth and development of shopping malls in Latin America underlines their speculative dimensions as key "settlement institutions," fostering and consolidating key linkages between neoliberal systems of production, consumption, and imagery.

In the past decade, reports by international nongovernmental organizations, journalists, and economists alike have registered the remarkable growth of the Latin American middle class, especially in larger countries like Brazil, Peru, and Mexico, where some of the most optimistic estimates put it at more than 50 to 60 percent of the population (Castañeda 2011; Castellani and Parent 2011). These groups correspond to what anthropologists have described as the "new middle classes," groups that—not unlike the new middle classes elsewhere—are considered to be more heterogeneous, more economically vulnerable, and more impoverished than what we associate with dominant definitions of the middle class in the United States and Europe (Heiman et al. 2012). Indeed, despite increases in social welfare in many Latin American countries, Latin America's middle class lacks key social benefits like unemployment benefits and job security and are highly reliant on the informal sector and the introduction of credit, which may threaten their ability to reproduce across generations (Kozameh and Ray 2012; Portes and Hoffman 2003). In fact, writers have remarked that Latin American middle classes are more appropriately described as "lower middle classes," or "emerging classes" as they are generally known by marketers, and that they have more populist backgrounds, culturally and socially, and are darker and more racially and ethnically mixed than previous middle-class groups (Castañeda 2007, 2011; Parker and Walker 2012; Moffett 2011). Their growth has also left untouched the area's high rates of income inequality, a situation that qualifies the relative economic prowess of the new middle classes as more marginal than striving and that has turned these groups into key actors at the center of social movements for greater democracy and social equity (Robinson 2010).

Yet these economic and social realities have not dampened the enthusiasm for the celebrated coming-of-age of the Latin American middle class. Instead "the middle class" is now evoked to support a range of neoliberal reforms, developments, and, most remarkably, new shopping malls. According to ICSC, Latin America is one of the regions undergoing the greatest investments. This development bonanza is especially evident in Bogotá, due to its recent political stability and the containment of violence away from the city's economic and cultural core. Acecolombia, Colombia's shopping mall trade association, estimates that Bogotá and medium-sized cities across Colombia are slated to receive investments of up to $4 billion, with seventy-six new developments planned, and it is projected that the number of shopping centers in the country will exceed more than two hundred by 2015 (*Portafolio* 2014c). Just in 2012, a total of twenty-five international retailers entered Colombia for the first time,[7] a development that is quickly transforming the urban landscape and consumer options for locals. Colombian shopping malls have also become a safe haven from crime and violence as well as full-service spaces where, in addition to shopping, visitors can pay utility bills, find child care, and attend Mass, concerts, and movies. Clearly, shopping malls are not merely offshoots of the emergence of and increase in new consumers. Instead, they are more fruitfully considered a primary medium helping to shape and bring new middle-class groups to light. This is also true for other parts of Latin America. As Marcelo Carvalho, heir of the pioneering Brazilian shopping mall family, explained to an audience of Latin American shopping mall professionals, "We call shopping malls 'therapy centers,' places where you can practice and exercise your identities."[8] As I discuss, for many people "exercising" these identities is not simply a matter of purchasing new commodities or a brand-new look in a modern shopping mall, but more significantly, of lingering and being seen in these spaces.

Insofar as shopping malls are at the vanguard of new urban planning developments and the reconstitution of urban space, we may ask if and how these constructions are helping to normalize the hypersecurity and surveillance measures that are common to most private developments (Caldeira 2000; Low 2004; Gregory 2006). We may also ask if shopping mall construction may have more to do with real estate speculation rather than with the needs of new consumers and what role they may be playing in shaping not only the lifeworlds, experiences, and attitudes of the new middle classes but also how these groups organize their day-to-day lives.

Shopping malls are at the forefront in the introduction and expansion of credit, raising questions about how they may be affecting attitudes toward credit and debt. Further, the ensuing privatization of space and the retreat from commercial street life and general decline in informal entrepreneurship raise concerns about the fate of informal vendors and microentrepreneurs, who have historically dominated the retail economy and sustained most economic development in Latin America (Fernández-Kelly and Shefner 2006).

In sum, I am interested in what we can learn about the emergence and workings of the "new middle classes" from an analysis of the very spaces of consumption that have been historically associated with the development and definition of "middle classes" throughout the world (Miller 1995; Veblen 1994; Williams 1991; Wilson 2004). To this end, I draw from ethnographic analyses of Bogotá's shopping mall industry and the city's new middle classes in order to examine how regional and national dynamics of race, ethnicity, and gender are mediating expressions and definitions of class and status and people's access and use of shopping malls. At the same time, I incorporate a larger comparative perspective drawn from regional meetings of the Latin American shopping mall industry to ascertain regional and global trends spearheading these developments and the regional boosterism around "middle classes" and consumption. In this way, while focusing primarily on Bogotá, I consider similar transformations taking place elsewhere in Latin America as it is imagined and commodified as a "coming of age" region, filled with untapped consumers. I aim to ensure an appreciation of matters of class and social inequality but also of the larger political economic processes that are not bounded by location or a particular nation-state.

Overall, I address the pressing need for understanding shopping malls in the developing world and the boom in retail in places like Latin America, China, and Russia, alongside the decline of the shopping mall industry in the United States (De Simone 2013, 2015; Halepete 2011; Stillerman et al. 2013). At stake are questions about the meaning of all this attention to "emergent markets" in relation to the globalization of the shopping mall industry. Finally, I raise concerns about the growing policing and surveillance of public space through consumption, where forces at work may involve not only exclusion, but dynamics of integration, shame, and intimidation concerning how people access and claim new spaces of consumption. I also examine how learning about appropriate practices for accessing the mall can entail the transmission of neoliberal dispositions among everyday people as they are actively reconstituted as "new consumers." I explore some key connections between consumption and class definitions and practices as a generative site to explore some of the larger neoliberalizing processes and transformations occurring in the developing world. This examination is central for understanding how new practices of consumption are affecting people's subjectivities, and also how they may be helping to shape our understanding of and larger debates on social inequality.

## CLASSING SHOPPING MALLS: MIDDLE CLASSES AND THE POLITICS OF CONSUMPTION

Questions of consumption and social identity have long been key scholarly concerns, but until now scholars of globalization have not examined closely the shopping mall industry in the developing world.[9] I am also in conversation with a growing interdisciplinary scholarship on space by bringing attention to urban planning issues and linking them to the speculation and privatization of urban space and the rise of tourist- and consumption-based developments (Dávila 2012; Irazabal 2008; Low 2000; Smith 1996; Gregory 2006).

A goal of this work is to thicken and bring nuance to the current literature on shopping malls originating largely from sociology, geography, and cultural studies by analyzing these developments as complex and contradictory rather than as undifferentiated middle-class consumer spaces (Farrell 2010; Underhill 2000, 2004). In part, this view derives from the extensive scholarship on shopping malls and spaces of consumption that has established consumption as a central practice shaping middle-class norms of consumer citizenship in the United States and Europe. Important examples include studies of the role of standardized consumption in the "Americanization" of new immigrants in the early twentieth century (Barth 1982; Ewen and Ewen 1992) and the influence of shopping malls on the development of the suburban landscapes of the 1950s North American middle class (Cohen 2003).

Although shopping malls in Latin America foster similar ideas of global mass culture and common citizenship through consumption, these processes are mediated by specific social and historical conditions. For instance, prior to the current shopping mall boom, the rise of consumption and the development of the first shopping malls in Latin America were a cornerstone of a variety of social modernization and urbanization programs throughout the region. In other words, consumption has been a historically contested development that was as central to worker-consumer politics in Argentina's nationalist populist politics of the mid-twentieth century (Milanesio 2013) as it was to right-wing military dictatorships that later enveloped the region and to ongoing neoliberal projects. In each period shopping malls have functioned as "artifacts of globalization" anchoring consumption and progress in relation to different political projects (De Mattos 1999; Ciccolella 1999).[10] As I discuss later, this linkage of shopping malls with modernization and progress continues to undergird the current boom in the development of shopping malls—even though there is also a rising tide of criticism about their multiple social costs.

We also need to unpack shopping malls' recognized role in representing, generating, and constructing "middle-class" dispositions, outlooks, and identities defined by consumption, whether these statuses are actually achieved or simply imagined. On this point, I suggest shopping malls are best seen as complex spaces of social differentiation, where a range of new identities and dispositions are being actively conditioned. In other words, the "middle class" is always more diverse than recognized by the category, and aspiring and emergent groups engage in relational practices of self-definition that belie simple associations of consumption with specific social identities. Ara Wilson's (2004) ethnography of the intersection between new consumer spaces like shopping malls and intimate economies of gender, sexuality, and ethnicity in Thailand is especially salient here. Her work demonstrates how shopping malls foster a dominant commercial transnational heterosexuality, especially through advertising, while also promoting spaces where the expression of alternative forms of gender and sexuality could be coded, and hence socially accommodated, as "different styles." At the same time, the plasticity that consumer culture seems to offer for expressing "middle-class" identities through consumption and self-styling needs to be critically assessed in relation to the contradictory role that shopping malls play in promoting the illusion of participatory equality while simultaneously imposing sociospatial constraints (Goss 1993; Miller 1998; Zukin 2005). Even visiting a mall is fraught with meanings when asserting the role of a prospective consumer is the most appropriate way to establish belonging and when variables of age, gender, and class mediate the extent to which one is welcomed or shunned (Chin 2001; Dávila 2012; O'Dougherty 2006). People's uses of the mall and how they establish belonging in these spaces and become familiar with the symbolic repertoire of consumption spaces, what has been described as "proletarian shopping," or engaging in the imaginary language of commodities (Fiske 2010), can thus provide key insights into people's changing awareness and experiences of consumption in relation to class. I ask how these insights translate to contexts like those of Bogotá and other cities in Latin America where class polarization is visible and where distinctions of class and status are embroiled in notions of modernity, race, and even morality. In other words, when the way in which one accesses malls becomes loaded with meaning about class and modernity and when purchasing disposable fashion at Forever 21 confounds dominant notions of *buena presencia,* or good presence, it is obvious that shopping malls are especially productive places to theorize issues of class under conditions of neoliberalism.

I complicate the findings of some initial studies on Latin American shopping malls that have suggested that, because many Latin American malls are located in urban centers—where they are accessible by walking or by public transportation—they are more democratic and open than the traditional U.S. suburban mall (Stillerman and Salcedo 2012). With a history of self-enclaving, self-walling, and urban repression compromising notions of public space in Latin America from colonial times into the present (Caldeira 2000; Low 2000), I can appreciate how the development of shopping malls in closer proximity to middling and popular classes could be interpreted as a sign of social openness and inclusion. In comparison to previous urban projects like private residential enclaves and luxury tourist and consumer outposts, shopping malls do function, market themselves, and appear as more "open" and democratic than many of these high-security private spaces. What is more, Latin American shopping malls are being increasingly developed in lower-class neighborhoods and in closer proximity to groups that never before imagined accessing these spaces and being targeted as potential consumers. In fact, shopping malls are often marketed and publicly touted as signs of the empowering of populations and communities that corroborate their worth as consumers who are "coming of age."

At the same time, while shopping malls are being developed closer to the popular classes the self-walling of elite groups continues apace. In fact, shopping malls are being developed within gated communities and outside urban centers of commerce, with one of the most popular types of new shopping malls involving mixed-use developments of residential and commercial spaces, which are marketed as bastions of security. Shopping malls in many parts of Latin America are also class-stratified, marketed to different consumers on the basis of class. In addition, even the most "populist" shopping mall is never as widely accessible as it may be reputed to be. Instead, shopping malls are rife with "invisible barriers," as an architect interviewed in Rivas's important new work on consumption in El Salvador put it: "The mall is 'free,' but there is something that says 'no,' something that makes some people feel out of place" (Rivas 2014: 131). This "something" is what architects recognize as "threshhold fears," or social constraints that limit people's use of and accessibility to a space that is supposedly open and geared to them.[11] The following pages provide examples of these invisible barries. Ultimately, I show that it is exactly shopping malls' presumed openness that makes them uniquely interesting for analyzing issues of class, identity, and consumption under neoliberal conditions. Because they point us to the seductive manners in which our imaginations about choice and access to the market can be so easily embroiled in projects of social exclusion and inequality.

Shopping malls' larger social effects need also be gauged against the processes of displacement they create and the pressure they place on the evaluation and upscaling of land. On this point, I show how shopping malls are becoming leading engines of growth in the development of middle-class outposts and residential enclaves, as well as key agents for land speculation, gentrification, and the revalorization of new urban frontiers. Chile, a pioneer of neoliberal development in Latin America, provides a pivotal example of what may be in store for the region. There, the influence of shopping malls on urban processes has seen the ascendancy of a new type of "retail urbanism," where retail developers become dominant in all types of urban design processes, from closing streets and reformulating public transit routes to valorizing properties and generating mobility conflicts (De Simone 2013: 37). Similar processes are at work in Colombia, where shopping mall developers exercise undue influence in planning decisions over and above city planning authorities, raising questions about their effects on the current and future state of urban governance across the region (Angotti 2012; Sassen 1999). Thus I suggest that the discourse of shopping malls' accessibility to the popular classes should be questioned while we remain vigilant to how people's spatial access to the city and their general influence on planning policies and urban politics are curtailed by the growth of shopping malls.

Last, I consider shopping malls vehicles to think about the workings of contemporary capitalism, fully aware that their development is neither the start of a process nor its culmination but rather a small part of a larger and unfolding story of imperial capitalism in the region. In this way, the boom in shopping malls is just one of the many outcomes of the spread of neoliberal policies in Latin America where the intersection of capital and land accumulation is made visible. Think here of mining, agribusiness, ecotourism, the spread of U.S. military bases, and more. The plantation is perhaps the very first example of a "settling institution," involving the accumulation of vast tracts of land and transnational capital that transformed Latin American economies.[12] It is not difficult to see the continuity from plantations to extractive agricultural estates, to shopping malls. My father used to remind me of this whenever we passed the current site of Plaza las Américas, the largest shopping mall in Puerto Rico, which he knew first as the site of one of the largest dairy farms on the island.[13] Growing up in Puerto Rico, an early laboratory of export processing zones, I also bore witness to the transformation of sugar fields into industrial zones and into housing and commercial developments, as if the obsolescence of each use had been carefully planned and considered. Indeed, I hope to bring light to the fickleness and planned obsolescence that investments in industries requiring massive land grabs involve, as they simultaneously shape and consolidate extractive and unequal economies and relations that are enduring.

However, unlike other development engines of growth that are affecting neoliberal development across the region, whether it be mining or agribusiness or urban and suburban housing developments and residential enclaves, shopping malls are predicated on notions of openness and consumer citizenship that demand special consideration insofar as they directly interpellate middling groups as participants in global consumer culture and modernity. We see former prisons, detention centers, and sites of terror being turned into tourist sites and shopping malls in many Latin American countries as they transitioned from dictatorships to neoliberal democracies; Montevideo's

Punta Carretas shopping center is one of the most well known examples of this trend (Draper 2012).[14] For nothing indexes the political "opening" of Latin American societies like the commodification of the past through consumption. In other words, we should never lose sight that shopping malls are not simply tools of neoliberal development or speculative land grabs. They also involve affective regimes that have an impact on people's imaginations and dreams in ways that make them far more powerful than many other land-intensive developments.

The dynamics at work in Bogotá and many other Latin American cities parallel a growing turn in the study of global middle classes that provides interesting insights and directions for examining these groups (Ariztía 2012; Heiman et al. 2012; Liechty 2002; O'Dougherty 2002). One key insight is the diversity of middle classes that may coexist and conflict with each other, given that they may hold different subjectivities around gender, politics, race, and styles of consumption. Most significantly, these groups' origins contrast with middle classes of the past in having grown up amid neoliberal reforms, which raises questions about whether these conditions have instilled among these groups a more general orientation to market ideologies and logics of individualization that normalize consumption and precarity as defining characteristics of how the term *middle class* is understood (Han 2012; Heiman et al. 2012). Another insight is the centrality of styles of consumption and of immaterial and material aspirations and lifestyles as a defining characteristic of new middle classes. Having seldom originated from previous middle classes, these groups often have to learn the most "suitable" ways to navigate new cultural codes and practices of consumption, demeanor, and style with which to exercise their identities and express new "statuses," whether objective, aspirational, or imagined (Heiman et al. 2012; Liechty 2003; Tible 2013).

Indeed, leaving behind single-variable analyses of class that defined it as a static category or strictly in relation to people's differential access to means of production, or resources, or statuses, anthropologists have for some time analyzed class as a social project for establishing boundaries and social hierarchies relationally and across groups. As a social project of culture making, class is actively produced and projected through symbolic, discursive, and material behaviors and practices, as well as through aspirations to upward mobility (O'Dougherty 2002; Ariztía 2012; Freeman 2014). The chapters that follow show evidence of many of these insights particularly of the transformations involved in defining the middle class based on consumption. For instance, I evidence a broadening of the groups that may be considered to belong to "middle classes" but also a downgrading and expansion of the types of consumption associated with middle-class belonging. Thus, for instance, the new middle classes in Bogotá are less likely to be defined in relation to traditional references such as higher education, formal employment, or home ownership and more likely to be defined in relation to accessing a modern shopping mall, whether for shopping or simply for leisure.

The intersection of consumption and social identities is far from a new topic in Latin America. It has been examined in communications and media reception studies, where scholars have analyzed popular culture and mass media as a key space for mediating processes of modernization and the creation of urban-based identities (Martín-Barbero 1993; García Canclini 2005). Thus insights from this research are relevant for thinking about new spaces of consumption as key areas for analyzing issues of social mobility and inequality as well as for theorizing the new meanings that emerge from their use by new publics, akin to what occurs with other aspects of popular culture. For instance, popular "reconversions" of uses and meanings of the mall are especially interesting as references for class and identity in contexts of rapid change when traditional referents for defining class are in flux or disappearing. By bringing attention to people's engagement with spaces of consumption, I hope to thicken dominant analyses of class in Latin America, which have generally ignored emergent groups or have revolved primarily around statistical analyses, providing few insights into how people live and define class in their daily lives. Indeed, most of the studies on the middle classes in the region have looked at these groups primarily through historical or sociological lenses (Milanesio 2013; Gilbert 2007; López and Weinstein 2012). One notable exception is Chile, whose history as a laboratory for neoliberal reforms has launched important contemporary studies on consumption and the material expression of the contemporary middle class (Ariztía 2012; Méndez 2008).

My interest in Bogotá derives from a visit to the city after attending a conference in Medellín where I presented my previous work on shopping malls in Puerto Rico. I learned that Colombia was undergoing one of the fastest rates of shopping mall development in Latin America: the number of malls tripled between 2003 to 2014, from 60 to 196.[15] When the Free Commerce Treaty (TLC) took effect in May 2012 Colombia was receiving a massive flow of investments and imports that were helping to boost the shopping mall industry while having lethal effects on local industries and fueling debates about the costs of globalization and the availability of cheap imported goods. Colombia is also an exemplary case to study because of its existing class polarities. Given the large inequities between rich and poor in the country, discussion of the new middle classes takes on added meanings about the ways in which inequalities are being refashioned and reconfigured by the sudden attention to the middle classes on the part of marketers and investors. Colombia is also especially noteworthy because of its history of conflict and civil war, which has strengthened the role of shopping malls as bastions of security and refuge for middle classes.

Steeped in a history of political violence, internal conflict, and population displacement, Colombia at the same time was in the midst of much-anticipated peace talks between the government and the Revolutionary Armed Forces of Colombia (FARC) that put the end of the fifty-year conflict within reach. In this context, the violence coexisted with rising expectations that the country would see a greater opening and globalization. And almost everyone I talked to agreed that this process would undoubtedly bring the country even closer to the United States. Colombia is already one of the staunchest U.S. allies in the region and one of the largest recipients of U.S. military aid and financial assistance, particularly since the 2000s, after the spike in aid specifically directed at the War on Drugs and terrorism, two key concerns of the United States after September 11, 2001 (Cepeda 2010). Thinking about shopping malls in Colombia thus offers an opportunity to appreciate the linkages between the growing economic investments in this sector and the country's strategies of political alignment with U.S. and global capitalist neoliberal policies. The latter are visible everywhere, such as in the number of transnational companies that are establishing themselves in Colombia, thereby heightening the demand for leisure and consumer spaces both for expats and for transnational-oriented middling groups and consumers.

Finally, Colombia is a unique case for analyzing the globalization of shopping malls because many of them are still under multiple ownership rather than held by a single developer or investor, as is the global standard for the industry. Colombia is thus considered a challenge to international industry "best practices," which recommend the single ownership of shopping malls by a mega developer or investment trust, making it a a revealing case for examining the land politics involved in the globalization of retail and shopping malls.

On this subject, this work is in dialogue with anthropological research on land politics, ethnicity, and race in Colombia, including studies of the development of Afro-Colombian movements in relation to the politics of space (Wade 1995; Escobar 2008). In particular, my work directs attention to the politics of space unleashed by the rise of consumption-based developments in the country's major and intermediate cities. These have been a direct outcome of governmental efforts to counter the country's internal conflict through securitized constructions and through marketing efforts to attract international investments in the country's creative industries, especially in the realm of TV and media production, and now shopping malls (Rincón and Martínez 2013). In the past decade Colombia has emerged as the darling of global investors, an assessment I became skeptical of given my recent work on neoliberal urban development in Buenos Aires and Puerto Rico. On the island, I came to see that ideologies of "overconsumption" had been mobilized to justify the unabated growth of shopping malls, despite Puerto Rico's dire economic condition, while in Buenos Aires, the boosterism around the city's "coming of age" veiled the fact that it was tourists and expats, not locals, who benefited.

Thus what follows is also informed by concerns of my previous research on the marketing of identity among Puerto Rican and Latino/a consumers, on the making of the Latino/a middle class, and, more recently, on ideologies of consumption in Puerto Rico and Buenos Aires. For the story I tell is not unique to Bogotá or to Colombia or to any specific city in Latin America. In fact, shopping malls are developing into one the most important engines of growth in peripheral cities across Latin America, with developers turning to small and medium-sized cities in search of new development frontiers, including cities with as few as 30,000 to 60,000 residents.[16] Shopping malls are being developed and planned in the most secluded highland regions and even in communities in the Peruvian Amazon that are accessible only by airplane or by river (Bird Picó 2014b). In other words, what I present is a slice of a much larger unfolding story. This work may also speak to developing contexts beyond Latin America where shopping malls are expanding rapidly and guiding discussions about urban planning and development and the "new middle classes."

Chapter 1 provides an overview of some of the macroeconomic and political trends that are leading the way to new shopping developments across the globe. I link the shopping mall industry's profitability to three key immaterial processes involved in its development and growth: the financialization processes that have transformed shopping malls into a tool for real estate investment and speculation; the growth of neoliberal urban planning policies that favor mega developments; and the public boosterism that links these developments with the coming-of-age of different countries in Latin America and beyond.

Chapter 2 explores the professionalization of the industry around U.S.-centered "global" conventions and the historical regimes that frame Latin Americans' involvement in the industry. In particular, I call attention to how the state of the Latin American shopping mall industry and its professionals have become mediums to communicate hierarchies of power that position Latin America as always premodern, despite its current development of grander and glossier shopping malls than those in the United States.

Chapter 3 turns to Bogotá, Colombia, as a case study to analyze on-the-ground transformations unleashed by the development of shopping malls in the region, particularly in regard to debates over space and urban development and to the effects that shopping malls and their reliance of imported goods are having on people's livelihoods. I also discuss how shopping malls are affecting the informal economy and eroding the historical connection between local production and consumption, which has sustained middling groups for decades, thus ironically shrinking opportunities for some of the very groups that it seeks to target as consumers.

Issues of class and consumption are the focus of chapters 4, 5, and 6. Chapters 4 and 5 position the debate over middle-class groups' access to and use of the mall in a larger discussion on social inequality that anchors their entry to these spaces within ongoing processes of class differentiation. I examine who these emerging groups are, how they are defined, and how they define themselves in opposition to other groups and classes both in the present and in the past, and what role consumption and shopping practices may play in these definitions. I also examine people's shopping and retail histories, with attention primarily to young and professional women, detailing how their shopping habits and practices (whether in local markets or in modern malls) may have changed during their lifetimes and how these practices and changes intersect with their real or imagined social mobility. I analyze these dynamics in relation to the continued reproduction of a highly classist bogotano culture against which the consumption of the new middle classes is consistently being gauged. Chapter 6 develops these themes by looking at the effects of *pronta moda,* or fast fashion, while considering how middle-class fashionistas consume and maneuver through the sudden availability of imported fashion. I raise questions about what it means for young professional women and by extension for many middle-class people across

Colombia and the region when middle-class ideals and upward mobility are so closely linked and increasingly limited to the realm of consumption. I note that the issues at stake are not limited to the primarily female shopping mall visitors who inform this chapter. They implicate all of us who are left with the activity of shopping, and fashion self-styling, as a last resort for exercising ingenuity and choice.

The concluding chapter explores the politics of space in contemporary shopping malls and how issues of security intersect with popular demands for accessing space in a context when shopping malls have become a premier venue for contesting matters of equity and citizenship rights. From Brazil's *rolezinhos* organizing youth flash mobs in shopping malls to expose racism in Brazilian society to university students in Puerto Rico taking over shopping malls in order to challenge tuition hikes to die-ins in Minnesota's Mall of the Americas as part of the #BlackLivesMatter movement to Bogotá LGBT youth organizing "kissathons" to challenge homophobia, this chapter evidences the politicization of shopping malls and the many battles over equity, space, and citizenship that are currently being waged inside and through these private spaces. Battles around shopping malls are suggestive of a rise in consumption-based social movements in contemporary societies, but I call attention to the classist foundations that often limit these struggles to underscore the continual need for broader movements and politics.

# ONE

# The Immateriality of the Mall

## FINANCIAL REGIMES, URBAN POLICIES, AND THE "LATIN AMERICAN BOOM"

When one thinks of shopping malls, it is stores, brands, sales, fashion, customers, and the activity of shopping itself that quickly come to mind. What one soon learns, however, is that these are but a fraction of the many interrelated areas that come together in the thriving international business of shopping malls. There are countless ways to make a profit in and from shopping malls, all of which go beyond the point of purchase and are mostly invisible. From research companies marketing the use of GIS and computer Apps to find the best retail locations to new ways to collect intelligence on consumer behavior, from architects and designers building the next award-wining sustainable "green" design to security companies to signage and social media marketing companies, shopping malls are at the center of a complex set of industries and service providers that have little to do with any actual good sold but everything to do with the success and profitability of the shopping mall and the retail industry. And at the heart of it all is the purchase, development, and leasing of land, or in industry terms, the acquisition of "footprints"—the core and most profitable activity and the most invisible.

This chapter looks at three immaterial regimes that have facilitated the spread of shopping mall construction throughout the world by sustaining the acquisition of "footprints" while simultaneously downplaying the centrality of this material practice to the shopping mall industry. These regimes are the financialization processes that have transformed shopping malls into a primary space for investment and speculation, the growth of neoliberal urban planning policies whereby shopping malls are seen as key "worlding" mechanisms for branding a city's image (Roy and Ong 2011), and the boosterism surrounding the coming-of-age of Latin America whereby countries and regions are compared and even made to compete against each other as the most "primed" for business and development. I start by examining the financialization of the industry in the United States through the development of real estate investment trusts that have opened the path to private investments in the business of shopping malls in Latin America and globally. Key to financialization processes is the erasure of place and of physical references like bounded communities in favor of abstract models that foster the integration of markets, which we see in the creation and development of global real estate investment trusts (Martin 2002). I suggest that it is only by understanding these processes and their centrality to this industry's operations that we can fully appreciate why claims about the "end of the mall" are largely deceiving and why and how the "global" has become the sexiest new terrain in the world of retail real estate.

I then turn to the rise of neoliberal urban planning in Latin America and how it has contributed to the growth of shopping malls, looking at the example of Bogotá. Not unlike the industry's turn to financialization, urban planning has been lauded for opening opportunities in the market and for expediting the modernization of space. I show that urban planning has become one of the most important forces furthering the immaterialization and financialization of space at the core of the uneven accumulation of land and resources that are so central to the business of shopping malls. Last, I look at how both processes are maintained by an ongoing boosterism that has overtaken discussions of urban development in Latin America, where development's ill effects, consequences, and failures in one region are easily erased by stories of the coming-of-age of another. The result is that in the past decades Latin America has become poised to be the new frontier for opportunity at the same time that the inequalities and the short-lived gains of neoliberal developments, whether it be inflation or social strife and protests, and recession have become visible everywhere.

## THE FINANCIALIZATION OF THE MALL

That the business of shopping malls is ultimately about the business of retail real estate, where the retail component is largely a secondary element, may be surprising but not when we consider the materiality of shopping malls and the profitability of establishing footprints in industry terms. Like few other real estate projects, whether multifamily homes or commercial office space, shopping malls require massive amounts of land. Their developers covet strategic locations that are the most valuable in real estate terms and constitute a relatively stable and durable asset that in good times can yield a steady stream of income in rents and in slow times can be valuable to speculators. In the words of Milton Cooper, CEO of Kimko, one of the largest international realty corporations:

> This is the asset class that has the largest proportion of land value to total value, because you need parking, and the buildings are modest, one-story buildings, they are not expensive, not too much capital cost involved. So that you own the land. And concepts come and go, and they'll be problems in retailing and in America, but one thing that happens in America no matter what we do our population grows by 3 million people a year and at the end of 10 years, it's as much as Canada, or Australia, so over time it is a wonderful business.[1]

What Cooper's comments make clear is the primacy of real estate over retail. Stores may open and close, but sooner or later the land on which a shopping mall sits will be in demand, even if for new uses. In the world of retail real estate, "tenant" is synonymous for whatever business or organization leases a space in the mall. The idea is that retail real estate is not limited to retail and that the same land can and will accrue value for a variety of uses.

This is perhaps one of the basic tenets of gentrification and land valorization, that they are central to cycles of disinvestment and devalorization that create the possibility of future profitability and reinvestment (Smith 1996). Devalorization is also central to processes of accumulation in times of recession, or to what Harvey (2004) has termed "accumulation through dispossession," in which the credit system is a key element. This is exactly what has happened with shopping malls, whose ownership in the past two decades has become concentrated in the hands of a few industry giants. It is estimated that the top one hundred owners of retail real estate control around two billion square feet of retail space, of which more than 50 percent is concentrated in the hands of the ten largest firms (Retail Traffic 2010). Simon Property Group, the largest real estate investment trust, almost doubled its size between 1998 and 2008, a pattern of consolidation followed by other industry giants (Bodamer 2008). Most recently, the 2015 failed yet highly publicized attempted merger of Simon-Macerich, two of the largest mall REITs (real estate investment trusts) in the United States, points to the continued consolidation of this industry, this time involving the acquisition of Class A upscale malls, which are considered the only category of shopping malls that are outperforming regular malls in the United States.

Moreover, shopping malls involve intricate life stages, with diverse opportunities to profit in and from them: the initial point of purchasing the land, building and developing the infrastructure, managing and leasing space to stores or selling space in the mall as a marketing vehicle in and of itself. In other words, there is a temporality to different types of returns and many different opportunities for diverse stakeholders to get involved: investors, banks, pension funds, individuals, developers, stockholders, governments. The latter are especially interested in these developments to increase their rent rolls through construction and sales taxes and, in the developing world, to regularize jobs and formalize economies traditionally dependent on informal markets. In slow times, retail real estate can always profit from speculation and calculated investments, especially in core markets and areas that are on the rise. This means that while in retail terms an "empty box" may be understood as a sign of declining consumer confidence, in retail real estate terms this same vacancy can mean an opportunity to bring "the highest and best use" to any specific location—in other words, a higher-paying or a different or more attractive mix of tenants. But even if such tenants are nonexistent, somewhere out there is a lucky developer and builder who has already walked away with profits from building the mall. Thus, while the media may bemoan the death of the mall in the United States, some industry leaders believe that the recession has only made the business of shopping malls more profitable for those at the top, who are now able to accumulate an inordinate number of properties.

To understand this paradox, we need to consider the financialization regimes sustaining the industry and the fact that most contemporary shopping malls function and are organized as REITS that own and manage pools of shopping mall properties, making shopping malls into prime candidates for financial investment and speculation. A U.S. invention under President Dwight Eisenhower in the early 1960s, REITs were "reinvented" in the 1990s as publicly traded companies that have spurred the financialization of real estate (Martin 2002). And shopping malls (retail real estate) quickly became a specialty market. REITs are commonly lauded as vehicles for democratizing real estate markets, allowing people to invest in real estate who would not be able to do so individually; but their popularity stems from the fact that they allow the industry to enjoy tax-free status on most of its earned income that is distributed and divided to shareholders. This makes REITs the biggest winner since taxation is effectively shifted from the corporation to individual shareholders. This finance structure also maximizes and lowers the costs of capital for the real estate business organized as a REIT, strengthening its clout and competitiveness in acquiring real estate. As the manager of a hedge fund explained, "The benefit of the REIT is that you can pay more for the same property than you can if you were not a REIT. As a REIT, I can afford to bid more. So as these REITs have come in, the value of the real estate has gone up because they don't pay taxes. Guess what? They can pay a lot more for the same property, 35 percent more, so the REITs are far more competitive in acquiring properties." This explains the growth of Simon Property Group and other giants like General Growth Properties, Developers Diversified Realty, Kimco Realty, and Jones Lang Lasalle that, organized as REITs have become the dominant players controlling most of the most coveted locations in the strongest and healthiest shopping malls, all of which are increasingly becoming global players.

As REITs, shopping malls function as pawns in a larger portfolio of commercial properties, where the liability of a failing shopping mall is evened out by the profitability of another. Alternatively, a REIT can mitigate losses by converting shopping malls to new uses and, increasingly, by investing in new developments in new and emerging markets. Finally, as REITs, shopping malls have attracted new types of capital such as investments from pensions funds and other nontaxed organizations, thereby avoiding double taxation, and investments treated as "bonds," which provides a low but steady yield that still surpasses the low interest rates that have been offered by banks since the 2008 recession. REITs or similar instruments are now a common financial tool for acquiring real estate value in over thirty countries, including in Latin America. Chile, Brazil, and Argentina in the 1990s and Mexico more recently have developed their own version of this financial mechanism, for example, Fideicomisos de Infrastructura y Bienes Raices (FIBRAS) in Mexico. The recognition of REITs and their counterparts has brought about a rapid wave of investments, easing and opening up the path to real estate developments, most visible in the growth of shopping malls and consolidation of their ownership.

These changes have been fast and expedient. The rapid transformation of the shopping mall industry in the United States after the introduction of REITs is a case in point. Previously, the industry was composed of family- and privately run businesses operating on a regional basis. After the building spree of the 1970s and the downturn of the real estate market in the 1980s, the industry as a whole suffered from a lack of capital (Tubridy 2006). Thus when Kimco Realty Corp. went public in 1991, the industry noticed. Kimco was not the first shopping mall company to turn to the public market, but it was the largest and quickly set a precedent (Tubridy 2006). Within a few years, REITs were operating across regions, as the acquisition of shopping malls became a national endeavor (Baker 1997). Malls also got bigger; those built between 1998 and 2000 were 70 percent larger than those opened a decade earlier as competition led more diversified offerings (Tubridy 1998). Most significantly, REITs led to the standardization and "professionalization" of the industry, promoting research in the field of retail real estate. As Richard Sokolov, president and chief operating officer of Simon Property Group, put it, "The public process made the industry far more transparent, because for the first time, companies were not privately held so they were disclosing publicly things like lease terms, and rents and top tenants, and square footage of properties, and as a result there was much more information out there both for companies to analyze their performance relative to other companies but also for investors to analyze companies' relative performances versus other companies."[2]

REITs helped to immaterialize the shopping mall industry by turning it into a matter of financial indicators such as rent-to-sales ratios and flows or complex formulas for researching tenant mix or a market's demographic. In this regard, the industry has seen the rise of the same type of "techniques of calculability" that have become central to financial capitalism for managing and, most important, "exploiting" risk across different industries (Appadurai 2013). Never mind that industry leaders are the first to admit that standardized measurements are difficult if not impossible to achieve given the lack of a common measurement for calculating success and value in different operations and comparing results across companies. What the growth of research and metrics assures, however, is the consistent erasure of the materiality of the land—its access, ownership, and control that are at the heart of the business. In other words, with the advent of research, it is abbreviations like GLA (gross leasable area) and ROI (return of investment) and terms like Cap rates (capitalization rates) and recapture rates, along with other "measurable" real estate finance terms, that dominate industry lingo and make it unintelligible to outsiders, hiding the fact that the industry is ultimately all about the acquisition of real estate, or footprints.

One area that is not so easily veiled, however, is in regard to the leasing process with retailers. Shopping malls still depend on retailers to rent their space, even though retailers depend just as much on leasing agents, brokers, and managers to gain access to the most coveted locations. And just as with any piece of real estate, it all comes down to location. Retailers seek locations with the best rent-to-sales ratio and "attributes" such as visibility and proximity to transportation, banks, and "attractive" populations in terms of income and education, such as those who are 50 percent and above in educational attainment and income. Shopping malls, for their part, seek rent-paying tenants but also those that provide the best "tenant mix" to sustain synergy between the stores and the upscale identity most seek to project. Who courts whom, however, is connected to the larger political economy of the industry. Generally it is developers and shopping malls leasers who have the upper hand, though retailers' relative power is also affected by the health of the economy and by local conditions.

I set out to study shopping malls in 2011–15, at a time when the industry had reached a saturation point in the United States. The recession, the rise of Internet sales, and low consumer confidence had halted the U.S. industry's rapid growth, which at its peak, in the 1980s and 1990s, had seen more than sixteen thousand shopping centers built. This was also the time when super-regional shopping centers (i.e., larger than 800,000 square feet) grew popular with shoppers.[3] By the late 2000s, especially right after the 2008 recession, however, the U.S. industry was in a highly defensive position, facing an excess of properties in prime locations and a constant public relations battle to defend shopping malls as a thriving concept and as "America's first and foremost marketplace" against the increasing visibility of dead malls.[4] Specifically, the industry was grappling with fears about the end of brick-and-mortar stores and the realization that the real growth spur for this industry lay elsewhere, in global markets in Asia and Latin America, where shopping malls were being developed at rates unheard of for decades in the United States.

The uncertain mood was palpable at the 2013 New York National Conference and Deal Making and Global Retail Real Estate Convention in Las Vegas, Nevada, the annual meeting of shopping center industry professionals and the prime site for networking and deal making in retail real estate. That year, over 33,000 attendees involved in leasing, financial services, and retail as well as the government sector gathered to make deals but also to hear optimistic presentations about an industry that had been touted as "better than ever" since the start of the recession. The exhibit halls were packed with suits, reflecting the heavily male dominated industry, and the atmosphere was rushed and intense. No one lingered, despite the attractive candy and food displayed by exhibitors.

Still, uncertainty and defensiveness were palpable in the presentations, which centered on how best to maintain the continued importance and relevance of the mall, sparked with calls for federal legislation to require out-of-state Internet retailers to collect sales taxes so as to level the playing field for brick-and-mortar retailers. Over and over, speakers reminded industry professionals that some of the top Internet sellers are in fact brick-and-mortar retailers—Staples, Target, Wal-Mart—and that many goods and services cannot be bought on the Internet. But the argument that was heard loudest and most often is that brick-and-mortar stores reign supreme both in building a product's brand and in creating and providing customers with "irreplaceable" experiences.[5] As Brad Hutensky, ICSC chair and president and principal of Hutensky Capital Partners, stated during his luncheon address at RECon (Real Estate Convention) 2013 in New York City, "You can't buy a fitted suit over the Internet. You can get all the movies at home, but it's not the total experience; at the theater when they laugh, you laugh. We want experiences. How many women do you hear say, 'Hey, let's come over to my house and shop the Internet together'? They don't do it. They say, 'Let's go to the mall together,' 'Let's have lunch,' 'Let's see people.' That's an experience, that's part of the human condition. You don't buy ice cream or haircuts on the Internet."

I will have more to say about this emphasis on experience as the inalienable component for evaluating the relevance of shopping malls and how it serves as a euphemism for a highly securitized, raced, and classed isolated state of being. The point here is the larger context in which to understand the interdependency between retailers and shopping malls at a moment where retailers were turning to Internet sales and limiting their brick-and-mortar footprints. In real estate terms, this meant that shopping malls were highlighting their role as *destinations*, entertainment centers and experience builders, to underscore the source of the mall's continued relevance and value. But this also meant that developers were largely courting retailers, or in the words of a leasing agent, "Very few retailers are paying for their steak dinners here. They get wined and dined here." And just as she said, retailers were present at RECon's deal-making conferences. But they were not as visible as leasing agents.

Leasing agents made up the majority of the over one thousand exhibitors present, and the ones with the most intricate and glitziest free-standing exhibitions, as if their "footprints" and the amount of space rented in the exhibit hall were an indicator of their prowess in the world of retail real estate. The largest exhibitors were also the busiest and the most sought after, and, according to a retailer I spoke to, for obvious reasons. As he noted, "if you're a retailer you want the 'big guys' to want to work with you because they control all the best locations that could make or break your brand." The "big guys" are of course the Simons and DDRs of the world, whose holdings include the most coveted commercial real estate locations.

In sum, many shopping malls are failing and closing in the United States. But the invisible world of REITs demands that the industry's health be accounted for through larger frameworks some of which may seem contradictory and even counterintuitive. One example is the well-known industry claim that the United States is "saturated" and that despite all the supposedly empty shopping malls, the industry is plagued by a lack of "prime space." Consider the statements by Daniel Hurwitz, chief executive officer of DDR, which owns and manages shopping mall properties in Puerto Rico and Brazil as well as the United States, during a visit to CNBC News to address the myth of the "death of the big box.".[6] He explained to the audience that the closing of a big box store like Best Buy is far from a sign of doom but rather a "blessing in disguise"—an opportunity to market the space where little is being built and "demand is outstripping supply." The hosts were perplexed, as was I when first confronted with the idea that there may in fact be "demand" despite all the stories of empty stores in the news and that "failure" may in fact be "success" in industry terms. Hurwitz, however, was unrelenting in his emphasis on real estate speculation and the desire for prime space and location as the true motor of the industry, which means that even in slow times the competition for prime locations continues apace.

The important question is, how does one define "prime location"? The idea that there is always scarcity and competition over space is dependent on the industry's narrow definitions of "prime locations," prioritizing access to a density of consumers, especially upscale shoppers, and transportation. It is only these types of locations that are most sought after by retailers and that are saturated by malls, not the universe of possibilities for developing retail and commercial development. In fact, the industry's bias toward "prime space" and high ROIs is accompanied by an almost total obliviousness to other sites and communities that provide possibilities for development and may even be in need of commercial developments. This was one of the most striking disparities on display at RECon Las Vegas, which was also attended by city officials representing depressed towns in the U.S. Southwest. Some had been coming for years; others were so new to this corporate-driven space that they had come totally unprepared, without the must-have business cards that are exchanged robotically as a mode of introduction. They were eager to learn how to attract retailers and developers to their cities and municipalities and ready with government entitlements and offers of expedited review and approval processes for developers, among other incentives they felt were more necessary than ever to attract malls and retail within their communities. "We want anything," is how one official for the city of San Luis, Arizona, put it. "We are among the largest agricultural providers in the nation, but we only have Walgreens and McDonald's."

It is from these officials that I learned about the giveaway of over $30 million by the depressed city of Harlingen, Texas, to Bass Pro Shop, the giant outdoor/sports store, which included the naming of a street "Bass Pro Drive" to increase the visibility of the store's location. The store promised the community a destination point to attract tourists and traffic from nearby towns, but the city is still paying the bill while awaiting the promised economic development. In fact, a study of Bass Pro–anchored projects found that despite winning over $500 million in taxpayer subsidies from other municipalities across the United States, the mega store had repeatedly failed to deliver economic development and tourism, leaving instead towns with high levels of debt and fiscal stress (Connor and Stecker 2011).

Here lies one of the most puzzling aspects of the shopping mall industry: all the excitement over Latin America, Eastern Europe, Asia, and India and anything "global" as new frontiers for development while border communities in Texas, Arizona, and elsewhere in the United States cannot get one major store to open in their area even after extending extraordinary conditions to shopping mall and big-box store developers at the cost of residents and taxpayers. Obviously, then, it is not lack of land on which to build more malls and box stores that is affecting industry trends. Instead, it is saturation of the most coveted areas as narrowly defined by the industry. This alone is a leading factor pushing the industry to go global in search of new frontiers for prime-time locations in emerging cities, especially those where they can secure locations close to transportation and a high density of prospective shoppers and where they can bet on higher rates of revenue for their invest ments. A North American evaluator of commercial real estate property who was living as an expat in Bogotá when I met him spoke to these issues when explaining the advantage of making deals in Latin America relative to the United States. A native of Arizona, he initially found prices in Mexico and now in Bogotá too expensive compared to prices back home, until he realized that the comparison should be made to other global cities, not Arizona. As he explained, "Bogotá is one of the most densely populated cities in the world. So if you compare it with other dense cities like New York, the price is cheap." He also pointed to the higher rates of return that investors can expect because there is less competition than in the United States, and to the fact that while buyers may have to show up with cash to purchase in Latin America, there is an overall shorter diligence period for closing a deal.

Félix, a self-described "colored Latino" of Ecuadorian background who had worked at a North American investment company making feasibility studies for Latin American markets, was more skeptical when assessing Latin America's "sexiness" to investors: "The people making deals are old white guys, and the fact is that they don't want to go to Latin America; they think it's too dangerous and too difficult. They want to make local deals. But they go [to Latin America] because this is the only place where they can get a decent rate of return." Average rates of return in the United States for shopping mall projects stand at around 5 percent, but in Latin America, I was told, a project can yield 10 to 12 percent or more because of the higher risks involved.

Another impetus for the industry's turn to globalization is the "burden of permits," or the consent and regulation around the use of space, including zoning and urban planning laws, that place limits on the repurposing of spaces and may affect the industry's solvency and flexibility. Discussions of the death of the mall in the United States revolve around the development of alternative uses, such as converting or cutting up boxes for nonretail uses, including educational or health care facilities, megachurches, call centers, or government offices. From the perspective of many retail real estate investors, however, this strategy requires consents and permits that can devalue the structure's assets and involve many different stakeholders; it also limits candidates for repurposing to those in the most attractive locations or those that demand less invention and investment.

Jose Legaspi, a leader in repurposing shopping malls, had a lot to say about the lack of vision in developers' decision to repurpose a mall or to flee. The Mexican-born former advertising executive and founder of the Legaspi Company, has become an industry leader by turning dead malls into Hispanic cultural centers, courting Latinos through culturally relevant shops and events and by including local retailers as community anchors. One of these repurposed malls is La Gran Plaza in Fort Worth, Texas, which was acquired in 1991 and converted into the "largest Hispanic-themed mall in the U.S."; it now claims to have 90 percent occupancy as well as "an official Mariachi" to "enhance its appeal as a family destination."[7]

Legaspi minced no words, stating that most "contingencies" and excuses for not repurposing malls are "mumbo jumbo." In his view, the issue is that corporate America is too lazy and too scared of the changing demographics of the American consumer, especially of the Latinization of American landscapes, to engage in the necessary transformations to make retail relevant for the twenty-first century. Thus, instead of transforming malls to fit the needs for changing communities of consumers, most investors prefer to pack up and leave. Legaspi added, "They think consumers don't want them, instead of finding out who the new consumers are and what they want." In this context, perception—of more opportunities abroad rather than in their backyards—becomes the reality and another sign of the racial biases involved in many retail real estate decisions. Legaspi has shown that making a shopping mall relevant demands a transformation of the concept of the mall to make it more culturally and community relevant. In contrast, in Latin America shopping mall developers do not have to retrofit their formula: the same old thing can be presented as flashy and new to new consumers. In this way, despite being better acquainted with urban planning processes and zoning legislation in the United States and more familiar with its base of consumers, developers often perceive more "obstacles" than opportunities in the United States vis-à-vis the relatively "new" and "unencumbered" terrain they supposedly find in Latin America. Add to this the pull of urban planning policies and the ascendancy of neoliberal urban reforms, and we can more fully appreciate the added lure that Latin America represents for investors.

## ON THE IMMATERIAL PRACTICES OF URBAN PLANNING

The design, development, and construction of shopping malls is linked to urban policies that support and value their construction, and nowhere is this more evident than in many developing countries where shopping malls have become a common feature of "worlding" practices and the quest for recognition as world-class cities (Roy and Ong 2011). In particular, shopping malls are at the forefront of the type of enclave urbanism, or segregated planning, that has characterized much neoliberal urban development throughout Latin America, where exclusive enclaves are carved and safeguarded, exacerbating social and spatial inequalities (Angotti 2013; Caldeira 2000). Scholars warn us that these enclave developments are not entirely importations from the United States but rather are linked to long-standing colonial and neocolonial hierarchies of race, class, and region and patterns of segregation. Nevertheless, their growth has certainly been expedited by neoliberal urban developments, by new types of financial regimes fostering private investments, and by a lax planning environment that since the 1990s has dominated neoliberal urban policies throughout the region.

Market-enabling policies have been nurtured by the dominance of top-down master planning devoid of popular and community consultation and also by the decentralization of planning governance in many Latin American countries (Irazabal 2009). With decentralization, municipalities and cities can make ad hoc land use decisions, a context that makes for a hospitable context for developers with resources. An Argentine developer I met at a Latin American shopping mall training course in Mexico City put it in simple terms when he explained that big developers can get away with anything while smaller ones get tangled in bureaucratic red tape and permits. Another Argentine developer corrected me when I asked him about the role of urban planning in the region, saying I should speak about the "lack" of urban planning instead. The discovery by *New York Times* investigative reporters that Wal-Mart had used bribes to change zoning laws in Mexico City, allowing it to build in one of the most densely populated areas without a construction license, urban and environmental impact assessments, or a traffic permit may sadly not be that uncommon in Latin America (Barstow and Xanic von Bertrab 2012). Stories like this point to the dominance of private developers in the urban planning process and to the neoliberal urban planning frenzy that has become so prevalent in the region.

A contrasting view celebrates the construction boom in the region and neoliberal urban planning policies for fostering "creative" cities and "open spaces," without consideration of the uneven development that is occurring. This is especially the case in Colombia, where cities like Bogotá and Medellín have been lauded in international circles for democratic, open, and successful urban planning at the same time that the country and its large and medium-sized cities have become the sites of the largest expansion of shopping mall centers across the region (Cifuentes and Tixier 2012).[8]

Like many other Latin American nations, Colombia has been a center for experimentation and development of transnational urban policies. In the 1950s Bogotá housed the Organization of American States International Housing and Planning Center to train housing officials throughout the Americas and was also the site of Ciudad Kennedy, the largest public housing project built as "self-help housing" under the Alliance for Progress, now recognized as one of the first semiprivatized housing models and a precursor to neoliberal housing policies (Offner 2012). In the past decades, however, a number of reforms have helped anchor Colombia as a globally recognized and celebrated example of urban planning that is economically viable, inclusive, progressive, and "benevolent." In particular, Bogotá has become a global model for "best practices." It is visited by planners, designers, and city officials intent on learning about what has been described as its own brand of "pedagogical urbanism"—an urbanism that has relied on the promotion of open and public spaces and public investments to foster greater accessibility by popular sectors to the city through improvements in public transportation and the creation of bicycle and pedestrian routes (Berney 2011; Galvin 2011). These developments followed a new constitution (1991), which gave local authorities more autonomy and awarded Bogotá a separate governing structure that facilitated the creation of development policies and projects, as well as the solidification of urban policy around the goals of enhancing competitiveness and attracting economic growth, echoing the rationale for neoliberal urban planning around the globe (Galvis 2011). Branding and marketing campaigns for the city, for example, "Invest in Bogotá," which in 2009 was ranked by the World Bank as the "best investment agency of a developing country," and international press coverage praising Bogotá as a model for urban reinvention helped to hone Bogotá's cosmopolitan identity and the general equation of Bogotá's good image with its "good" urban governance (Castro 2013; Galvis 2011; McGuirck 2014). Closer analysis of Bogotá's urban planning policy, however, highlights the paradox that its supposedly more open type of urbanism was consolidated through an increase in enforcement and policing and that most of the investments for creating and maintaining open spaces were highly uneven and directed to more affluent sections of the city (Valenzuela Aguilera 2013; Berney 2011). The Transmileneo, the massive public transport system in operation since 2000, is a good example. While it features direct exits to some of the major shopping mall developments, it does not reach all sections of the city, in particular the poor communities in the southwest around Bosa and Ciudad Bolívar. These residents have to rely on a feeder system to reach the Transmileneo that many people dismiss for its poor service and unreliability.

Critics have also pointed to the powerful implications of urban governmental policies that help redefine urban middle-class ideals to matters of "access and redistribution to recreation and public space" rather than access to necessary services and infrastructure (Galvis 2011). In this context, "the old developmentalist middle-class ideal, ... of providing every family with the means to have 'house, car and schooling,' are replaced by definitions of middle class in relation to ideals of access to public space, and to enjoying the boosterism of living in a global city" (Galvis 2011: 148), or even access to malls. My informants also complained about the uniformity and sanitization of public space, a product of security concerns that led to construction of public areas and parks that were built alike and primarily of cement.

Most notably, Bogotá's new urban planning was accompanied by policies of market enablement that reinforced the role of private development in urban planning, particularly in regard to mega projects such as malls (Ortiz Gómez and Zetter 2004). Thus a study comparing the development of shopping malls in Mexico and Colombia found that both countries offered an exceptional urban planning environment where developments were the exclusive domain of private developers and largely excluded from official urban planning considerations and purview. Yet, in contrast to Mexico, the study found that Bogotá, which lacks a tradition of control and regulation, has been more lax and supportive of private sector development, especially throughout the 1990s, when the private sector enjoyed considerable liberty, until 2000, when the city approved its first citywide urban plan (Plan de Ordenamiento Territorial, or POT) (Lulle and Paquette 2007). The authors note that this plan is likely to spur the growth of more shopping malls by facilitating developments that conform to the city's master development plan but not necessarily to the needs of communities. And this seems to be exactly the case with most shopping malls built after the passage of POT, or before the new guidelines, but now facing scrutiny for the first time.

Key examples of the inability of the urban government to control the reach of shopping mall developers are the many stories of shopping malls that were supposedly built in compliance with new standards for construction but nevertheless ended up in the middle of major urban planning disasters and debates. One example is the much-discussed traffic congestion created by the building of Titán Shopping Mall, one of Bogotá's largest, which opened in 2011, even after it had supposedly developed a traffic plan approved by transportation authorities (Secretaría Distrital de Movilidad). In addition to not accounting for the pressure they add to the already congested Bogotá traffic, shopping malls are known for ignoring the spillover effect they create in neighboring communities, whose streets become alternative entryways for people trying to avoid traffic jams. Shopping malls are also blamed for attracting informal vendors and for obstructing pedestrian traffic. Each time, shopping mall managers respond to criticisms with predictable public relations assurances that they complied with all government requirements and are looking into new ways to solve the problems, but instead their efforts expose the ineffectiveness of privately led urban planning (El Tiempo 2008, 2012).

The clout of private developers in urban planning and public space became evident during recent debates over the expansion of Unicentro, Bogotá's first modern shopping mall, inaugurated in 1976. At issue was Unicentro's plan to build a new office tower of twenty-five floors with five hundred parking spots in an area that is highly saturated, which residents complain that the shopping mall proceeded to do without community consultation or meeting the new POT requirements for new construction. As challengers of the project explained, Unicentro resisted developing a traffic and impact plan for the new construction on the grounds that the project was solely "an expansion" that should follow the same terms of its original building license issued in 1974, as if the area had remained unchanged since the mall was first built. Apparently Unicentro had secured several previous construction permits from the city on similar grounds, hence their surprise when its plans were met with heavy resistance.

Urban planning advocates I spoke to described Unicentro's position as an exemplary case of the way urban planning worked before the 2000 law, when there was a lack of legal instruments to hold developers accountable and the construction of shopping malls seldom considered the community impact or complied with modern norms. This case is also especially important because it launched Bogotá's first large-scale protest against a major shopping mall in the city, which happens to be one of the most symbolically important shopping malls to date. Not surprisingly, its opponents were the affluent residents of the immediate community, a mostly upscale neighborhood with links to powerful groups in the city that were concerned about the devalorization of their properties and the commercialization of their residential enclave just steps from Unicentro. With resources and contacts in key city organizations and government planning offices, including the Personería de Bogotá, the Secretaría de Habitat de la Alcaldia, and the Contraloría General de la Nación, these powerful players brought a level of scrutiny and contention unheard of for these type of projects, setting an important precedent as the first community group to face up to and win a ruling against a shopping center.[9]

I met with the Multijunta, the home owners' organization leading the opposition to Unicentro's plans and learned about the difficulties faced by any community group seeking to challenge a shopping mall development, even when it counted among its supporters seasoned urban planners, professors, and elected officials with the cultural capital and resources to hire the necessary consultants and lawyers. Multijunta had been struggling for six years and though they were proud of their success in preventing Unicentro from starting construction, they were disheartened at what was obviously a long, uncertain, costly, and uphill battle with the mall.

It is interesting that the group was not contesting Unicentro's right to build but rather its adherence to urban norms to mitigate environmental and social impacts, including parking, providing public community space, and creating a mobility and transportation plan. The group had seen their neighborhood change since the advent of Unicentro, with neighbors turning their residences into commercial uses as they were unable to compete with the commercialization of the entire area, and they were fed up with Unicentro's inordinate power to determine the fate of their community. One of the members shared his frustration by noting that norms and urban planning are *"una absoluta carreta"* (an absolute lie) where shopping malls are concerned. In his estimation Bogotá was an informal city first and foremost, where, as he put it, "50 percent of the city developed outside the norm, while among the remaining 50 percent that supposedly developed under the norm 50 percent violates the norm and the other half does not use it." A year later, I found the group visibly tired and frustrated and left doubting their resistance would continue.

The irony is that shopping malls are such a profitable business that even when they do comply with any official urban requirements and demands, the costs entailed represent an insignificant fraction of their overall profits. So admitted the developer of Bogotá's Gran Estación (built in 2006), who complained at length about the "unreasonable" demands extracted by the city to build the mall. In his view, shopping mall developers were facing conditions that were "too trying and difficult," especially having to work under left-leaning mayors like Enrique Peñalosa and the even more maligned Gustavo Petro, whose urban plan for the city, Bogotá Humana, was the first to seek control of mega developments by imposing greater demands on developers. In particular, this developer bemoaned having to pay a licensing fee of 20 million pesos, approximately a mere $10,000, to the city, the first time a shopping mall had been asked to pay such a fee, and having to build two main avenues to the mall, as if this investment in infrastructure was outside his responsibility. Yet from his office's high-rise window in the very tony Zona

Rosa it was obvious that these "unreasonable requests" from the city had done little to harm his profits. As he enthusiastically reported, the project had grown tenfold in value in the less than ten years since it was built.

One reason shopping malls are seemingly immune to government scrutiny is because they have historically functioned as key worlding mechanisms to mark the newfound "globality" and modernity of many developing cities. According to Roy and Ong (2011), the construction of mega projects that break with local standards and position a city as a true "global city" can function as key worlding mechanisms for branding a city or a country under conditions of neoliberal development. What the case of shopping malls reveals, however, is that these structures have long been at the forefront of globalization strategies prior to the current boom in construction. Not for nothing was the launching of Unicentro in 1976 advertised with the assertion, "Today, Bogotá is more of a City," tying Bogotá's upgraded status to the inauguration of its first shopping mall while furthering the association of shopping malls with "development" that continues to date (El Tiempo 1976).

One powerful advocate of this view is FENALCO, Colombia's national merchant association and one of its oldest and largest organizations. In the association's magazine, *Centros Comerciales,* shopping malls are regularly praised for being engines of growth, for helping to regularize the economy, and even for "creating pleasant and livable spaces that reflect a clear identity and define the personality of a society" (*Centros Comerciales* 2012: 4). Foremost, shopping malls are lauded as the best place for tourists to get to know and experience Bogotá, where they can feel safe while buying souvenirs, tasting traditional foods, or just browsing the hallways "enjoying the scenery of the people" (4). In fact, the city of Bogotá has recognized shopping malls' tourism and image-making potential by placing tourist information booths in selected shopping malls.

In addition to projecting safe and sanitized pictures of Colombia to tourists, shopping malls are recognized by FENALCO for their role in setting the standards of "good living" for locals, touting them as the place where local middle classes can not only find entertainment, information, and activities for leisure but also and most important stand on an equal footing with consumers worldwide. This last point is reinforced by *Centros Comerciales'* coverage of some of the most renowned shopping malls in the world—Beijing, Austria, or Dubai—alongside Colombian malls.[10]

FENALCO's leading economist was just as exuberant in his praise of shopping malls as its magazine. He described Unicentro as "Bogotá's pride" and one, if not one of its most important, tourism icons: "You know how New York has the Statue of Liberty as its emblem? Well, Bogotá has two: Montserrate and Unicentro."[11] In equating Unicentro with Montserrate—the famous tourist site of the historic seventeenth-century chapel on Montserrate hill, a traditional symbol of Bogotá—the economist could not be more clearly enthusiastic about the symbolic and cultural power of shopping malls. But even more fantastic was this economist's projection of how Colombia would look twenty years from now if it continued to develop at its current rate. It would be a Colombia where everyone would be fluent in both Spanish and English, have access to the Internet, make purchases on their smartphones, and drive their own cars, in other words, "a global metropolis, not unlike New York."

### THE LATIN AMERICAN BOOM: CYCLES OF BOOSTERISM AND BUST

In the summer of 2013, the *Financial Times* seemed to confirm the economist's vision of the future when it described Colombia as "the most Anglo-Saxon country in Latin America" (Rathbone 2013). The piece did not point to the country's multilingual abilities but to Bogotá's red brick and mock-Tudor architecture, as well as to the country's clean record in foreign debt, long democratic tradition, and considerable economic stability despite a history of conflict. It touted a "New Colombia" filled with prosperity, young innovators, vibrant nightlife, and safer streets, adding to previous stories in *Fortune, fDi Magazine,* the *New York Times,* and other publications calling Bogotá a "cultural capital" and one of the fifteen best new cities to do business in (Hammer 2012).

Anyone who had been paying attention to Latin America's economic coming-of-age in the past two decades, however, would immediately see echoes of previous stories singling out a particular country as the new "business nirvana" and the next frontier for growth. In the mid-2000s it was Argentina, and in particular the city of Buenos Aires, that was praised as an attractive venue for investors by the international press, in stories hailing the country's quick turnaround after the 2000 economic crisis. Commentators went on at length about Buenos Aires's European feel, echoing Colombia's "Anglo-Saxonness," as if to communicate a racial and ethnic makeup that would be welcoming to foreigners and ease any race-based fears about settling or investing in the city (Dávila 2012). By 2012, however, it was stories of inflation and social strife that occupied news on Argentina. Brazil, the region's giant, which has topped the Global Retail Development Index and other indicators of emerging market investment opportunities for years, is perhaps the perfect example of the cyclical rise and fall of Latin America's regional economies. After seeing dizzying rapid growth throughout the 2000s, by the summer of 2013 Brazil was the site of major social revolts spurred by government expenditures of billions of dollars for stadiums for the World Cup while public services like education, transportation, and health floundered. The revolts exposed a history of public infrastructure disinvestment that had accompanied the government-sustained financing of the private sector, putting a halt to the country's unabated and much celebrated growth that had remained unchecked for years. The vulnerability of Brazil's miracle was made apparent by a rise in inflation; a decline of 23 percent in Brazil's stock market index, "the largest of any large country"; and a negative rating by S&P immediately following the protests (Lattman and Romero 2013).

Indeed, as I write this, the fault lines of neoliberalism are everywhere evident throughout the region: in Chile's student protests demanding accessible education, in Brazilians' outrage about the construction of mega projects for the World Cup while the infrastructure for locals dwindles, and in the continued pink socialist stance of many governments in the region. Even Colombia, one of the United States's most loyal partners in the region, saw massive demonstrations in the summer of 2013 when peasants led a national strike against the TLC, government privatization policies, and the destruction of the agrarian economy. Signs of a weakening economy were already evident by 2015 with the drop in petroleum prices and the rise of the dollar relative to the declining Colombian peso (from around 1,800 pesos to the dollar when I started my research to 3,200 pesos in August 2015), exerting pressure on all exports and commodity prices and auguring a general recession that many were still unwilling to acknowledge. And who knows which Latin American country will be the next to have an up- or downswing and what lessons if any will have been learned.

Any marketing spin demands the systematic erasure of history, and this process is as quick to erase periods of decline, stagnation, inflation, and recession following any previously celebrated growth as it is to identify a new country or region as the "new" business nirvana. In the four years I attended shopping mall conferences and gatherings I heard contrasting assertions from experts about what country or countries I should look into, since Chile and Peru "were already developed," or assurances that Mexico is where it's at and where all investment is going or that it is smaller countries like Guatemala and Ecuador that will be poised for growth. I began to appreciate that these predictions were fed by market developments that were as fickle as the arrival of one major retailer in one country that made it seem as the "hot" new market, or the development of a REITs-type financial mechanism, or the privatization of pensions in one country that seemed to open up the path for new investment. Political conditions also factored in. The growing interest in Colombia, for instance, is directly tied to its conservative and pro–North American politics and history, relative to neighboring Venezuela and other seemingly more "socialist" countries. As the president of FENALCO put it, "For the Americans we are like South Korea, their friendly state next to Venezuela." Robert Dragoo, the real estate investment evaluator living in Colombia, could not place more emphasis on the centrality of macroeconomic and political factors. After scouting for business in the region, he had chosen Colombia because it was on "the right path," that is, with free trade agreements and an emphasis on opening up markets, in contrast to "socialist" countries like Argentina or Venezuela but also because the United States has a history of assisting Colombia with security and "making its presence known." He is referring to the continuous stream of U.S. military aid to Colombia, increased in the 2000s with the start of Plan Colombia, which involved a commitment of approximately $1.6 billion in military aid, making the country the third largest recipient of U.S military aid (Aviles 2006). This investment was accompanied by an almost doubling of Colombia's military spending between 2000 and 2010, turning its army into a global exporter of military training and technology (Schipani 2013).

Marketing overviews of the region, however, seldom highlight the structural factors that make different countries stand out, focusing instead on the "positive" social and economic indicators that are supposedly shared throughout the region. Industry advocates point to the region's faster and steadier rates of growth relative to Europe and the United States: 3.1 percent in 2012, compared to the average 2.2 percent for the rest of the world, and to its resilience after the global recession.[12] Relative to the United States and Europe, Latin America also has a younger population that is largely urbanized and densely located in large and medium-sized cities, making them easy targets for consumption at shopping malls.

Most important, Latin America has seen the growth of the so-called new middle classes, groups with some discretionary income and clamoring for new formats for shopping. This is another topic for which it is difficult to distinguish myth from reality. Camilo Herrera, a renowned Colombian market researcher, said, "It's difficult to know if there are more middle classes than in the past because the fact is that we did not talk about those groups, or look into those groups." Still, whether these groups are "new" or newly discovered, marketers point to a growth in average per capita income throughout the region, a decrease in urban unemployment, and low household debt-to-income levels, especially in comparison to the United States. In addition, improvements in education and health, alongside a decline in inflation and the introduction of credit, have increased the purchasing capacity of many middling groups. It is important to remember, however, that these groups are defined in very flexible and capacious ways, especially from the standpoint of those who are investing or representing these groups to investors. This was one of my most surprising findings: despite the buzz about Latin American new middle-class consumers, most experts I spoke to recognized that these groups are more marginal and vulnerable, and newer, than they are willing to openly acknowledge. As a Latin American representative of Prudential Bank explained, when the industry talks about middle classes, they recognize that they are talking about groups that are relatively new to shopping mall and modern consumer spaces. In sum, these are groups that have interacted with the informal economy and informal markets and have little history and experience with shopping malls.

> The competition for a shopping mall is the street market, which is how people typically interacted with the market. We are talking about the lower and middle classes, which are the great majority. What you've seen in the past twenty years is the expansion of the middle classes, who want middle-class things, and they want to shop at Wal-Mart, at a place that is clean, professional, with quality products. Wanting to participate in the middle class and in consumer activities is what is considered middle class and what is driving the shopping malls and pushing the informal economy out.

I will have more to say about who these middle classes may be later. Here I want to point to their vulnerability and to the preeminence of new types of consumption as a defining element of these groups.

Latin America is also considered a new frontier for growth because it is buffered from the "ills" that have affected malls in developed economies, primary among them, Internet sales. In fact, during his address at the 2013 RECon Latin America congress in Chile, ICSC's president pointed to Latin

Americans' "digital backwardness" as one of the characteristics that make Latin America so valuable, claiming—wrongly, I may add—that it will reputedly take 140 years for the area to reach the level of penetration by computers and Internet technology that exists in the developed world. In his view, these are consumers who are more reliant on brick-and-mortar stores, including of course shopping malls, than people elsewhere in the world.[13] Finally, investors are attracted to Latin America because it is considered an urbanized continent consisting of many "countries of cities." Not only are urbanization indexes high throughout the region, but most major Latin American countries have major and medium-sized cities—as in Colombia, which has over one hundred cities with at least fifty thousand residents. Such high levels of urbanization represent an added draw for developing shopping centers in proximity to a high density of consumers.[14]

For whatever reasons, at the 2012 Latin American RECon congress industry experts announced the construction of 200 new malls in Latin America during the next two years; and overall investments in Latin America were projected to reach a record $10.3 billion in 2011, up 27 percent from 2010 (Bird Picó 2013). Industry estimates circulated at the 2015 RECon projected that the number of shopping malls would increase from 196 to 280 in Colombia, from 584 to 700 in Mexico, and from 511 to 700 in Brazil, all unaffected by inflation or economic setbacks (Rodríguez Barrera 2015).

For their part, Latin America shopping mall professionals I spoke to both feed into and revel in the optimism about their industry. Some consider this attention well deserved, since their industry developed for the most part independently of global investors and retailers. Consider this statement by Alfredo Cohen, director of Venezuela's Constructora Sambil and developer of Sambil Malls in the Dominican Republic, Spain, and Puerto Rico, as he proudly reflected on the industry's growth before fellow Latin American developers in Las Vegas: "Ten years ago we would talk about North American franchises that don't come to our countries, and the fact is that they never came, but we developed our own franchises, which are very successful, as is the case in Colombia and Chile, where we have so many stores. We developed our own retailers, and we're taking our brands and stores to other countries and are transculturalizing our brands."

As Cohen stated, shopping malls and retail brands had been operating in many Latin American countries for decades, gaining their current standing thanks to their marginal position and invisibility to the global community. Cohen went on to describe how his business had benefited from Venezuela's political isolation and lack of competition from international investors, acknowledging the potential threat posed by new interests seeking to get a foothold in Latin America. Implicit in his statement is the realization that the new global interest in Latin America may backfire by threatening or limiting local entrepreneurs' involvement and control of the shopping mall and retail industries back home.

Indeed, while Latin American developers worked essentially in isolation when national shopping malls first developed, the industry is far from invisible today. At the same time, it is difficult to obtain an accurate picture of capital directed at shopping mall construction and management in the region because it is not consistent, unilateral, or always visible. Most transnational REITs work through local partners—companies in charge of permitting and local taxes, which are in a better position to tap into local talent and knowledge about locations and make contacts in government and the private sector across the region. Planigrupo, a Mexican company with long experience building shopping malls in Mexico, has worked with global giants like Kimco, GE Capital, LaSalle Investment Management, and Walton Street Capital (Inmobiliare 2013). In Brazil, shopping malls were at first built with funds from private investors and public pensions, but soon enough it saw global corporations such as General Growth Properties, DDR, and Westfield partnering with Brazilian entrepreneurs and swelling the funds for local construction (Cutait 2013). The developer of Gran Estación shopping mall claimed to receive upwards of two business solicitations a month from investors abroad seeking local partners in Colombia.

Signs of globalization are also evident in different sectors of the industry. International design and architectural firms like Callison have opened offices in Mexico in order to tap into local talent and save money in creative designs that, in turn, are being marketed to the rest of the world.

Retailers are also contributing to the shopping mall boom by building and leasing new stores for their franchisees. In 2012 the Global Retail Development Index reported that Starbucks doubled its store count in Brazil; that Gap and Banana Republic opened in Chile; that luxury brands such as Gucci, Chanel, and Prada opened in Mexico; and that retailers like Sephora, Payless, Guess, Giorgio Armani, Adolfo Dominguez, Wal-Mart, Adidas, Zara, and Levi's are also opening up all over Latin America, joining the retail giants Forever 21, H&M, and Victoria's Secret, among others (Callieri 2013).

The advent of a global retailer is of special note, because with the exception of luxury retailers they seldom open just one store in one country. Their arrival demands that they create "brands" and streamline the distribution, warehousing, and permit processes by opening up a series of locations at once, pushing for the construction of more retail space to accommodate their brands' needs. In fact, while local Colombian stores tend to average 50 to 100 square meters, global chain stores demand thousands of square meters, far above the size of most retail locations, hiking the demand for prime real estate locations wherever they seek to settle.

There has also been an increase in capital flows responding to the privatization of pension plans and the development of new REIT-like mechanisms that foster investment in real estate, such as the new capital development certificates (CKDs) issued by the Mexican government that encourage pension funds to invest in real estate projects and infrastructure and the FIBRAS. These mechanisms are quickly transforming the financialization of projects by providing a steady flow of financing in real estate, which has boosted construction and heightened investments in shopping centers. Most significantly, through this development, many workers in Latin America and elsewhere are becoming investors and stakeholders in shopping malls, even if unbeknownst to them, as their pensions funds become regular investors in shopping mall REITs. The result is that the region is seeing capital flows at rates previously unseen or unheard of. This was the assessment of Tim Gifford, a senior vice president of the Global Capital Advisory Group, which specializes in transborder transactions exceeding $200 million and has offices throughout Latin America. During a presentation on Latin American markets at RECon 2013 Las Vegas, he calculated that the region had seen capital flows in the thousands of millions in the previous twelve months, a trend that he envisioned would grow in the years ahead, especially in the area of retail real estate, which now makes up a third of all investments. Canadian, Australian, North American, and European pension funds were all key players according to Gifford, as are China and Singapore. And then there is the continuous cross-regional investment in shopping malls, including Venezuela's Sambil building in the Dominican Republic and Puerto Rico; Chile's Mall Plaza and Parque Arauco shopping malls opening branches in Colombia and throughout Latin America; and Chilean big-box stores such as Falabella, Ripley, and Cencosud opening in Peru and Colombia. Other big players include Cinepolis from Mexico, which has opened up megaplex movie theaters in shopping malls throughout Latin America; and the Colombian construction company Conconcreto, which is building malls in Guatemala at the same time that Guatemala's Spectrum Group is building malls in

Colombia. Often, these expansions are assisted by global capital investments, which remain veiled from view, as is the case with Chilean shopping malls developers who trade as public companies in the market. As a result, Colombians may recognize that Chileans are building malls in their cities but not the additional foreign interests and investments behind such developments.

Notwithstanding the obvious signs of confidence and certainty signaled by all this growth, fear and uncertainty about the industry's effect and future are also very visible. Some of my informants recognized and spoke out about the growing disconnect between all the hype and the state of the business. One real estate investor professional candidly admitted that he expected no "immediate payback" from all the new investments and developments in Latin America. In his view, investors should act with an eye to gaining a foothold and obtaining a presence in a market with long-term interests.

Latin American industry professionals are also concerned about the rapid hikes in the price of land and the stress it puts on local economies. Some wondered if Latin American cities had reached the level of saturation in the construction of shopping malls and whether and for how long local brands could resist the entry of new global brands. The rapid growth of FIBRAS in Mexico, in particular, was a hot topic of debate because it had brought a flow of investments into the country over and above the projects available. This situation was linked to a rapid increase in the value of land and to a boost in the development of new projects, as well as to rumors about the specter of a retail real estate bubble. In addition, the example of the U.S. shopping mall industry loomed large, as both a model and a warning. At its height, the U.S. shopping center industry grew practically unchecked form the 1970s to the last recession at the unsustainable rate of 110 percent while the population grew only 47 percent, leading to the current excess in dead and unused shopping malls.[15] Many wondered if Latin America was slated to repeat this same fate and how long would it take for it to experience the same problems of saturation. This is not surprising given that Brazil, a pioneer in the development of shopping malls, is already beginning to be haunted by the reality of overbuilding and "ghost malls" (Dickinson and Jelmayer 2015).

At a local forum on the state of the Latin American shopping industry during RECon 2013 Las Vegas an audience member expressed concern about the unsustainably aggressive prices for real estate by asking how much new capital it would take to create a bubble in land prices. Carlos Lecueder, an experienced developer from Uruguay who had been building malls in

Uruguay, Argentina, and Paraguay since the early 1980s, added a valuable historical perspective to the future prospects of the industry: "What happens when there's so much foreign investment? The currency falls, and the prices go up. This is what happened in Brazil and now in Uruguay, and we become too expensive to the world, and then investment falls. The problem is the rise in prices." Lecueder was speaking to a room filled with Latin American industry professionals, where people seemed to momentarily put a brake on their overenthusiastic stances to raise key questions and concerns about their industry and its future. I noticed that his peers in the room were listening intently, and for a moment there seemed to be recognition and identification, a sense of awareness that he was describing a domino effect that was already being experienced and that could be reproduced easily throughout the region. But the moment of introspection was just that. It was time for the next conference, and the attendees wrapped up the meeting with smiles, congratulatory handshakes, and hugs.

# TWO

# The Globalization of Retail and the Rise of Shopping Mall Professionals

Six years ago you had to "rent a crowd" for any international session at RECon. Today, it's almost the opposite, often with standing room only.

**IAN THOMAS**, *principal, Thomas Consultants, Vancouver, quoted in McLinden 2013*

While these developers speak many different languages, they all speak the language of retail.

**BRAD HUTENSKY**, *chairman, ICSC*

A common industry tale is that the International Council of Shopping Centers was called "international" to welcome the few Canadian attendees present when the trade organization for the shopping mall industry was founded in 1957. For little about the shopping mall industry and the everyday business of its trade organization would be truly international for decades. There were inklings of interest in internationalization in the 1970s, when the recession pushed the organization to seek European members, which led to the first ICSC European conference in Paris in 1976. But it was not until 1990 that the ICSC began to venture outside the West, holding its first World Congress of Shopping Centers in Hong Kong. In the early 1990s the first ICSC/Asia Conference, the first Mexico Symposium, and the first Caribbean Conference were held.

Attention to Latin America in the 1990s was spurred by international agreements like the North American Free Trade Agreement (NAFTA), which lowered restrictions for foreign investments and provided a great impetus for foreign developers at a moment when there was a general slowing of the industry's growth in the United States. Still, interest in Latin American markets was not regularized until 2009, when the RECon Latin America conference was initiated, joining other regularly held regional international congresses, RECon

Asia (formerly Asia Expo, 2006) and RECon Middle East and North Africa.[1] The new global outlook was reinforced by ICSC's third president, Michael Kercheval, who had previously worked with global and Latin American markets.[2] This vision was bolstered by the hiring of Jorge Lizán as director and then vice president of business development in 2006 and as the first ICSC staff member to focus specifically on Latin America, until his departure in 2014 to launch a private consultancy business. Born and raised in Mexico, Lizán had had worked at Carrefour in Mexico and then at Yum! Brands (Pizza Hut, Taco Bell, KFC) in the Caribbean and Latin America after leaving a career in architecture to complete an MA in global management in Arizona. But his love of travel and "anything global" made him a perfect fit for ICSC. Lizán is widely recognized for turning around the state of the Latin American shopping mall industry. Not only did he help develop RECon Latin America, expediting ICSC's expansion into Latin America, but he was central to the industry's growth in India and other parts of the developing world.

The result is that in the past decade, the "International" in the International Council of Shopping Centers is slowly being backed with substance. The global impetus was visible at the organization's 2013 Las Vegas Exhibition Hall, where commercial property development companies flaunted maps of the world with markings of their international footprints, and where you could meet developers from Europe, Canada, and China. References to the global also appeared frequently in the program, which included sessions on China, Asia/Pacific, the Middle East, and Latin America. Most notably, at the Global Delegates Breakfast, attended by over five hundred people, retail was touted as a catalyst for development and improved living standards across the globe. Panelists from India, Dubai, South Africa, and Mexico spoke optimistically in the same language—the "language of retail"—at a session where collaborative agreements between the ICSC and industry councils representing the Shopping Centers Association of India, the Shopping Centre Council of Australia, and the British and French Councils of Shopping Centers were signed. The session was moderated by Lauralee Martin, ICSC trustee and CEO of Jones Lang LaSalle, one of the largest global retail real estate companies, active in over seventy countries, whose slogan, "Real Value in a Changing World," brought home the simple message that in these changing times "real value" is to be found abroad.

But it was a general address by ICSC chairman Brad Hutensky that stated most clearly the new direction, touting an international membership of over 20 percent and the global as the new frontier of growth.

It became quite apparent that the opportunity in retail real estate development, which has slowed in the U.S., is exploding elsewhere. While only one enclosed mall opened in the U.S. in 2012, more than 40 new malls are scheduled to open in Brazil alone over the next 24 months. . . . Amazingly, 11 of the top 14 cities in the world ranked by retail construction in progress are in China. In the Middle East, Latin America, and elsewhere, new malls are being rushed to market, with each one striving to be more innovative than the next, to meet surging demand from a growing middle class with new discretionary income that is ready to shop.

All this attention to the global in the first international organization for the shopping mall industry does not mean that shopping malls were not already internationalized or a global phenomenon. Nor does it mean that shopping malls across the world had developed in total isolation from the United States. As early as 1947, North American retailers such as Sears had opened stores in Mexico, and beginning in the late 1960s shopping malls modeled after North American malls began to appear in some of the largest Latin American cities, many of them anchored by Sears (Campbell 1974; Moreno 2003). In fact, some of the most important shopping mall developers from Latin America, such as Mexico's Eduardo Bross from Planigrupo, Venezuela's Alfredo Cohen from Constructura Sambil, and Brazil's Sergio Andrade de Carvalho from Ancar Ivanhoe, had been regular attendees at ICSC conferences, where they honed their skills in the industry's best practices and the language of retail.

Attendance at ICSC conferences by these giants of the Latin American industry also served as the impetus for the establishment of shopping mall associations in Latin America. This is the case for ABRASCE, Brazil's national shopping mall council, which Carvalho founded after his first trip to RECon Las Vegas in 1976, a trip that was decisive in pushing him toward the then-nascent shopping mall business. As he explained, his background in banking made him hesitant to jump into the shopping mall business until he saw President Gerald Ford give the opening speech at RECon that year, an unquestionable sign that shopping malls were a legitimate business. Carvalho's three children are still involved in Brazil's shopping mall industry, and they received training and held internships in the United States through ICSC networks and mentors.[3] Notably, developers from Spain, Turkey, and other parts of the world share similar stories of having been influenced by the international organization even before its outlook was attuned to the global.

Indeed, educational and professional development are two of the most important components of ICSC's mission and a primary driver for advancing what Margaret Crawford (1992) has called the "science of malling," or the quest to create generic malls through standardized practices about shopping mall development advanced in meetings, certification programs, and research, as well as through advocacy and publications. ICSC RECon's regional meetings are all about promoting a global language of best practices for financing, managing, and running the business, and for those seeking additional training, the meetings are increasingly complemented by an educational component, including a series of classes on leasing strategies, design and construction, and any other hot topic of the day, such as the use of social networking. The ICSC also holds the Global John T. Riordan School for Professional Development, operating since the 1980s but later named for ICSC's second president and lifetime trustee and one of the most passionate believers in ICSC's global educational program. Riordan had been a schoolteacher and had previous experience developing standardized educational testing before joining the shopping mall industry, skills that he put to use in developing a standardized curriculum for shopping mall professionals.

The school operates in various countries on a rotating basis, providing students with the opportunity to learn about all facets of shopping mall development, building, leasing, and operations. Students are also assisted in obtaining certification titles in five different "specialties"—Leasing, Management, Marketing, Development, and Executive Leadership—after passing competitive exams that the website announces can be taken in up to four hundred locations worldwide. As early as 1963 ICSC instituted its University of Shopping Malls, which since 2004 has been housed at the prestigious Wharton School. The school has always drawn international students, but I was told that their numbers have increased to 20 percent of the student body, representing up to twenty different countries.

Notwithstanding its growing international presence, the ICSC's educational program remains unabashedly U.S. centered. As a coordinator for the University of Shopping Malls explained, "[The curriculum] is all U.S.-focused content about best practices and universal concepts you can incorporate. We have a very popular class on mixed-use developments and other general best practices in the U.S. that you can use throughout the world. If we have any global content it is directed to U.S. investors, not the other way around." Reviewing the brochure, it is obvious that the language of retail is all about "CAM, tenant mix, and footfall," or how to negotiate common areas maintenance and operations fees, obtain the best mix of tenants, and secure the largest number of visitors; in other words, how to run a shopping mall the way it has historically been done in the United States.

Riordan, for his part, was adamant about the need for standardization and the key role education can play to achieve it: "You have to stick to your guns about certain basics. There are things that are permanent. If you're talking about management, then there are just a few ways in which you could do development and successfully lease and manage commercial properties over time." The irony, however, is that industry experts will also tell you that there is no such thing as a uniform practice or standardized method for measuring success in the industry; it can differ from company to company in different sectors.

Indeed, I found that the "best practices" taught by ICSC often clashed with the ways shopping malls had been operating for decades in Latin America. In other words, in contrast to the ICSC chairman's optimistic statements, national retailers have been modeling their projects after U.S. and European malls without necessarily speaking the same language of retail. This is the reason for the sudden interest in the global on the part of industry promoters. A globalized landscape for investments demands conformity in language and practices, or at least a common space for negotiation that is recognizable among global retailers and investors intent on entering developing markets. In this regard, the strongest impetus for the educational turn is the need to translate shopping malls into the financial instrument they have become in the eyes of global investors. The idea then, is to see them as an "asset class," as they are regularly treated in most industry meetings. Or in the words of Riordan, the goal is for shopping malls to be considered a "management concept," not solely a building.[4]

What follows examines ICSC educational mission and educational programs to suggest that they are best considered as key "globalizing" projects integrating individuals, communities, and countries into the world economy of shopping malls and retail. Whether by opening up investment and encouraging global trade or by instituting new social and cultural regimes that are more conducive to investments, capital increasingly operates through entities like the ICSC that are central to spreading neoliberal governmentalities across the globe. Much has been said about global nongovernmental organizations (NGOs) or institutions like the World Bank or the International Monetary Fund, entities that are more directly involved in the "structural adjustment" of a country's economy or that work through social movements or actors in civil society. In both instances, scholars have exposed the "coloniality of power" and knowledge that are reproduced by many international NGOs, which tend to be invested in the paradigm of development, in which modernity and globalization are defined around narrow and hierarchical Western-dominated constructs.[5] The developing world, in turn, is presented as unable to fully attain modernity and hence as permanently lacking and in need of instruction and guidance (Escobar 2011; Woods 2006; Medeiros 2005). Writers have also paid attention to the new types of identities and subjectivities of class, demeanor, ethnicity, and more that are encouraged and disciplined among local actors who participate in NGO programs, where subjects are often constructed around narrow conventions linked to their areas of interest, whether it is ethnic entrepreneurs or "authentic" indigenous intellectuals (DeHart 2010; Hale 2006).

Outside of the developmental institutional machine, however, the rise of neoliberal capitalism has also seen the advent of a variety of technocratic and professionalizing global organizations focusing on the private sector that are just as important and effective as NGOs in spreading neoliberal governmentalities and colonial hierarchies of value. In fact, these professionalizing entities are not too different from development regimes of the past, which sought to remake the world as knowledgeable according to Western standards of modernity (Gibson-Graham 2006; Escobar 2011; Mitchell 2002). In my view, professional entities like the ICSC are especially interesting for placing a developmentalist focus on private ventures and businesses like shopping malls and for their role in professionalizing global capital-centric conventions that make U.S.-based business models and managerial practices the dominant reference for specific lines of work. They do this by creating a new set of "experts" in narrow fields of knowledge in particular industries, in this case, shopping mall development, management, and marketing, that are not only presented as "true" and applicable to every context, but also a prerequisite for entering the world economy of retail.[6] Foremost, the educational and professionalizing impetus contained in these strategies almost always guarantees the ranked and differential positioning between those who are "in the know" and those who are not.

At the same time, Latin Americans are far from new entrants to capitalism, which was consolidated by U.S. imperialism and its extractive economies in the area. Neither are Latin American entrepreneurs unfamiliar with North American business and entrepreneurial practices. These have a long history in the area, partly shaped through exchanges between the United

States and Latin America. A growing literature on the global circulation and social transfer of policies regarding security, housing, and urban planning attests to these types of relationships. A pertinent example is the University of Chicago's economics department's scholarship programs for Chilean students, which ushered in the ascendancy of market economics in the region, leading to what Greg Grandin (2006: 188) has termed the "third conquest of Latin America," the privatization of state enterprises from railroads to telephone companies.[7]

In this context, the key issue is accounting for the dominant categories and processes reproduced by the institutions and discourses of capitalist modernity—for instance, by the ICSC curriculum—but also for the coexistence of differences in regard to practices, interpretations and possibilities, among those that are positioned as forever backwards and in need of modernity's know-how. These warnings are especially relevant when grappling with the operation of a global school on shopping malls in a region where neoliberal capitalism has been restructuring old binaries around strict class divisions and the United States as *the* imperial threat. Having penetrated most Latin American industries, neoliberal capitalism has seen the rise and development of transnational capitalist classes in every sector of the economy, especially in new sectors such as the service, technology, and creative industries, whose interests are aligned with the global economy. One outcome of this is that strict binaries between the U.S. and the Latin American economies and interests are challenged, complicating the development of resistance movements as compared to when U.S. imperial interests were concentrated in particular extractive industries or an identifiable "multinational" corporation (Robinson 2008). In other words, capital-centric industries like shopping malls in Latin America are not always seen as "importations" or threats to local industries. Organized and embraced as "national" products and industries, they are often instead seen as signs of a city's or a country's ascendancy and modernity, even when they may in fact challenge other local and national industries, specifically, local retailers.

The key point here is that neoliberal projects and policies in Latin America are often intersected by particular national ideologies, with each powerful paradigm reinforcing the other through marketing discourses of boosterism and coming-of-age. For instance, commentators, politicians, and development enthusiasts continue to tie the region's aspirations for upward mobility to the marketing and circulation of new developments while interpreting their growth as signs of "the success" and endurance of Latin American countries and economies. Specifically, against the specter of a larger global economy that is seen to be in recession and decline, many neoliberal projects in Latin America are charged with political significance, signs that, despite recent problems, the region is undergoing a coming-of-age. As I discuss later, these attitudes were common among the Latin American professionals/students participating in one of ICSC's global courses that is the focus of this chapter. But they were also evident in the statements of pride in Latin American malls that I heard from developers as well as local visitors. I recall the many shopping mall visitors in Bogotá who, when I approached them about my project, wanted to hear what I thought about Colombian malls in comparison to those of the United States. After seeing many disappointed faces when I responded that there were too many malls in Bogotá, I learned to limit my reply to, "Malls here are bigger and better," the only response that was met with satisfaction and that would break the ice. In this way, globally oriented Latin American shopping mall professionals operate both as agents of globalization and as national and regional boosters through their very promotion of the global business of shopping malls. These dynamics, however, are accompanied by the reproduction of hierarchies of evaluation within the structure of ICSC training and professionalization where Latin American professionals are positioned as backward, corrupt, or lax or careless about details, hence in need of professionalizing standards and methods of transparency that only North American best practices can impart.

## THE GLOBALIZATION OF THE SHOPPING MALL "PROFESSIONAL"

In the summer of 2013, I had the opportunity to attend the ICSC John T. Riordan Global Professional Development School in Mexico City to take courses in the tracks on Development, Design and Construction, and Administration, Marketing, and Leasing. I met students and interviewed some of the professors and was able to get a sense of the global industry's impetus toward standardization and of the negotiations that take place among Latin American shopping mall professionals. I jokingly told friends that I was attending the shopping mall version of the School of the Americas, the famed school where Latin Americans were taught counterinsurgency methods from the 1940s on. I was not that far off. Just as the School of the Americas trained scores of political leaders in the political arts of warfare, counterinsurgency, and terror during the Cold War, the ICSC school has produced key leaders in the dominant political arts of the twenty-first century, those of seduction, consumption, and shopping, while providing key space for intraregional deal making and networking.[8]

Experienced ICSC members make up the school's staff, most of them certified in one or more of the organization's specialty tracks. They teach without pay on a voluntary basis, reputedly for their "love of teaching and the profession," though at least one individual confirmed that the position gives him recognition and visibility in the profession and in the ICSC leadership structure, in addition to networks and potential job opportunities. Another individual explained his decision to teach by saying that he might need a job sometime in the future. The Latin American school was initially taught by North American shopping mall professionals, but at the 2013 version in Mexico, North American staff were the minority: only two among the diverse Latin American faculty, which hailed from Venezuela, Mexico, Panama, Puerto Rico, and Argentina. All were male and at least fifty years old, making up a selected cadre of longtime industry professionals with a history of involvement in the ICSC. Certification is relatively easy for experienced North American professionals many of whom can pass the certification exams just by studying the ICSC materials, but for many international professionals these courses are key, not necessarily to "learn" the industry, but rather to acquire the "right" global industry language and terminology.

Still, my cohort of about one hundred students was quite familiar with U.S., or "global," standards for building and managing shopping malls. This is not surprising given that they were among the most globalized professionals in the industry, as was assured by the steep course registration fee: $1,575 for ICSC members and $1,875 for nonmembers (bear in mind that ICSC membership is $800 for companies and $125 for individuals employed by member companies). In addition to this fee, participants or their employers had to pay for transportation and lodging at the tony Sheraton Maria Isabel.[9] Participants were quite homogeneous in terms of race—white and light-skinned—and class—upwardly mobile and elite. Many had families with ties to banking, business, and shopping malls in their home countries. The classes were also very segregated by gender, according to the subject matter being taught: male students enrolled in the Development, Design, and Construction course; women were concentrated in the Marketing track.

All the students were highly experienced in their professional areas of expertise. For instance, my sixteen or so mostly male classmates in the Development,

Design, and Construction course included architects, civil engineers, and developers from Guatemala, Argentina, Mexico, Colombia, Chile, and Venezuela with at least three years of experience in the business and the majority having at least six years. Most of them had built and designed a shopping mall in their respective countries or had been involved in different capacities in one of these projects. One student, a Mexican architect, had just finished designing a nine-story shopping mall in China; another, an engineer from Mexico, worked for Planigrupo, one of Mexico's largest developers; the Argentine student had twenty years of experience in the industry, and a Colombian student turned out to be a major developer of shopping malls in medium-sized cities throughout the country. The Guatemalan student had built and introduced franchises for global brands like Dominos and McDonald's in Guatemala.

I note their previous experience and knowledge because the content of the classes seemed to mostly ignore it. Instead, I found that the classes were all about providing an overview of terminology and best practices that were primarily based on U.S. practices, with little consideration of students' backgrounds or the applicability of these practices in the Latin American context. This was especially evident during the classes taught by the two North American professors, whose presentation focused on conveying concepts and content geared to passing the ICSC certification exams and drawn primarily from Wikipedia or North American professional organizations like the American Institute of Architects. At lunch, I was surprised to discover how little these professors knew about Latin American malls. One did not speak Spanish, while, with two exceptions, everyone at the table spoke English fluently and graciously did so to accommodate him. The insularity of this instructor was obvious in his surprise at learning that our Mexican architect classmate was working globally and his inability to keep up with the conversation at the table. My lunch mates were bragging among themselves about the types of amenities and entertainment choices that are regular offerings at Latin American malls: re-creations of snowflakes or sandy beaches for children during holidays; bowling alleys or temporary skating rinks; amenities like gardens and fountains; innovative architectural features such as spiral-shaped hallways. But the North American professor could only bring up the example of Minnesota's Mall of the Americas. Lunch had turned into a contest of which country had the best and most original malls, and the North American professional was slated to lose.

Gaps between U.S. "best practices" and terminology and Latin American concepts and general practices were also evident during the Spanish-led classes. However, these were taught by Latin American professors, who were generally more sensitive to pointing out and bridging differences between the curriculum and "the way we do things in Latin America," always referring to "Latin America" as a monolith despite the many regional differences that came to light during discussion. In addition, there was a stark difference in the level of discussion and participation—almost nonexistent in the classes taught in English and simultaneously translated and quite common in those led in Spanish. This was in part because Latin American professors recognized students as their professional peers and addressed them accordingly.

Overall, the Latin American professors appeared far more "global" than their North American counterparts. For instance, because they were familiar with shopping malls in different Latin American countries and beyond, they were able to discuss examples from a variety of places. They were also able to distinguish between practices drawn from and mostly applicable to the United States and those that would make sense in Latin America, which they pointed out throughout their classes. They also seemed to show genuine interest in learning from students' experience in their respective home countries. For instance, Jose, a Spaniard with extensive work experience in Puerto Rico and Venezuela, talked excitedly about what he had learned from working in Venezuela, praising their imaginative building designs and the success of a model that relies on small stores and boutiques rather than on the big boxes typical of the North American model. Students wanted to hear about how Chileans built museums and libraries in their shopping malls, a model that turned out to be quite lucrative. Chilean malls can deduct up to 50 percent of monies spent on cultural contributions, and by placing libraries within malls they increase their value as destinations, expand the number of visitors, and generate goodwill in ways that far exceed any initial investment in building these spaces.

Students were surprised to find that parking was not a topic in the "global" curriculum, where it is treated as a free amenity. In contrast, parking is of paramount importance to most Latin American shopping malls. While many malls are indeed in close proximity to bus and transportation routes, their accessibility by car is controlled by the privatization of parking spaces, an outcome of security concerns. Issues of constructing, managing, and keeping parking areas safe, as well as creating luxury parking amenities for select customers, are at the forefront of concerns of many Latin American shopping mall professionals but entirely missing from the U.S.-based curriculum.

Still, it was the ICSC curriculum, not the expertise of the "global" participants at the school—the Latin American teachers and students—that was considered the proper conduit of globalization. Such a curriculum was presented as the means to establish a common global language of retail and essential to making the industry relevant and translatable across locations. This is how a thirty-four-year industry veteran who had been teaching for over twenty-four years, including at the Wharton School, and one of the first global teachers for ICSC—he had previously taught in Singapore, Mexico, Panama, and Hong Kong—put it when explaining the importance of the school and its certification exams: "The whole idea behind the certification program is that if you're certified we can take you from one property and put you in another property and within a very short time you should be able to reorient yourself and perform. Regardless of where you are, there are principles of shopping malls, of managing and leasing, that you'll know." In other words, the goal was the global reorientation of local industries to ensure that they would be ready and nimble candidates for global investments or, one may imagine, for future takeovers and consolidations.

The primacy given to the curriculum over and beyond any local knowledge among the students was also at play during a lesson differentiating formats for shopping malls. A student was confused by the distinction between a "neighborhood mall" and a "community center," two of about ten official formats that the ICSC recognizes for malls, which the PowerPoint presentation linked to square footage and the region it services. His question prompted a clarification from one of the Latin American teachers: "All of this comes from the U.S. model. They are things to think with. You have to put it in perspective." But one of the North American professors sitting in the back of the room insisted that "these are global designations" and that if they are the ICSC accepted terms for these malls, then they are indeed the globally accepted classifications. In other words, these were the categories students needed to learn to pass exams and certifications, and whether they made any sense given local conditions was unimportant.

At a session introducing ICSC's educational program during the 2014 RECon Latin America conference in Cartagena, one of the speakers, a Latin American professional certified by the ICSC, acknowledged that more than anything new, the educational and certification programs were about "restructuring what you know and putting it in a way that will be in concert with the global industry." "We teach the language of expansion," specified the presenter, as his PowerPoint presentation flashed all the titles he had received in ICSC certification programs right after his name.

But it is the inapplicable aspects of ICSC's "best practices" that exposed their differences from the everyday operation of many Latin American malls. ICSC teachers emphasized the need for "rigorous research" prior to each stage in design, development, and construction and went on at length about the "D and B Report," or the Dunn and Bradstreet Report, a U.S. rating system that professionals use to get performance reviews about architects and contractors. They further stressed the importance of using forms and checklists like the "AIA A305," developed by the American Institute of Architects to keep track of the work records of particular contractors. But my classmates pointed out that it is almost impossible to get accurate data about contractors and similar businesses in their countries and questioned the accuracy of any record that is ultimately based on voluntary data. Choosing and composing work teams based solely on reports and information obtained from the Internet also did not strike my classmates as more trustworthy than drawing on well-known personal and social networks.

The lack of statistics and information on demographics and markets in most Latin American countries hindered collecting the type of market reports that were considered "reliable" by ICSC standards. In Latin America, even determining the accessibility of a location can be challenged by cultural factors, including visible and invisible barriers of class, race, and history, that were nowhere acknowledged by the professors but that everyone else recognized as decisive. For instance, a lesson on site selection for building a mall focused on the particularities and physical attributes of a building site and how they can aid or impair construction, but my classmates noted that there is no such thing as "perfect terrain" if that terrain is located in the "wrong part of town," far from the residences of and inaccessible by the middle classes. In all, my classroom peers agreed that market research in Latin America is unable to rely simply on maps or secondary research, as teachers argued was regularly done in the United States. Instead, research demanded fieldwork that would test routes and accessibility on the ground and, most important, account for the many invisible yet key cultural variables of race, class, and status that distinguished a "good" from a bad location. Latin American professionals also seemed far more aware of the social meanings of their malls and what they communicated to visitors in terms of class, upward mobility, and status. For instance, the Latin American professionals were surprised when presented with ideas about how to search for tenants to occupy temporary stands and kiosks in their hallways. This is never necessary, one noted, since temporary tenants always come looking for them. Their task, then, involves selecting tenants that fit best with their mall's identity. In other words, I found that Latin American professionals felt that any new mall would be of popular interest; for them the key issue was therefore not one of marketing but rather of targeting and attracting the right type of businesses and constituencies.

Courses on developing the best tenant mix for a mall focused on the importance of securing a large big-box store to serve as an anchor. In fact, ICSC classifications for different types of shopping malls are based on the number, size, and type of stores that serve as anchors. My Latin American classmates pointed out, however, that there are very few options for anchor stores in their countries and that many stores operate as monopolies, limiting or eliminating any choice on the part of the developer. As a Mexican classmate explained, "If you're putting in a mall and looking for an anchor, you'll have two options for a department store, Liverpool or El Palacio de Hierro, and two for a movie theater, Cinemex and Cinépolis, and they want months of free rent or detrimental arrangements to come to your space." In many instances, large supermarket chains have filled the void but have not solved the problem of one or two companies dominating the format and limiting the options.[10]

Latin American shopping mall professionals also lack a diversified pool of stores to occupy their malls. As the next chapter shows, many local brands and retailers have been badly hurt or eliminated by the introduction of global brands and the increase in imports. Few can generate the sales necessary to pay rent and maintain a presence in a shopping mall. In fact, the search and competition for global brands and stores to fill in their spaces and distinguish their malls—as the only mall that has a Forever 21 or a Victoria's Secret, for instance—has become one of the greatest threats to the dwindling indigenous retail sector across the region. More and more, it is Forever 21, Zara, H&M, Payless, and Nine West that occupy malls, limiting the ability of shopping malls to differentiate themselves from one another and creating competition instead over who can bring the next "new brand" or global product to their mall.

In particular, Latin American mall professionals were facing a new reality in which, in order to survive, they have to limit their dealings to global brands and retailers (most of them North American and European fast fashion chains), the only ones in a position to pay and commit to signing a long-term lease. What is more, global brands such as H&M and Forever 21 are exploiting their symbolic role as markers of fashion and modernity in many Latin American countries by demanding free rents and even payments from shopping malls for the "privilege" of having them. This has placed many Latin American shopping malls in competition with one another over which can attract the trendiest global brands, reproducing a modernist developmentalist logic that relies on local malls extending "benefits" to attract global brands by making it so attractive for them that they have gains even if they end up selling very little or nothing at all. This explains the bonanza of global brands, including luxury brands, that are now populating many Latin American malls. The press often touts the arrival of these brands to individual Latin American countries as a sign of their affluence, ignoring the fact that these brands often flock to Latin America because of the extremely beneficial conditions they are being extended to open stores there, not necessarily because of these countries' economic profiles or the affluence of its residents. As a shopping mall manager explained, "It's like they are getting free advertisement for their brand just by opening up a store in a Latin American mall." In fact, many international brands are known to be settling and signing long-term contracts as a way to gain an advantage as "pioneers" over other global retailers or to keep competitors out.

In sum, Latin American professionals face more uncertainty around the ability to attract the right mix of stores than is recognized by the ICSC recommendations for achieving the best and most balanced mix of tenants. The curriculum assumes the existence of a more diversified pool of prospective stores and retailers ready to populate a mall, a more even field for malls and retailers when negotiating contracts and leases, and situations where there is not such dependency on globally imported brands as currently exists in most Latin American malls. The fact is that Latin American shopping malls are operating at a disadvantage relative to global retailers, and this too sets them apart from U.S.-generated "best practices."

A class on advance strategic leasing was another instance of the gaps between U.S.-based industry trends and how malls operate in many Latin American contexts. The class revolved around the "best practice" of negotiating stores' leases based on their pro rated sales, calculated in relation to specific categories of retail and taking into account that some stores move more merchandise than others. But my Latin American professional classmates felt this idea would not work in their malls because most retailers do not like to share data on their sales for security or financial reasons. In addition, in Latin

America many shopping malls cannot just terminate a lease to put up a more "fashionable" or appealing tenant, because lease laws are often more protective of commercial tenants than those in the United States. Consequently, many shopping malls are awash with vacancies, with store owners preferring to hold out for global brands to pay higher prices rather than rent to local retailers whose tenancy could slow the mall's "modernization" and opening to global brands.

Differences between U.S. and Latin American practices were also evidenced in regard to the value and ownership patterns of land. As a student noted, "The difference is that they don't care about the land, and for us everything is about the land." Here it is important to remember that due to a lack of financing, the first Latin American malls built in the 1970s and 1980s modeled their designs after U.S. malls, without adopting the U.S. finance structure or model of operation based on leasing. Most were initiated by elite family dynasties, landowners and heirs of previous feudal economies, which were the only ones with the ability to find financing and credit at a time when there was little access to global financing, and these families still control their businesses and most of the land (Bird Picó 2006).

For instance, Hernando Casas, the architect of Bogotá's Unicentro, drew inspiration from a West Palm Beach mall he visited during his honeymoon, reinforced by a "initiation trip" to learn about shopping malls in the United States and Europe along with the developer Pedro Gómez. The team reportedly visited and studied over fifty malls (Valencia 2008). Other professionals I spoke to shared similar tales of field trips to U.S. malls, especially those in Miami, which they scrutinized in search for ideas. What the developers of Unicentro and similar shopping malls across Latin America did not copy, however, was the single property and leasing model dominant in the United States. With limited international financing available, the dominant tendency in many countries in Latin America and in the developing world was for a developer to acquire financing from individual store owners and buyers. The developer would then build but leave management to individual store owners and merchants. The latter were free to decide what to sell, when to open, and how to operate their businesses day to day and come together as an association to decide matters pertaining to the use and maintenance of the mall's common areas.

Most significantly, in this model retailers became effectively involved in both the business of retail and in real estate, given that as owners they could also rent their stores to other retailers if they so wished,—in direct opposition of the U.S. (or the ICSC's "international") model where most retailers lease space within a mall that is centrally owned and managed (most often by a REIT). The ICSC (2014) has canonized this single ownership concept, even defining "shopping malls" as "a group of retail and other commercial establishments that is planned, developed, owned and managed as a single property." In contrast, many Latin American shopping malls still follow a "condominium," or horizontal property, model, similar to that of a residential condominium project. This model provides greater freedom to retail owners but creates chaos in the view of international investors and ICSC practices. From their standpoint, this system hinders the ability to gather information on sales and retail health, as individual retailers have no incentive or pressure to disclose it. The industry's prescriptions on what is the best or most "appropriate" mix of tenants also go out the window when such decisions are taken individually, without considering the identity and financial health of the mall as a whole. The condominium system is also criticized for its lack of flexibility. In a leased mall, a store can be moved at the will of management, and spaces can be rented to new retailers to ensure diversity and balance in retail offerings; in the condominium model, there might be three shoestores next to each other competing for the same customers or a "shoddy" establishment next to an up-and-coming business, diminishing its status. In fact, some of the oldest shopping malls like Unicentro still display the traditional organization of retail that is common in street-level commerce, with stores selling the same products concentrated near each other.

Throughout the region, the advent of international financing and investment has challenged the common property model, which is now almost extinct in some countries, and new malls are being built and managed as single properties. Remnants of the old model linger, especially among shopping malls built before the 2000s, that is, before the current financialization trend that turned shopping malls into vehicles for international investments (Rodríguez-Barrera 2010). Most notably, this model is still dominant in Colombia, where it is seen both as the biggest impediment to foreign financial investments and as a buffer to the survival of many national retailers.

And then there was the elephant in the room: the issue of corruption and the many *mordidas* (lit., "bites," bribes) and *cuotas* (quotas) that are almost de rigueur in the development of any project. The subject was finally brought up during one of the question-and-answer periods. A student asked the professor to clarify the category "soft costs" in relation to the totality of a project's cost, which prompted a response from the most picturesque character in the class, a seventy-two-year-old developer from the Mexican city of Querétaro who attended the seminar with one of his sons who had been urging him to develop a mall. His response: soft costs are *"las vacaciones del alcalde"* (the mayor's vacation). Everyone began to laugh, except for the Chilean students, who made a point of distancing themselves from the conversation by noting that corruption was a problem in "some countries" but not in theirs.

In the past decade, Chileans have moved to the "pinnacle" of the symbolic hierarchy of globalization in Latin America, having been at the forefront of neoliberalization processes. During the seminar, the Chileans highlighted the modernity of their industry and distanced themselves from anything that hinted at backwardness, like the spirited discussion of mordidas. But this class was led in Spanish by one of the Latin American professors, and the atmosphere was more open and jovial, so everyone else quickly joined in the discussion. Most acknowledged that "mordidas," "cuotas," or whatever they may be called in people's home countries were a must to "liberate" or "expedite" permits, the alternative being that permits would fall by the sidelines or take years to be issued. Such payments were not only of monetary value; they included requests for specific projects that the city or mayor could then present to his constituency as the product of "people's taxes at work." A Guatemalan peer made everyone laugh when he told tales of a city official who asked him to build a public project in exchange for a building permit but requested that his workers wear city uniforms to further the charade that it was the city, not the developer, that was building the project. In these instances, it was the government that was exposed as corrupt for stealing the monies that should have paid for projects built by developers, which is not at all surprising given that I was in a room full of developers. I was obviously less likely to hear about the many "giveaways" they regularly obtain from government officials or about how they benefit from their country's public infrastructure. The informal tone of their discussion, however, left no doubt about the close ties that exist between developers and their specific regional and national government bureaucracies.

Payments to narcos in exchange for security were also not easily discussed in the open, though they were a common concern that did not fit "best practices" for accounting for shared fees and maintenance costs. A Mexican shopping mall owner raised this issue with great frustration and disappointment because no one could respond to his plight, beyond acknowledging that these payments had become a regular part of doing business. Also left unremarked was the reality that many shopping malls in Latin America served as outlets for money laundering. Yet my Colombian informants confirmed that shopping malls are commonly among the properties seized by the government when a narco or drug money launderer is caught. In fact, the entry of the Chilean department store Falabella into some of Colombia's most coveted shopping malls, including Unicentro, was made possible by the government confiscation of Almacenes Casa Estrella, formerly owned by Grupo Grajales, because of its owners' links to narco-trafficking (El Tiempo 2008). The San Andresitos, a series of discount stores and outlets where locals find imported and contraband merchandise, named after the Caribbean duty-free island, have also been linked to money laundering and narco-trafficking. The arrest of the Clan Báez, known as the czars of Bogotá's San Andresitos, is one of the many examples that speak to the intersection of the business of drugs and that of construction. News of the arrest reported their descent from "businessmen and investors in construction projects to extraditable by a federal court in Florida" (El Tiempo 2011). This construction-narco connection was common lore among my informants in Colombia who were quick to see evidence of *lavaderos* (money laundering places) everywhere, especially at the sites of upscale stores that never had clients or whose merchandise never seemed to move. I was not able to follow up my informants' perceptions, though I found enough evidence to support them. For instance, scholars have documented that it was not until 1996, decades after narco-traffickers began to purchase and register through legal means their illegally seized and violently acquired lands, that Colombia enacted a law extinguishing the ownership of properties that were unlawfully acquired (Reyes Posada 1990, 1997). Consequently, much of the real estate investment by narco-traffickers has become "normalized" and difficult to distinguish, especially in urban areas, where investments are smaller and less visible and there has been less research on land laundering compared to rural areas (Ballvé 2012, 2013; Reyes Posada 1990). In this context, my informants' perceptions show an awareness of the high degree of speculation involved in the shopping mall business. Their suspicions were generated not only by their experiences and past history but also by the displays of wealth that the advent of luxury stores represented across cities that remain highly segregated and economically depressed.

I could go on contrasting the standardized curriculum to the much more revealing and lively particulars I learned from my classmates about the actual on-the-ground workings of this global business. I found that the class had become a minefield of false dichotomies around "best practices" linked to the North American industry and its professionals while the Latin American industry always appeared, or was presented, as requiring correction and guidance. But first we must consider how the curriculum and the specific course were experienced and interpreted by the Latin American professionals, the students. As I listened to them I realized that the course's content was largely meaningless and secondary to their primary reason for being there: not so much to learn as to be certified as a global shopping mall professional. For instance, the students/professionals told me that they found value in learning about concepts they already applied or understood because it validated that they were already "acting global" in their business. Many welcomed learning "the official lingo" and adding some additional concepts to "talk the talk" while obtaining validation as professionals by participating in a global course under the ICSC banner.

Learning to "talk the talk" was perhaps one of the most important lessons, not only because it anchored their belonging in a community of privileged "industry" experts, but also because the new terminology was loaded with neoliberal meanings and worldviews about how the industry should work.[11] Some examples include the regular treatment of shopping malls as an "asset class," a "product" (of real estate), or a "management concept" and the preference for referring to "experiences" and "brands" rather than mere products to whatever was discussed as the subject of a sale and a purchase. The regular reference to shopping malls as "investment" products is especially significant because it naturalizes the REIT business model of the United States. Since their introduction REITs-type investment tools have revolutionized how shopping malls are built and managed in Mexico, but this is not yet the case in Colombia, making the assumed financialization of the shopping mall industry a projection that has a lot more to do with the needs and imaginations of the global retail real estate industry than with the everyday realities of local professionals.

New ways of looking at shopping malls were conveyed by spirited pep talks about the importance of the business and the yes-you-can aphorisms and attitudes liberally dished out by the professors. "To be early is to be on time. To be on time is to be late, and to be late is to be left behind"; "Amateurs practice to get it right. Professionals practice until they can't get it wrong"; "The opposite of success is not failure but not trying"; "You're not renting space to your tenants, you're providing them with opportunities" were just a few of the aphorisms thrown at students by the ICSC professors eager to instill something more powerful than knowledge: an attitude. The veteran North American teacher explained to me, "One of the things that we are doing is stretching students' understanding of what the business is, to give them the full picture of their business. We're pushing them to think differently." Professors felt they needed to instill more strategic thinking in Latin American professionals, who were seen as primarily task oriented, an assumption that devalued the backgrounds and experiences of the Latin American professionals.

My observations, however, countered these assumptions. Latin American professionals had ample knowledge and experience to share, which they did either spontaneously or when their participation was fostered in classes. Some felt that their cutting-edge concepts and formats should be adopted internationally. In particular, Latin Americans took pride in their innovative mall designs, in contrast to the somber white boxes that we associate with shopping malls in the United States. They also marveled at the greater number of community events and cultural programs that are common in many Latin American malls. Some expressed skepticism about learning lessons from representatives of what they saw as a failing industry, relative to the current success of shopping malls back home.

However, these alternative perspectives were silenced during the course. The common view was that the Latin American shopping mall industry is a direct outcome of the U.S. shopping mall industry and that it stands at a lower evolutionary stage relative to the United States. Accordingly, Latin Americans are slated to experience the same problems unless they learn the "right" lessons by "right" professionals. In particular, Latin American professionals were assumed to be lacking in the technical "know-how" and competencies that could only be obtained through ICSC guidance. So stressed one of the professors, who praised Latin American designers for their architecturally interesting and out-of-the-box projects while bemoaning the lack of quality control that he perceived had accompanied the recent construction boom in shopping malls in the region. In his view, Latin America was filled with malls with a lot of "wow factor" but with little quality control. He recalled a shopping mall tour in Chile that he took accompanied by a North American professional who was astounded by all the structural faults he found in plain sight: "We couldn't believe it! They had spent millions of dollars building a mall with so many structural issues."

As one might imagine, the view that Latin American malls are "faulty" and "unprofessional" contributes to the industry's globalization by facilitating the entry of North American and international players, conduits of "true expertise" and professional ingenuity. Consider how a Miami-based North

American architect at the 2014 Latin American RECon described the preference for hiring North American architects by both his Latin American and North American developer clients: "They hire us because they want a building that looks good and that also has function and value, that's efficient. They know we'll investigate and find strategies and provide solutions. Our clients know that Latin Americans work differently. They know what they are getting when they hire us." Note his emphasis on function, efficiency, strategies, and solutions as qualities that were distinctive in his professional practice and missing among Latin American professionals.

The preference for hiring North American professionals was especially pronounced in market research, an area North American professionals helped pioneer in Latin America. Consider the example of Cleo, who had been working on Latin American shopping malls since the 1980s and is considered a pioneer in Latin American market research. Cleo attributed his success to classist attitudes toward research among many of his Latin American clients who preferred to hire him rather than become "tainted" by associating with the popular classes: "This research involves fieldwork, because most of the governments' stats are not reliable, so you have to do footwork. People I work with prefer to hire me than do it themselves because they'd be socially scarred to go to these 'hoods . . . like they'd lose status. I go to sites with my bosses, and they're totally disoriented [because], they've never been there. . . . I don't care about being in these spaces. I don't have to deal with what my friends or family may say."

Without denying that Cleo benefited from Latin American shopping mall professionals' elitism, it is important to note the level of expertise attributed to him on account of his being North American. In fact, a Mexican researcher and competitor to Cleo shared his frustration that many of his clients often hire both of them, as if to corroborate the research produced by Mexican companies. As in this case, I found many North American professionals who benefited from the aura of "efficiency" and expertise afforded them and their work on account of their North Americanness. In fact, North American professionals have become a strong presence at Latin American shopping mall industry conferences, searching for jobs and opportunities in the region.

In this regard, the ICSC's educational programs validate a troubling yet dominant view about the state of the booming Latin American shopping mall industry as "cultural creative" but "technically faulty," as if reproducing nineteenth-century nationalist/imperialist binaries circulated about the inherent cultural attributes of a homogeneous United States and a homogeneous Latin America. I immediately thought of the Hispanic marketers I met almost twenty years earlier whose ads trafficked in similar colonial-based hierarchies about Latin Americans' supposedly stronger cultural core and spontaneous spirit in opposition to Anglo-Americans' more technical and rational nature (Dávila 2012). In other words, shopping malls were acting as the latest surface on which to stamp and reproduce old imperial epistemological regimes where "culture" (in the form of aesthetic innovation in the design of malls) functioned as the only means of for claiming any kind of superiority among Latin American professionals.

Latin American management practices were seen as especially faulty from the standpoint of the ICSC. Whereas the ICSC fosters "tracks" and specializations that break up the business of shopping malls into different expertises, giving rise to a variety of mutually distinct professionals/technicians, in many Latin American countries most professionals work as jacks of all trades, mixing areas or work that the ICSC considers totally unrelated. Under the U.S. model, then, Latin American professionals' breadth of expertise was dismissed as a possible asset and treated as the source of their lack of technical expertise and attention to detail. Latin Americans' supposedly top down, family dynasty, and hierarchical structure, which results in a few people making decisions at the top, was contrasted to the more "democratic" U.S. practice of allotting decision-making positions according to expertise, where everyone is held accountable and family and personal relations do not matter. As one teacher put it, "There may be a lot of national pride in these malls, but as long as you have a limited number of people at the top, which may or may not include family members, when you have that type of inbreeding, you limit yourself. . . . So there's a lot of focus on interesting concepts and design, you saw it in Mexico, one design was better than another. There's a lot of trial and error, but if they're blinded by the status of their company they're going to be blind."

Of course, the instructors' strict dichotomies between how Latin Americans and North American professionals run their businesses are naive. For years scholars have noted that the intimate and the economic and business realms are never mutually exclusive or in direct opposition to each other and that capital always draws strength from and reproduces itself through close-knit relations, whether they be of family and kin relations or highly nepotistic institutional relations like those of the Ivy League (Ho 2009; Zelizer 2007). Ho's (2009) ethnography of Wall street reminds of the social relations of race, gender, and class that inform the purportedly emotion-free world of New York City investment firms, a world she exposes as a highly closed circle where only elite universities are harvested for prospective recruits. In fact, the ICSC itself serves as a breeding ground for the type of close-knit relations that the teacher discussed above felt hindered Latin Americans' ability to make proper business decisions. This same teacher encouraged students to engage in networking and deal making and shared stories about how he had met some of his business partners at previous ICSC events. And let us also not forget about the "global" course's male-only faculty: a revealing example of the preponderance of personal and social relations and gender biases in the industry and of its narrow content focused on U.S.-centered concepts.

Then there is the ironic and very real fact that the global shopping mall industry profits from the same so-called premodern practices and family and network relations among Latin Americans' ruling elites that it bemoans. In fact, the "synergy" that characterizes partnerships in Latin America is one of the greatest motives behind U.S. investors' preference for engaging in global over local investments as they seek greater effectiveness and faster returns on investments. As one U.S.-based developer who works both in the United States and Latin America explained, "In Latin America it's not about the 'know-how,' it's about the 'know-who'—who knows the president, the senator, and the mayor." The same applies to mordidas, which in fact are a key component of how the industry is increasingly organized as a "global" operation. Not for nothing the international exposé of Wal-Mart's use of payoffs and bribes to acquire land permits to build in Mexico implicated corporate officers in the United States, who initially buried the investigation (Barstow and von Bertrab 2012).

Finally, the type of binaries and hierarchies of professional value that circulate in in the shopping mall industry were displayed in the flagship event of the Latin American shopping mall industry. At the 2014 RECon Cartagena, for instance, panels on industry trends, concepts, and best management practices were dominated by professionals from Toronto, the United States, and London. It was these "global" professionals who were positioned as experts imparting specific knowledge and information about the latest in industry trends. In contrast, Latin American professionals were concentrated in panels on the state of the local industry, where the subtext was always the marketing of the region and its unlimited opportunities for growth. The marketing subtext of these panels was acknowledged by one of the local speakers who jokingly admitted he had been warned to be vague and not say too much about the local industry "lest they keep everything." His comments drew laughter from an audience well aware of the many international attendees vying for business in Latin America.

To conclude, the turn to "professionalization" is on. All the Latin American professionals I spoke to described craving more professional development from ICSC and at least two of the Latin American professionals present at the course in Mexico shared plans to open similar educational programs in Latin America. What remains certain is that shopping malls are spreading rapidly throughout the region, and with them, management technologies that are moving the shopping mall business and Latin American societies toward closer synergy with the interests of the global economy. Global entities like the ICSC will continue to play a key role in the region, both professionalizing the field and training its professionals.[12] Most important, the globalization of the shopping mall industry exposes how an entire economic sector can generate and reproduce ideas about the relationship between culture and capital, as well as provide a space to reinscribe hierarchies of modernity through the old-fashioned but always effective tools of learning and training. Yet the magnitude of the global endeavor cannot be apprehended without an understanding of how shopping malls are developing in particular places and locations. It is to this subject that I now turn.

# THREE

# Retail Wars

## ON THE POLITICS OF SPACE AND INFORMAL WORK

Colombia was repeatedly mentioned as the hottest new market by industry experts; the number of shopping centers has tripled since 2003, and there are many more in the works. At the same time I was told that Colombia is an unusual case. Most shopping centers there operate under the condominium model, horizontally owned by multiple merchants, a common practice in the developing world but one that has been almost eradicated by the globalization of the shopping mall industry and its preference for the single-ownership leasing model. A vivid example is Unicentro, where as of 2013 its 312 locales had close to six hundred owners, 30 percent of whom are the original merchant-owners.[1] Consequently, global developers and brands seeking to conquer Colombia find limited room to negotiate for significantly more square footage. Developers and retail real estate professionals have tried to sidestep this obstacle by building "modern" shopping malls following the industry's dominant leasing method. However, these have been largely relegated to intermediate-sized cities; prime commercial real estate in Bogotá remains inaccessible and highly contentious.[2]

In addition, the price of commercial property in Bogotá's upscale shopping malls is $100 to $300 per square meter, one of the highest in the region and the world, spurred by historical and contemporary factors (*Portafolio* 2014). Among these are the enclaving by elite sectors of the city stemming from Colombia's long history of civil war and the use of the construction business and of commercial real estate for laundering narco-trafficking money (Muller 2004; UIAF 2013). Because of its illicit nature, narco-trafficking is difficult to document, though it is important to remember the example of one of Unicentro's largest stores, presently occupied by Falabella, formerly linked to the narco-traffic and confiscated by the state. More recently, global investors, ranging from Colombians living abroad to investors from declining economies in Europe to neighboring Venezuelans looking for a pro-U.S., "safe" haven for investments, have contributed to hikes in real estate prices (Gomez Kopp 2013). But the biggest culprit behind Bogotá's high prices remains the concentration of landownership in the hands of a few elite families, not unlike the problem of arable land, with 52 percent percent of farms estimated to be owned by 1.15 percent of the population.[3]

Many Colombian retailers entered the business of shopping malls by helping to build them and by investing in the purchase of space. This practice was essential because of a lack of credit and financing. However, it was also fed by long-standing attitudes and ingrained cultural practices that have historically tied ownership of land to security and ownership of a home or a locale to the most secure investments, over and above banks. As one person put it, in locals' view "owning a home is not richness but not owning is poverty." The practice of purchasing space in shopping malls has led to its concentration among the most successful national merchants. Many of the first Unicentro owners, for example, went on to purchase and acquire stores in new shopping mall developments with the result that it is not uncommon to see the same stores in malls in close proximity to each other or even a store with two locations in the same shopping mall. Arturo Calle, one of the largest and most influential Colombian owner-merchants is reputed to own over 45,000 square meters of commercial space in the country, primarily in shopping centers and centrally located areas. Consequently, a spot in a shopping mall is highly coveted and expensive. Many former merchants function as landlords of their original locales, while some of the most successful national merchants, like Mario Hernández, who heads the renowned luxury leather brand, have become savvy real estate investors and important partners in the development of new shopping malls, such as Hernández's Centro Calima. As he explained, "It's like McDonald's. We have two different businesses: the real estate property and the brand. Outsiders think that we're backwards in the topic of shopping malls, and we're not. We're in the vanguard, we're used to purchasing our locations. In the U.S. they have the Simon Group, but we have too much terrain already gained over them."

In other words, not unlike the global shopping mall industry, commercial real estate in Colombia is highly concentrated, but rather than in the hands of global REITs like DDR or Simon it is in the hands of Colombia's elite commercial families. Still, their control is contested and in flux. Increasingly, it is European and Chilean investors such as Casino (Exito), Plaza Mall, and

Cencosud (Falabella, Home Sentry, and Jumbo) and European brands such as Inditex (Zara, Bershka, Stradivarius) that are the leading speculators in the ownership and leasing of shopping malls by developing and purchasing major anchors and large commercial surfaces, as well as the spread of credit and new types of consumption.

This means that Colombia is slated for war, as Fernando de Peña, executive vice president of Mall Plaza in Chile and one of the biggest investors in Colombia, put it at an ICSC panel in Las Vegas on Latin American developments, with more and more interests keen on breaking the traditional condominium ownership model in order to ease the entry of global brands and investors. Similarly, more and more interests are keen on opening up Bogotá for private shopping mall development, whether by expanding the city's outskirts or by reclaiming previously disinvested areas as new areas for growth.

Shopping malls are at the forefront of this urban reclamation process. In the late 1970s the development of Unicentro shopping mall on 124th Street spurred development away from the city's traditional center of La Candelaria and 26th Street toward the north, becoming the leading axis for the development of what almost forty years later is known as the imaginary landmark for the upscale "north." People can recall that visiting Unicentro was akin to a field trip to a rural location, a far cry from its current densely populated area. Today, new shopping malls like Salitre Plaza, Titán Plaza, and Centro Mayor are similarly gentrifying agents but on a much faster scale. Built in strata 2–4 regions, as many of these new malls are, they are at the forefront of the city's gentrification by attracting new developments, including administrative offices and new housing developments catering to higher strata. And in Colombia it's all about class, which is really what the strata system represents, as I discuss later in greater detail. For now, strata are geospatial categories that are linked to the price of rent and to services subsidized by the state, which in turn are popularly associated with class, with strata 1–2 placed at the bottom, 5–6 at the top, and 3–4 largely associated with "middle classes." Hence when most shopping mall developments select strata 2–4 to build their new malls, it is evident that they function as one of the most important forces spearheading the city's upscaling and gentrification.

The more I learned about Colombia, the more I realized what a productive example it provides for analyzing the effects of globalization that are being expedited by shopping malls. Among these are questions of urban planning and space, the homogenization of brands and retail formats, and access to the economy of brands, as well as issues related to the introduction and standardization of new types of consumption and their effects on the informal sector. In what follows, I address some of these issues, paying particular attention to how they intersect with matters of class and with imaginaries of upward mobility, all of which are foundational to the business of shopping malls throughout the world.

## THE WAR FOR SPACE

Forty years after Unicentro became the model for shopping mall–led development, shopping malls are Bogotá's primary engine of urban growth. And no one evidences this pattern of growth better than Pedro Gómez, or "Pedro Trancones" (Pedro Traffic Jams) as he is also popularly known. Since 1968 Gómez's company has developed sixty-four urban projects, with more in the planning stage. Shopping malls have been at the forefront of the company's approach to, as touted in its logo, "a better way of living." Gómez began building in the city's north in the 1950s, right after the "Bogotazo," the popular riots of 1948, when the lower classes rose up after the murder of the populist presidential candidate Jorge Eliécer Gaitán, destroying buildings and commerce. Since then Gómez's influence on Bogotá's urban development has been so powerful that in forty years his developments have not only moved the city's residential and commercial center from the historic district to the north but also started to reclaim previously disinvested areas closer to the center. This is the case with his newest projects, Multicentro and La Felicidad, located in the hot area of growth, Avenida Boyaca between Thirteenth and Twenty-Third Streets, in Occidente, adjoining barrios in the west like Salitre, Fontibón, Modelia, and Hayuelos, which range primarily between strata 2 and 4.

Inspired by urbanist ideals of building self-sufficient "cities within cities" developed by Lauchlin Currie—a World Bank economist and consultant who then served the city and national government in Colombia—Gómez's projects have followed a similar pattern of building residential enclaves with services that would also offer higher levels of security (Reyna 2008). But it was the development of Unicentro that best embodied Gómez's urbanist ideals for an enclave where one could find all the city's offerings in a single place, without *desplazamientos* (displacements, referring here to the need to commute), that is, a city inside a city (Reyna 2008: 91). Unicentro led to the building of apartments and private homes in the nearby area, developments that helped consolidate the dominant model for middle-class living around a residential/commercial urban complex where convenience and hypersecurity stood at the core. The residential neighborhood next to Unicentro is still considered among the most secure areas in the city—a cluster of high-income residential towers, each enclosed with its own private security at the entrance, with signs announcing Alto Voltaje, warning about the ubiquitous electric fences.

After Unicentro, the price of commercial square footage would change forever, as the shopping center became the medium whereby space accrued value in the form of convenience and hypersecurity. Commercial space in a shopping mall has since remained more expensive than outside it, even if located in the same sector of the city. One person who lives in the vicinity of Unicentro told me he purchased a commercial property a couple of blocks from Unicentro whose value is $8 million pesos per square meter, compared to a minimum of $50 million pesos per square meter inside Unicentro. This speaks to the level of real estate speculation inside the mall and to a value accrued not only by its promise of security but also by what is perceived as authenticity. In particular, making a purchase inside a shopping mall is recognized as the surest way to acquire "authentic" products. As a customer at Unicentro explained, "It's cheaper to buy in the street, but it's safer to buy in the shopping center. In the street you don't know if what you're purchasing is new or stolen or fake." This view notwithstanding, "authenticity" can be problematic, as I learned from a taxi driver who told me tales of picking up Unicentro retailers and taking them to San Andresitos to buy contraband and counterfeit goods to sell at triple their value in their "legitimate" stores.

Shopping malls have also served as catalysts for some of Bogotá's busiest commercial and tourist developments, including the upscale Zona Rosa in the north spurred by the Andino, Atlantis, and El Retiro shopping malls and its opposite, the popular and frenzied Primero de Mayo in the south, dominated by bars, discos, and motels steps away from Plaza de las Américas. Alternatively, shopping malls have opened the path to new residential areas emphasizing green spaces, suburban living, or "country houses without exiting the city," as in the case of Santa Fe shopping center and other developments extending the city's perimeter to the north and, more recently, La Felicidad, consisting of seventeen thousand new residences and a shopping center.

Two notable trends emerged from analyzing Pedro Gómez's developments over the past forty years: a growth in the number of private developments from 1998 to 2008, coinciding with the new citywide emphasis on public space and transportation aimed at opening up the city and reclaiming public space instituted during the Enrique Peñalosa mayoral administration (1998–2001); and a marked emphasis on enclosed commercial-residential enclaves so people can avoid desplazamientos (Reyna 2008). These trends point to a rise in residential enclaving alongside the "opening" of the city and serve as reminders of how neoliberal development ends up feeding itself by creating the conditions that demand more development. Consider, for instance, how the construction of new shopping malls has led to more traffic congestion on major highways, hence to greater demand for more residential enclaves containing commerce and services nearby. In other words, mega shopping malls tend to create the very conditions that inform and demand more enclaved residential developments in order to limit the need for desplazamientos, which is how people regularly speak about the difficulty of having to commute from one sector of the city to another. Consequently, shopping malls have contributed to an increasingly chopped up and segregated city.

Because of their long commutes to work during the week, people generally stay within a particular region for leisure, entertainment, and commerce, avoiding venturing to other sectors of the city unless they must or as a form of *paseo* (stroll). On weekends, however, malls are where lower- and middle-income families gather, leading to their being referred to as "clubs for the poor." This is when malls become the places to be: to spend the day, walk around, eat ice cream, take kids to kiddie rides, and, for those with sufficient financial resources, have lunch and see a movie. Indeed, at Titán I met families that had traveled over an hour on the Transmileneo to see the mall and spend the day. Higher-income families, in contrast, are more likely to go to their social clubs (casas de campo) or limit their shopping mall visits to the luxury ones in the Zona Rosa. For instance, a resident of Nogales, one of the most exclusive communities, told me she had never even set foot in Avenida Chile, a middle-class mall that was much closer to her residence than the Andino and Retiro luxury malls she regularly patronized. She also knew exactly when to avoid visiting a mall: "at the start of the pay period and at the end of the month [when people get paid] and on weekends."

In fact, very wealthy Colombians are not different from their counterparts in the rest of the world in regard to their disdain for shopping malls, or at least in posturing this disdain publicly. An example of this position is the 2013 newspaper column by the poet and writer Piedad Bonnett, which predictably criticized malls' promotion of consumerism and the culture of idleness and entertainment that made people favor malls over "real" public spaces like parks, plazas, and streets. The column launched a public debate over the issue, with one rebuttal challenging the existence of free and accessible "public" space in Bogotá and praising malls for being more open than many of the neighborhoods in the north where "even bakeries can reserve the right to admission" (Acevedo 2013; Bonnett 2013).

The fact is that shopping malls are of little use to Colombian elites, who have private clubs to linger at on weekends and can afford to travel and shop in Miami and New York. In Colombia, the Spanish clothier Zara is among the "top" fashion designers one can find at a mall. Consider Diego, who lives in stratum 4 in Chapinero, a gentrifying middle-class neighborhood,[4] and has considerable discretionary income thanks to a high-paying federal government job. Diego was an avid mall shopper when I first met him. But after a trip to New York, where he was able to purchase what he described as two years' worth of brand-name clothing and shoes, he gave up shopping at local malls. Instead, he planned to save money for another shopping trip: "I can save $700 for the ticket, stay with friends, and with $700 more purchase a new wardrobe of brand-name clothes." He was especially proud of the Kenneth Cole shoes he had seen in a Bogotá mall for 400,000 Colombian pesos (around US$200) and had purchased in New York for $78, or 148,000 pesos, and more excitingly, at an original Kenneth Cole store. Almost everyone I spoke to who was identifiably upper middle class and had good jobs in the business or government sector was eager to share stories about shopping in Miami or New York and offer their own shortcuts to stockpiling luxury products, whether it was goods purchased in stores nonexistent at home or at the same stores but at a fraction of the price. It is not surprising that a study of global shoppers at the popular Miami Dolphin Mall found that Colombian travelers are the second most frequent visitors, right after Brazilians (Bowden 2014).

The Dolphin Mall, in turn, delights in its Latin American and other international visitors, whom they cater to with discounts, transportation, and more. I visited Miami's Dolphin riding one of the mall shuttles that link some of the major area hotels with the mall and marveled at the services that were offered. At the entrance to the mall I found a well-staffed visitors' center flashing exchange rates for international currencies and offering coupon books in multiple languages, more akin to an international airport than a mall. The coupon book looked like a passport. It was validated with a "passport stamp" by the attendant, who handed me a booklet in Spanish even before I finished uttering my greeting. But it was the sound of Spanish and Portuguese being spoken everywhere, the crowd of Latin American shoppers

towing large carryon bags to accommodate their purchases, and the ubiquitous stands selling extra luggage to the most zealous shoppers that made clear
the importance of international visitors. In fact, the greater availability of
international flights connecting Latin America and Miami makes a trip to
Miami considerably cheaper than a trip to and from a neighboring Latin
American country.

Returning to Bogotá, shopping malls are limiting the city's ability to control urban planning. This matter was especially at play in debates over Mayor
Gustavo Petro's proposal for the new Plan de Ordenamiento Territorial and
the prospect of a recall election, which resulted in his removal from office and
then reinstatement in what became a national and international scandal.[5]
Petro, a former guerrilla and a left-leaning mayor, had been elected by a narrow margin in a highly contested race—in recent elections Bogotá has
selected candidates on the left, countering the national political preference
for ultraconservative and neoliberal presidents like Álvaro Uribe and Juan
Manuel Santos—and was in the midst of major urban reforms when the
debate over his governance was unleashed. Critics pointed to a lack of citizen
input on the POT, but it was the plan's populist and "socialist" measures that
were of most concern to upwardly mobile groups and powerful organizations
representing commercial interests and the construction industry. Among
these measures were the creation of a less segregated and more inclusive city
by constructing housing for the very poor in central Bogotá; the elimination
of strict zoning ordinances (and distinctions between strictly residential and
commercial space) to encourage more mixed developments; and, most significantly, a provision that projects of over 10,000 square meters provide 35 percent of their space for housing for the very poor. Measures to hold large
developments accountable for the costs of public infrastructural needs, highways for instance, to limit parking, and to accommodate informal vendors
were also especially contentious.

Noteworthy the mayor's contested plan represented the first and most
aggressive attempt by any city administration to limit the ability of large
commercial developments like shopping malls to benefit from the city's infrastructural investments, with little to no payments or giveaways. Developers
were not used to this level of scrutiny. Titán's direct access from the new
Transmileneo line on Boyaca Avenue was a notable example of a major governmental giveaway that I was told about by Octavio Fajardo, undersecretary
of urban planning and a big proponent of the POT: "Everyone knows that
investments in infrastructure lead to a rise in the value of the land. Why

should it be Titán Plaza instead of a public project that benefits from such major public investments?"

Urbanists and activists I spoke to also identified real estate valuation as another way for megaprojects to accrue value. It is not uncommon for differences to exist between the value of land in the official property register and its commercial rate in the market. What is less common, however, and I was told makes real estate so attractive for money laundering in Colombia, is the common practice of using the always more modest property register figure in all "official" transactions while pocketing the difference in the price at which a property is sold and paying less in taxes. As one person explained, "In New York an apartment is worth this, and will be worth this price everywhere, but here you never know what the real selling price is." Urbanists also pointed to the practice of buying land in strata 2, 3 ,and 4 locations and at depreciated rates, only to develop, build, and sell projects as stratum 5 or 6, particularly residential homes.

Needless to say, the POT gained many political foes representing the business, construction, and shopping mall industries. These groups predictably complained of the potential negative effects of stricter regulation on job creation and the opening of new businesses, not unlike neoliberal development advocates repeatedly argue elsewhere in the world. Still, the more I heard about the plan, the more it became obvious that fears of class mingling dominated the public debate, taking attention from key proposals that would finally address the city's ability to place some limits and controls on major developments. Specifically, the proposal to build housing for the lowest income groups in the city's core raised fears about crime and the need for more policing, while the proposal to build mixed-use commercial properties was smeared as a proposal to insert brothels in high-class shopping centers like Andino (Unidad de Investigación 2013; El Espectador 2013). Fajardo, from the city's urban planning office, was clearly frustrated by the symbolic war being waged over their proposal, a war they seemed to be losing against the powerful interests that had historically dominated development. He feared that too many class-sensitive issues had been raised, hitting at the heart of Bogotá's culture of appearances and upward mobility. What's more, some proposals, such as those aimed at limiting the amount of space dedicated to parking, were criticized by poorer sectors of the city. As he explained, it is not only upwardly mobile groups—who like driving from self-enclosed residences in their private vehicles to their private parking spaces and destinations—who protested but also poorer residents, for whom owning and driving a car is an aspiration, one being made possible by new credit and leasing programs.

Class dynamics also play out in regard to the valuation of land and the displacements of locals. Colombia's strata system to some extent helps buffer residents from gentrification but only by keeping a ceiling on residents' expenses for public utilities and services according to strata. However, this system has no bearing on tax increases resulting from a property's valuation or increases in the cost of living. In 2012 this issue was the subject of hearty protests that galvanized residents from strata 1–5 in a common struggle when they received tax bills they could not afford to pay. People demonstrated by burning their tax bills to underscore the great inequities and irregularities in the estimation of taxes that represented increases in the value of property but not in people's ability to pay. These disparities were especially evident among residents of lower strata like Bosa (stratum 2) and Engativá (stratum 3). The demonstration ultimately led to a decrease of 54 percent in the cost to citizens and to the exemption of the poorest sectors but not to a revamping of the failed procedure for estimating payments.[6]

But not everyone is unhappy about the high prices. Gladys, a longtime resident of La Candelaria, a neighborhood that has become popular among tourists and has seen an influx of new restaurants and hostels, was excited about the new Swiss bakery that had just opened near her street. "It's a sign of progress that even with the lack of security in this sector we have a Swiss bakery like this one," she explained, well aware that tourists could afford it and Colombians could not. She was also aware of land speculation in the area. She had received offers from the nearby University of the Andes for her home and was sorry for her elderly neighbors whose daughter sold their house for double the price without informing them, effectively displacing them. But she was staying put. As a longtime resident of a historic district where public services are charged at stratum 1, she did well and felt no need to raise the 400,000-peso ($200) rent she charged a local Laundromat for a small space she purchased with her secretary's salary and with which she now supplements her retirement pension. But she could not guarantee that her daughter would not sell the house and displace the Laundromat and other residents in the future.

People are entirely unprotected from increases in the costs for everyday consumption. There are significant disparities in Bogotá between the cost of average consumer products in different sectors and at different stores, an outcome of the overvaluation of the north relative to the south. A taxi driver who lives in Bachue, a poorer enclave in the north, sandwiched between higher stratas, offered as an example the drink he had just purchased: "I paid 3,000 pesos for this drink. They are taking back what we save in rent by overcharging for the things we consume." Workers from strata 1 and 2 who work in the north are especially hurt by the upscaling of the north and other tourist sectors of the city, which makes already expensive areas even more expensive. Two security officers in Alto Chapinero explained, "In the south they charge you 4,000 pesos to do your hair, in the north they charge you 24,000 and they do the same to your hair, and a roasted chicken is 12,000 in the south and 35,000 in the north, because the north is the north and they charge you more." Both showed me the lunches they bring from home to avoid paying for meals during working hours.

The disparity in prices means that a food basket of milk, eggs, bread, rice, and other basic groceries costs at least twice as such in a higher-stratum barrio store than in a popular barrio store (*Portafolio* 2014b). And not surprisingly, this was one of the loudest arguments against Petro's proposal to build housing for the poor and the displaced in barrios in the north. In contrast to the many openly classist arguments against Petro's proposal that were also raised—that the poor do not "belong" in the north, do not know how to behave, are prone to crime, and so forth—the "matter-of-fact" statement that the poor were simply unable to afford prices in the north became a favorite argument, being seemingly more reasonable and judgment-free (La Silla Vacia 2014). What remained veiled was the history of class privilege that sustained the normalization of different price points.

## THE STANDARDIZATION OF SHOPPING AND THE DISAPPEARANCE OF WORK

During my visits to Bogotá I stayed in Barrio Porciúncula in Chapinero, next to the Avenida Chile Shopping Center (formerly Granahorrar), built in 1982 and revamped in 2010. During my first visit, the mall struck me as quaint. It still had some of the original stores, including clothing and shoe stores whose suppliers were local factories and workshops and where clerks offered to tailor or custom make whatever you could not find in the store. There were also popular trinket and souvenir shops, of the kinds that make shopping mall professionals cringe with horror, next to medium-priced and high-end stores like Totto, Vélez, and Mario Hernández that are omnipresent in Colombian malls.

But just in the span of a year, there were noticeable changes. At least one independent designer had fled the mall, pushed out by prices that had almost doubled for most of retailers I spoke to. Some longtime establishments had seen their locales "requested" by the original owners, and there were empty shops everywhere. Up to twenty-two locales had been emptied, and not because of a lack of interest in the mall. I know of at least one designer/retailer who offered to pay 3.5 million pesos, or $3,500, for a small space but had been turned down. Rumor had it that owners were hoarding retail space awaiting offers from global brands. The latter would likely demand that the small spaces be modified and adapted but were certain to pay and bring in more revenue. The new Ishop was an example: it had acquired the spaces occupied by a number of different owners and merged them to create a grand new store.

Successful retailers and development enthusiasts in the government and retail sectors I spoke to saw little cause for alarm in these trends. In their view, it was just a natural progression that shopping malls become the exclusive domain of modern global brands and retailers; shopping malls were not the place for quaint mom-and-pop stores or new and unproven or independent ventures, and their disappearance from shopping malls should instead be seen as a sign of the local economy's maturity and growth. In fact, shopping mall developers have become extremely selective: they now sell and lease only to recognized *marcas,* or established brands, or to investors representing or in association with global brands, eliminating the opportunity that newcomer merchants once had to invest or to at least claim a spot in a new development. We might suppose emerging middle-class consumers would be excited to see the arrival of more global brands, attesting to Colombia's progress, and welcome the lower prices that greater availability of products may yield. After all, why shouldn't Colombian malls exhibit the homogeneity and mainstream offerings that malls in the rest of the world do?

If we take shopping malls as indicators of wider trends in Colombia's economy, however, there are many reasons for concern beyond fears over the rapidly dwindling opportunities for merchants to invest in real estate and acquire commercial space. First, there is the rapid disappearance of important linkages between retailers and national industries that had historically fed the Colombian economy, not to mention anxiety about the many industries and jobs threatened by imported goods. In fact, what Colombia is experiencing is not dissimilar to the transformations undergone by Mexico after NAFTA, with new trade agreements that are destabilizing the rural economy and tying Colombia's economy closer to the United States. The effects of globalization and the liberalization of trade on the transformation and decimation of local industries are documented outcomes that consumers are regularly told are worth enduring for the privilege of accessing "better," cheaper, and flashier products. Yet focusing on shopping malls to analyze the effects of free trade agreements provides an interesting perspective: we clearly see the substitution of high-quality products for cheaper products, or even for equally priced products of poorer quality, as well as the elimination of artisanal and local industries alongside the "walmartization" of the retail economy. In other words, the case of Colombia's retail sector shows that globalization and trade agreements represent only more trade, not necessarily better products, or better conditions for workers or consumers.

Colombia's malls have been distinguished historically by the presence of national retailers and brands: Arturo Calle, Totto, Mario Hernández, Vélez, Mussi, Studio F, Fuera de Serie, Armi, Tennis, Juan Valdez, and Onda de Mar are staples of most shopping malls throughout the country, an outcome of their early investments. As a result, Colombian shopping malls are quite homogeneous in their offerings; most have the same clothing stores (Studio F, Armi, Arturo Calle), shoe stores (Vélez, Mussi), the same coffee shops (Juan Valdez or Oma), the same fast-food stores (Corral or Frisby), not unlike many shopping malls throughout the world. A big difference, however, is that many of these brands are of Colombian origin, even though they may import parts and produce some goods elsewhere, especially China, and share space with European, North American, and Chilean stores. In part, this relatively high representation of national brands and retailers stems from Colombia's previous seclusion, which aided its development of national brands that are widely recognized across the region. In fact, Colombia represents an aspirational fashion hub in comparison to other Latin American countries, a place where, I was told, one can find high-quality products "just like you would find in Europe." These words were spoken by a Peruvian professional whom I met at a regional shopping mall conference who was taking advantage of her trip to shop for Colombian underwear and jeans, the latter well known for their quality and flattering design. My fashionista friends raved about the popular "butt-picker-uppers" by local brands such as Angel Jeans, which started in San Victorino but has since moved into Centro Mayor shopping malls, becoming one of the few local brands thriving in the current climate. Other product categories for which Colombian retailers have gained recognition across the region are swimsuits, shoes, and leather goods.

Colombia thus provides a sharp contrast to the case of Puerto Rico or Mexico, two Latin American countries with the longest history of involvement with North American retailers and the business of shopping malls. In these two countries, as in many countries in the region, there are few or no national retailers in shopping malls, and most retail and commercial businesses are owned or managed by North American franchises. In contrast, buffered for decades from the incursion of international brands, Colombian retailers were well positioned to develop strong franchises. As one retailer explained, "How could anyone develop Corral Burgers when you have McDonalds and Burger King from day one. Or Frisby or Kokorico if you had KFC?" Corral and Frisby are Colombian fast-food chains, for hamburgers and fried chicken respectively, that remain competitive and a mainstay in most shopping mall food courts.

In addition, it is not uncommon to find in many Colombian stores items that are still produced in local factories and workshops. Mercedes Campuzano, a thirty-year-old shoe entrepreneur from Medellín who has stores all over Colombia, said she had hired over two hundred artisanal shoemakers and proudly pointed out that each shoe sold fed at least seven Colombian families, a fact she often flagged when people questioned why her prices were higher than those of imported brands. Some start-up designers have also managed to secure space in shopping malls by renting from long-time owners at the edges of the current speculation. This has led to the coexistence of many established brands with many *marcas pajarito*, the unknown brands that many in the industry bemoan for lowering a mall's high-end profile, selling everything from party favors to corsets. Still, the days when local brands and merchants can find space in shopping malls are numbered. The muscle of global retail combined with governmental economic liberalization policies and international free trade agreements, most recently the TLC with the United States and the Pacific Alliance with Mexico, Peru, and Chile, are ensuring that this is the case.[7] The coming war over Colombian consumers, then, is slated to partly take place on the terrain of retail. Retail giants like Zara and Forever 21 have already made a huge impact on the retail fashion sector. Leather producers are suffering; most small merchants and designers I spoke to are suffering, not unlike the peasants who in summer 2012 called for a national strike against the TLC for its annihilation of all sectors of the Colombia's agricultural economy. In all, the Colombia I encountered during my research was a country being quickly forced open by trade agreements and bombarded with imported products with few to no protections for local producers and workers.

The state of the leather goods industry is a revealing example. I had the opportunity to speak to many national wholesale leather producers during the Tenth International Leather Goods Fair in 2013, a key event where leather producers from all over the country take wholesale orders from retailers. This year the event coincided with national discussions about the need to protect the industry from the effects of the TLC, and I found many people eager to talk. In particular, people were galvanized by a massive four-kilometer protest organized some months earlier by residents of Barrio Restrepo. This Bogotá barrio is traditionally known for its leather production, and many were eager to take to the streets to challenge the massive dumping of "Chinese" and synthetic leather products for which the TLC was partly responsible. The demonstration was fueled especially by the decision of large retailers like Falabella and Spring Step to stop buying their products and import them instead, effectively eliminating one the largest avenues for Barrio Restrepo leather products to reach consumers.[8] Mario Reyes, director of the association of microentrepreneurs, which was established in 2009 to challenge the effects of the TLC, recalled how their industry was almost decimated after Colombia underwent massive economic and trade liberation during César Gaviria's administration (1990–94). But in his view, today the challenges are far more daunting: "They started importing in 2003, but in 2009 with the TLC there is a lot more product, a hike from 3 million to 4 million pairs of shoes to 12 million to 13 million pairs in 2011, and this year 18 million pairs of shoes. The drop [in sales] has been too big in our sector." Mario was especially adamant about the need for legislation to curb contraband Chinese products, where importers declare products of lesser value than they are worth to save taxes.[9] His group has also called for an increase in the tax on imports, among other measures to protect the competitiveness of Colombian wholesalers.

Restrepo leather producers are arguably more vulnerable than other sectors of the leather industry because they produce more artisanal products, with "less value added" in terms of dominant fashion and design prerogatives. However, producers of high-end luxury leather goods present at the fair also complained about the effect of the TLC. They were especially affected by an increase in the export of the best Colombian hides to the United States and Europe, leading to a shortage of quality leather for local production. At least one producer complained about the inability to remain competitive because of his lack of access to technology. He could not take orders on the Internet or create a Web page for his factory, as could some of his competitors. The consensus among leather manufacturers—with the exception of brands like Mario Hernández that had restructured along global lines—was that the government had opened up the field but done little to protect the local industry.

Knitwear and textiles is another sector that had historically served as direct providers to national stores that has been greatly affected by trade agreements, and later I examine more closely the challenges presented by the hike in imported fast fashion. Even stores that advertised Colombian knitwear were selling products with "Made in China" or "Made in Madagascar" labels. Hence my surprise to come across Laura de Dios colorful artisanal knits at Salitre Plaza shopping center. It turns out that Laura had worked for seventeen years as producer-supplier for Shetland, Colombia's largest retail chain for knitwear and sweaters, until the company was sold, shifting its production model to more standardized imported products in 2010 and forcing Laura to go out on her own. For Laura, and many other local designers and producers, this was a huge blow; it represented not only the loss of one of her largest clients, but also one that had allowed some room for creativity and independent design. "My products become too *hipiosos,* too hippie-like," Laura admitted, meaning that it did not fit the Gap and Benetton model. I found her struggling when we spoke at the small workshop from which she runs her business, along with six female heads of families she employs. She said she was lucky to find a low-priced location at Salitre Plaza, a solidly middle-class mall in Occidente, but her monthly rent of 6 million pesos (almost $3,000), though low compared to other locations, was a struggle. Unfortunately, three years later after we met, I learned Laura had been forced to leave the mall altogether, unable to compete with the challenges of pronta moda, or fast fashion, and the costs of rent and keeping her workshop, added costs not faced by many of her retail competitors that had turned to the importation of products.

The growing favor for global brands was visible at RECon 2015 in Cancún, Mexico, where Latin American shopping mall managers could be seen openly courting global brands like Pizza Hut and Payless. The manager of a new mall in Manizales, a medium-sized city in Colombia, explained to me that she wanted "nothing short of Payless" for her mall, which catered to a relatively upscale consumer base of primarily strata 4 and 5. As she explained, local brands like Spring Step or Aquiles have price points similar to Payless but lacked the prestige she was after. The result is that global brands end up obtaining considerably better lease terms in shopping malls than do local retailers. In fact, local brands are the first candidates for eviction when a Forever 21 or Express seeks space in a Colombian or Latin American mall.[10]

Colombia's film industry is also worth considering insofar as the rise of multiplex theaters and their exclusive location in malls has turned a trip to the movies into a trip to the mall.[11] Multiplexes have become anchors in many shopping malls across the world, valuable for their ability to attract traffic and for providing what is considered one of the cheapest entertainment choices for middle-class families outside their homes. However, most Colombian commercial theater chains like Cinemark (North American owned), Cine Colombia (owned by the local Grupo Santo Domingo), and Cinépolis (Mexican owned) have begun to show Hollywood films exclusively, leaving only a limited number of screens in selected theaters for either local fare or international or alternative films. Hollywood films have long been dominant in Latin America. Media scholars have advanced different interpretations for this trend, acknowledging in particular the political and economic conditions that ease the distribution of Hollywood products (Miller 2007; Ross 2010). The rise of multiplexes, however, is an added threat to local filmmakers and films because they rely on commercial models that prioritize high turnaround (Acland 2003) and because they have distribution deals and formats that favor Hollywood blockbusters. Agreements between IMAX theaters and the Mexican company Cinépolis, one of the largest multiplex chains in the world, with theaters in Guatemala, Colombia, Peru, and even India, to build and develop more IMAX theaters in the region is a case in point.[12] In particular, Hollywood fare is seen as a more reliable and familiar formula for mall multiplexes than is the highly diverse landscape of national cinema. This is how Mauricio Vaca, CFO of Cinépolis, put it: "The problem is that few films from the national cinema are rentable. When programming films, you know what will work with Hollywood fare. You know how many films will be produced and the specifics of their release dates. But it is very difficult to calculate and determine which national movies will be released or have demand. With U.S. films there's a lot more information. You also have franchises and sequels, proven formulas and well-known stars." Vaca also underscored Hollywood's expertise in making *películas espectaculares,* with sound and special events that attract paying viewers to see films in the actual theaters rather than pirated films sold for 2,000 pesos on the street, as another draw that most national movies lack altogether.

In his analysis of multiplexes in India, Ganti (2012) linked their rise to the luxurification of audiences and of the viewing process, and similar processes are seen in Colombia and other parts of Latin America. In fact, countering the shrinking of movie audiences in the United States, where people are turning to home viewing and downloads, audiences in the developing world, who previously shunned visiting single-theater movie houses because of security concerns, are turning in hoards to theaters in shopping malls in search of luxury and security (Miller 2010; Ganti 2012), even though what they come to see is increasingly limited to the same standardized Hollywood commercial fare that dominates theater chains at most malls.

Finally, shopping malls and the globalization of retail are having severe effects on the informal economy, the historic stronghold of Colombia's economy that is still estimated to account for 68 percent of all workers (EFE 2013). Vendors around the peripheries of shopping malls have been especially hurt, while the shopping mall industry touts itself as a key vehicle for "formalizing" employment and bringing informal work to within the purview of "urban" norms. The irony, however, is that shopping malls are not eliminating the informal economy. Contrary to neoliberal policy dictums, scholars have consistently documented that neoliberal development, particularly measures advocating the deregulation of work, are launching processes of informalization alongside an expansion of the groups that gain their livelihood through informal means (Fernández-Kelly and Shefner 2006; Robinson 2008). What shopping malls are definitely affecting is the leverage and attraction of the informal economy among consumers and upwardly mobile groups and the rate of profit for informal vendors, who find themselves unable to compete with malls selling competitively priced and glossily packaged consumer goods.

Still, the persistence of the informal economy was widely recognized by everyone I spoke to. It even has an impact on what many locals still define as a *centro comercial*. For instance, as of 2015 the local branches of the ICSC and the local shopping mall organization, Acecolombia, count 196 shopping centers in Colombia, based on industry standards for structures of over five thousand square feet. However, this number is but a fraction of the *centros comerciales* and commercial structures that are scattered around the country and serve as venues for commerce with differing degrees of informality.[13] In fact, Acecolombia once tried to account for these structures but gave up, frustrated by the enormity of the task and the unreliability of information about their volume of sales and impact on the economy. As Carlos Betancourt, president of Acecolombia, explained, "Every corner became *centro comercial mi casa,* and it ran totally informally without administration, each opened and closed whenever it wanted, and no one knew even how many vendors operated on a spot!" Betancourt was especially frustrated about the spread of San Andresitos and the commercial district of San Victorino and many more commercial clusters throughout the city where hundreds of vendors gather to sell low-priced merchandise, most of it imported or smuggled at retail and wholesale prices. People come to San Victorino from all over the city, and sometimes from farther away, to supply their own stores and commercial businesses, getting there as early as 3 a.m. to take advantage of the *madrugón,* early bird sales, when the best prices and selection of wholesale merchandise is offered on selected days of the week and during the holiday seasons. At any time visiting San Victorino is like attending a massive street festival, where the high density of commerce and street vendors blend in with the commercial structures, making it almost impossible to tell them apart.[14]

In contrast, the spatial segregation of commerce, shopping, and street life away from public areas is one the most distinctive characteristics of new shopping mall developments in Colombia. Enclosed, without access to streets, and separated by private boulevards that add even more physical distance between the mall's boundaries and the public street, shopping malls create a segregated physical reality, entirely different from the normal boisterousness of the city as lived and experienced outside the boundaries of the mall.

Vendors who stock up on products in San Victorino to resell elsewhere, however, are finding it difficult to make a living. We may recall the case of Olivia Mostacilla, Michael Taussig's seamstress friend of forty years whose livelihood has been ruined by "the fashion industry and its cheap clothes from China" (2012: 52). My assistant Natalia also shared the tale of her mom who previously could purchase an imported blouse in San Victorino for 10,000 pesos ($5) to be sold at around 25,000 pesos at a local commercial center. In fact, just as the taxi driver had revealed, her mother had seen many upscale shopping mall store owners purchasing merchandise in San Victorino and stitching new labels in them to sell as their store's upscale brands. Recently, though, Natalia's mother has had to sell the same blouses for at most 15,000 pesos because of the aggressive sales that are facilitated by the growth in imports and the rapid turnaround of new merchandise that has followed the lowering of tariffs and taxes.

Browsing products at a shopping mall but purchasing the same or similar merchandise in San Andresitos or San Victorino was a common strategy among my informants, who were savvy enough about prices and offers available outside a mall to avoid paying its bloated prices. However, when prices at the shopping mall and on the street are similar, the shopping mall almost always wins out because of the prestige associated with it. In contrast, chaotic, popular, and filled with cheap clothes—many of them the type my middle-class informants would consider too trashy—San Victorino and other popular commercial sectors do not carry the aspirational identity of a modern shopping mall. In fact, the advent of sales and promotions are reshaping people's imagination of the mall—as a place that is no longer inaccessible and unaffordable, as a real option over an outlet or a San Andresito. Vendors like Natalia's mother are especially hurt by the massification of products. While shopping malls can increase prices on account of the names attached to their products, informal vendors end up competing with each other, lowering the profit ceilings for everyone.

The irony is that while shopping malls are decimating the profits of the informal retail economy they are also appropriating its marketing strategies. Two examples are early dawn sales and setting up racks with merchandise in the hallways outside stores to attract consumers.

Industry advocates regard shopping malls' attack on the informal economy as a welcome development. In their view, shopping malls represent an effective solution to the problem of informality by creating new jobs and new revenue for taxes that would otherwise be lost through sales in the informal sector. The other side of this picture, however, is not that rosy: retail jobs pay minimum wage, around 612,500 pesos ($306) a month with no commission or a small one, 1.5 to 3 percent, for work characterized by long hours and full days, sometimes including weekends. It is rare for a retail worker to earn more than one million pesos a month, even those selling high-end brands, whose base salary is lower and commission higher. Retail clerks I spoke to complained of long hours, working alone without help if they need to take breaks, and job uncertainty. They are often hired for a period of six months or a year to avoid compensation if they are let go. Commissions are deceptive, as sales goals may be impossible to achieve. Workers do not receive paid vacations, and some stores deduct the cost of merchandise stolen during their shifts. An attendant at a *pastelería* (bakery shop) said she could not even eat a small pastry without paying for it. An older retail worker who, unlike the mostly younger clerks I met, was more willing to dismiss the incentive of working in a mall admitted that she could be making more money selling *arepas* (cornmeal bread) in the street. But the police raids of vendors that were becoming a common sight during her daily morning commute warned her off selling in the street.

But there is an even more aggressive way in which the standardization of commerce is affecting informal commerce: actively seizing it. This is exactly what the megastore Exito, the country's largest retail grocer whose majority partner is now the French group Casino, is doing. Exito is the anchor in most shopping malls throughout Colombia, but it is an insignificant player among the popular classes, most of whom earn on a daily basis and purchase their groceries as needed. Camilo Herrera, a retail and marketing expert, estimates that six of ten Colombians get paid on a daily basis and have little purchasing power at supermarkets. For this group, buying in large quantities is a rarity, and it is small corner stores selling products in a piecemeal fashion—a cup of rice, a few ounces of oil, daily arepas—while offering convenience, familiarity, and easier availability of credit that are favored. Then there is the fact that many middle-class Colombians have little interest or need for the type of loading and storage consumption promoted by supermarkets. For many of them, buying in small quantities is not about lack of resources but efficiency and reduction of waste.[15]

Hence Exito's plan, presented as "collaboration" with barrio stores, or as CEO Claudio Mario Giraldo put it to a group of Wall Street investors in New York, "collaboration toward formalization." By turning small barrio stores into "associates" of Exito, which provides its products at competitive prices as well as technical assistance and marketing to the stores, Exito gains penetration in the popular sectors that had been out of its reach.[16] And for now, the barrio stores remain in the hands of their owners, who do not pay franchise costs for affiliation with Exito. However, many questions remain about the future of barrio stores when vendors are ready to sell and Exito would have a preferential place at the table. Exito's "association" with barrio stores is also likely to erode people's ability to acquire goods through more flexible ways, including bartering and negotiating prices or obtaining informal credit, more possible when products are sold informally and unpackaged than when they are individually wrapped and have barcodes.

I can't conclude a discussion of the standardization of shopping without considering the huge effect that the advent of big retailers and megastores has had on the spread of credit and credit cards and how this financialization contributes to these processes. For instance, since the advent of credit cards in Colombia, big box stores have seen an increase in sales, from 12.8 to 30.06 percent in the years between 2005 and 2012, while sales in barrio stores experienced a drop from 58.96 to 45.26 percent, pointing to the linkage between the availability of credit and people's likehood to make their purchases in big box stores (RADDAR 2012b).

In recent years credit cards have become ubiquitous in many emerging economies, with finance companies extending credit to emerging groups and betting on economies of scale and numbers. In Colombia, credit cards are relatively new, and their penetration is quite limited: they were introduced in 1993 and as of 2011 were available only to 16 percent of the population. Yet since their initial introduction, the rate of penetration has almost tripled (RADDAR 2012a), and anyone visiting a Falabella or Exito store would immediately know why. It is practically impossible to visit these large department stores without being offered a credit card on the spot, and more and more retailers are following this model by developing store-issued credit cards to ensure that consumers will purchase exclusively at their stores. Big-box retailers are in the lead in handing out credit cards based on customers' IDs, with little checking of credit histories, a trend that has introduced new consumers to the world of credit and financing but also pushed large numbers into a life of debt and bankruptcy. In 2001 Colombia's utility company launched "Crédito Fácil Codensa" targeting strata 1–3, which dispenses credit to people who lack a banking history and had never had access to credit based on their history of paying their electric bills. By reaching agreements with some of the largest retailers and big box stores, Codensa has been a key catalyst in the processes of diverting sales from local and smaller retailers to big-box stores like Exito, Home Center, and others.

Marketing has also aided the turn to plastic, forcing consumers to rely on prepaid cards to get bonus points and incentives. For instance, most kiddie rides in shopping malls are sold through credits dispensed through cards, which not only helps to further the use and handling of plastic as the primary form of payment but also serves as incentive for return visits to cash in whatever credit is left. Most movie theaters also accept "bonus" cards, which give viewers discounted prices. However, one of the largest chains, Cinecolombia, requires you to purchase the card for 10,000 pesos and credit a minimum of 30,000 pesos, the equivalent of two and a half movie tickets.

On and on, credit cards and bonuses in the form of plastic come with strings attached, especially handling costs that can range from $5 to $15 a month, a fee that is sometimes charged whether or not the customer used them. But even more powerfully, credit cards are transforming people's involvement with the dream world of mass consumption, allowing the poorest of the poor access to computers, washing machines, and even cars, among other standards of modernity, and the ability to purchase these goods in shining new spaces like shopping malls. In this way, Colombians are recent arrivals to the world of credit but also to the world of debt. In 2013, Colombians were estimated to have an average of 2.4 million pesos, or approximately $1.2 thousand in credit card debt per person, an amount that exceeds the average monthly income for most Colombian families (La República 2013). More troubling, people are accruing debt through the purchase of highly expendable consumer goods—with home electronics, clothing, and home furnishings the three major expenses, alongside education (García 2014).

The result has been a growing polemic over credit cards' high interest rates and their level of penetration and exploitation of poor families. The issue was even featured in one of the most popular editions of *Especiales Pirry*, a popular TV exposé, where Pirry joked that credit cards were handed out so freely that "if you don't pay attention they put it on your car window during a traffic stop, and don't be surprised if you open a soda bottle and credit cards come out of it." The special went on to uncover the exorbitant financing tariffs and fees that banks are charging Colombian consumers, not only for credit, but also for most basic banking activities, making banks, as Pirry poignantly joked during his special, *"la segunda colonización española"* (the second Spanish conquest).[17]

Analyzing the expansion of credit in neoliberal Chile, a country where each citizen has up to 3.5 credit cards, Clara Han (2012) describes how indebtedness was spread by its treatment as a sign of development and growth by governmental and international neoliberal pundits, ignoring the costs to citizens, which include the growth of surveillance through credit reporting systems and the spread of precarity and debt. Most important, she notes that while debt may be tied to individuals, it almost always implicates and affects entire households that may find themselves threatened with the loss of services (e.g., water and electricity), of homes, and even of their social standing and reputations. Han's account of Chile sounds very familiar, and from my observations of the aggressive marketing of credit cards, one that Colombians and other Latin American consumers unfortunately seem slated to repeat.

In all, the globalization of retail is having significant and lasting effects on Colombia's economic and social life, which are evident in matters of urban planning and space, as well in terms of people's daily lives and everyday economic subsistence. Shopping malls are presented as bastions of upward mobility and middle-class well-being. However, when shopping malls become such dominant players as I have shown to be the case in Colombia and likely in other developing nations across the globe, it is important that we inquire more critically into what roles they may be playing and what actions and social transformations are being effected by their growth. At the least, this involves asking whether they promote or, as I hope to have shown, hinder the social mobility and abundance that they so ably project with so much currency and illusion.

Kimco, one of the largest retail real estate companies, flagging its international footprint at the global retail real estate convention in Las Vegas. Photo by author.

This Bogotá bus names four shopping malls along its route, Andino, Granahorrar (Avenida Chile), Salitre Plaza, and Hayuelos, pointing to their role as urban landmarks. Photo by author.

Transmileneo exits that directly connect with shopping malls evidence the type of infrastructural benefits from municipal administrations enjoyed by many shopping malls. Photo by author.

Advertisement for Unicentro's inauguration, Wednesday, April 28, 1976. *El Tiempo.*

Empty storefronts and "For Rent" signs, like these in Avenida Chile shopping mall, are becoming a common sight, an outcome of the growing speculation on retail real estate. Photo by author.

Industry leaders meet in Cancún at RECon Latin America 2015. Photo by author.

View of San Victorino market during the madrugón, or "early bird" sale. The photo, taken around 5:30 a.m., shows the vibrancy of this local market. Photo by author.

Informal vendors flank most shopping malls, and their proximity indexes the mall's level of exclusivity. Here one can see vendors along Seventy-Second Street, directly in front of Avenida Chile shopping center. Photo by author.

Guards astride two-wheeled personal vehicles are a common sight in many shopping malls. Photo by author.

One of the many activities geared to attracting traffic in more popular shopping malls, this contest by City TV was filmed in Gran Estación in 2012. Photo by author.

Frequent and aggressive sales facilitated by the rise in imports are making shopping malls more accessible and a more attractive option than informal markets for consumers.

Family-oriented exhibition at Centro Mayor. Photo by author.

Families socializing and eating ice cream sit under the stairs of Unicentro. Photo by author.

Families strolling in groups, a common sight on weekend afternoons. Photo by author.

The fountain at Titán Plaza, a popular spot for families on Sundays. Photo by author.

A Coca-Cola promotion station serves as "free entertainment" for visitors. Photo by author.

Credit promotions are ubiquitous at most shopping centers. Here a promotion for a credit card by Ripley department store. Photo by author.

This young woman along Chapinero is wearing a style common among professional women; her red camisole coordinates with her red bag and shoes. Photo by author.

Mannequins in Avenida Chile display professional outfits. Photo by author.

More street fashion: office workers with straightened (*planchado*) hair wear color-coordinated shoes and jackets. Photo by author.

"Chiveado" products for sale alongside San Victorino. Photo by author.

Independent designers respond to imports by differentiating their products as "designed and produced in Colombia under the highest standards of design and quality." Photo by author.

Besatón at Avenida Chile, February 27, 2014. Photo by Hector Fabio Zamora. Courtesy of *El Tiempo*.

----

# Inside the Class-Stratified Mall

I only buy in Unicentro and Andino. I would never go to a shopping mall in the south.

**CAMILA**, *thirty-eight, licensed engineer*

It's easy. The rich people are in the north, the poor are in the south.

**JULIANA**, *thirty, private high school teacher*

The middle classes are everywhere fluid and capacious, and nowhere more than in the global South, where scholars and pundits have tended to define it in very optimistic terms. Such is the case in Colombia, where the middle class has become the subject of much celebration and debate. A recent study pointed to the "doubling" of the middle class between 2002 and 2011, from 15 to 28 percent of the population, a number that is estimated to grow to 30 percent in 2012 (Manchego 2012). Similar reports have been advanced by the National Association of Colombian Entrepreneurs, which also points to the country's growing urbanization, growth in per capita income, rise in purchasing power due to the extension of credit, and a lowering of prices for consumer goods, touting that in 2013, 91.7 percent of all homes have a television, 53.9 percent a washing machine, 42.2 percent a home computer, 35.7 percent an Internet connection, 94.7 percent a cell phone, 23.1 a motorcycle, and 13.3 at least one private car (DANE 2013).

When looked at closely, however, the same studies predictably admit that Colombia's 13.8 million supposedly middle-class residents pale in comparison to the 16.5 million living in poverty and the 1.38 million who are wealthy (Angulo et al. 2013; Manchego 2012). Another pressing concern is the arbitrary definition of the middle class used by international entities, such as the World Bank, that are often reproduced by local economists, where people with income ranging from $10 to $50 a day are considered "middle class," with little consideration of local living conditions and costs. Most important, the growth of emerging middle classes is often optimistically tied to consumption, as if the growth in the number of visitors to shopping malls and the purchase of consumer goods by groups never before associated with consumption do in fact signal an actual economic coming-of-age. Seldom mentioned is the extent to which these trends may be tied to the lowering of prices as result of the rise in imports, or to greater access to credit, or to the growth of shopping malls and the transformation of retail in closer proximity to popular classes rather than to the economic health or actual upward mobility of these groups. Also not explored is whether these developments are accompanied by any economic and income redistribution or a lessening of economic inequalities and, equally important, by greater rights and recognition of middling groups in greater society. The case of Brazilian flash mobs of rolezinhos taking over upscale shopping malls to expose the continued fissures of class and race that impair their right to space provides a welcome warning against the easy equation of greater consumerism with unqualified citizenship.

In this context, it is difficult to assess the extent to which middle classes are more of a construct than a reality, though for the purpose of this study some working definitions are in order. This chapter introduces some dominant definitions of the Colombian middle class, exploring how it is locally defined around the strata system. I also expose how issues of space figure in these definitions and how shopping malls have become loaded with meanings around class and social hierarchies, making them into a key space for class expression and differentiation.

## "IT'S ALL ABOUT STRATA"

Informed by some of the difficulties of defining "middle classes," I decided to focus on emerging middle classes defined according to local definitions that link social class to stratum, examining primarily informants who live and identify themselves as stratum 3, most of whom had some higher education and lived in stratum 3 or stratum 4 neighborhoods.[1] As noted earlier, stratas are geospatial categories related to the quality of one's home and to services subsidized by the state, in which a person of strata 1, 2, and 3 pays a lower percentage for services like electricity, water, and rent than does a person of strata 5 and 6. Residents of strata 5 and 6 pay a fee over consumption, while those of stratum 4 pay the assigned price for consumption. Strata are not class categories; you may find people of higher income and resources living in a lower stratum area to save on their living costs, though it is economically more difficult if not prohibitive for poor and middle classes to live in higher strata areas. Different strata areas can also adjoin each other in ways that make it difficult to associate stratum, class, and space. Nevertheless, strata categories have become consolidated into the dominant and most basic imaginary of how class is defined in Bogotá (Aliaga-Linares and Álvarez-Rivadulla 2010; Uribe-Mallarino 2008). This is so even though open discussion about one's stratum and those of other people was not common but functioned more as an invisible reference, especially among people of the middle classes who I found less likely to talk openly about stratum than were people living in poorer sectors of the city. Many of my middle-class informants felt that the mere talk of strata was "low class," with phrases like "se le salió el estrato," "his/her stratum kicked in" or "became noticeable," often used to reproach low-class or vulgar behavior or manners (Wallace 2014). According to this imaginary, being middle class and upwardly mobile places one above any "talk of stratum," itself conceived as a "vulgar" and debased topic of conversation. Camilo, my consumer researcher friend, put it in simple terms: "To move up a stratum is like improving your race. For the rich even talk of stratum implies poverty, while for stratum 6 stratum 5 is poor, and so on."

Generally, however, lower income groups are associated with strata 1 and 2, strata 3–4 with middle classes, and strata 5–6 with higher income groups, references and associations that are regularly made without full knowledge of people's background, income, or education or their actual class or the stratum in which they live. Most important, most of my informants recognized that these categories fall short of fully describing the income inequality and incredible disparity in wealth and resources that exist. For that, one would need to acknowledge the many people who live much below any official stratum classification, as well as those who live over and beyond the officially recognized stratum 6. Thus it is not uncommon for people to sarcastically— but revealingly—refer to "made up" strata in the range of minus zero to the thousands. In fact, strata have become so misleading and inflated that the city administration has been considering proposals to eliminate their use in favor of more accurate and precise means to determine people's socioeconomic standing, for instance, tying stratum groups to people's income rather than the quality of their homes. What these measures are likely to leave untouched is the popular fixation with indexing class and status differences in a society that is marked by deep social inequalities.

As reference, government statistics document that upwards of 32.7 percent of Colombians live in poverty. While poverty in Bogotá, 11.6 percent, is lower than in rural areas, where it stands at over 46 percent, it is still in double digits and not insignificant, and it likely underestimates the most abject poor (DANE 2013). In a similar manner, strata have become strictly associated with geographic area. In Bogotá, the south is generalized as an impoverished area, the north as a space of affluence, and the Occidente or western part of the city with middle classes and emerging groups, even though these groups are in reality more complexly distributed throughout the city. Consider the contrasting examples of Winston and Juan. Winston, a taxi driver, lives in stratum 2 Engativa and owns his own house and the car he drives to work and has some extra funds from informal side activities. He was probably one of the most well off middle-class informants I met and admitted he could well move to a better area but had become *emañado* (attached) to the easier life-style offered by a more affordable stratum 2 community. He said he did not care much about appearances, like others who had moved up and chosen to move, having to pay more in the process. Juan, a professional chef, for his part had grown up in a solid upper-middle-class neighborhood, stratum 5, going to private schools and colleges and even traveling abroad, but now lives in La Candelaria. This neighborhood is cataloged as stratum 1 because it is a historic neighborhood, not necessarily because of its lack of resources. In fact, both the presidential palace and the most exclusive private university, Los Andes, are located in this sector. La Candelaria has become a bohemian spot, attracting tourists and more educated, culturally oriented members of the middle classes like him who bemoan the elitism and push for "good" neighborhoods preferred by more traditional middle classes. In his case, he had purposely chosen La Candelaria as the site for his restaurant and residence well aware that neither his profession, *cocinero,* nor the neighborhood in which it is located is well regarded according to the social conventions of class held by many of the friends he grew up with as well as his family.

Aware that income and stratum are not always coterminous and that class is never a static construct but a project of differentiation, I also decided to include emerging groups more broadly, including residents from strata 2–5, who either self-identified as *clase media,* or middling groups, or were eager to share their views on these groups. In fact, not unlike what has been documented elsewhere, opinion polls indicate that more people self-describe as middle class than are accounted for by economic measurements, and this is the case in Colombia where in a recent poll 59 percent self-described as middle class, versus the 30.5 that are cataloged in this manner by the extremely generous standards of the World Bank (El Tiempo 2014a).

I also focused on groups whose household incomes ranged from 1,500 million to 4 million (roughly $600 to $2,000 whereas minimum wage stands at 612,000 pesos or $306.00), echoing the average of 3,378.395 for a household of four that marketers use to define middle classes locally.[2] While higher than the minimum income with which economists define "middle classes," this medium also reflects Bogotá's high rents and living expenses, not unlike in other global cities where living costs limit the reach of higher incomes.[3] In addition, all of my informants were regular visitors to malls, the site and surroundings where I recruited most of my informants. In particular, I focused on residents of Occidente and visitors to shopping malls there. This section of the city is recognized as a new stronghold of the middle class, an aspirational neighborhood for emerging groups, and the site of Salitre Plaza and Gran Estación, two of the largest and most popular shopping malls among emerging classes. I also did many observations and interviews around Avenida Chile shopping mall in Chapinero, an older and less aspirational mall, next to my research home base in the middle of a financial and administrative section of the city that attracts professional office workers, many from stratum 3 and hailing from all over the city during lunchtime and regular office hours. Comparative interviews and observations were also carried out in Unicentro, a premier upscale mall in the north (multistrata but primarily upscale) and Centro Mayor, one of the largest malls in the south, which is primarily strata 2 and 3.

However, I also kept in mind that the growth of "middle classes" has been accompanied by a simultaneous rise in the levels of inequity, whereby what has experienced the largest growth is not "middle classes" but the gap between the very rich and the poor. According to statistics from the Centro de Estudios Económicos Regionales, the wealthiest 10 percent of Colombia's population earns half of the gross domestic product, while the poorest 10 percent barely earns 0.6 percent (Correa 2013). Indeed, the power of the elite in Bogotá (and Colombia at large) is legendary and recognized even by the most humble residents who were as equipped to name the most powerful monopolies as were my most elite informants. The media and beverage monopolies of the Ardila Lülle family, owners of RCN communications and Postobón drinks, and of the Santo Domingos, owners of Caracol and Bavaria Beer, were repeatedly mentioned as examples of the type of mega monopolies owned by the most powerful families. Tatiana Santo Domingo, an heiress of the Santo Domingo clan who married Monaco's Prince Andrea Casiraghi, is even reputed to be wealthier than the royal prince she married. Also recognized is the power held by *abolengo,* or white creole, family names such as Los López, Los Posada, Los Urrutia, Debrigard, Ospina, Michelsen, Santamaria, Sanz, and more, sustained and reproduced across generations by private schools like Gimnasio Moderno, Nueva Granada, and Los Nogales; private universities like Los Andes, la Javeriana, and Universidad del Rosario; and country clubs such as Los Lagartos, El Country Club, and El Nogal, the latter all spatially isolated in the north. In addition, the continued hold of *roscas,* or socially sanctioned networks of nepotism, in employment and for accessing favors and resources at all levels of society and the growing demands for travel and education abroad among the upwardly mobile continue to present strict barriers to social mobility against which the "gains" of middle classes remain modest at best.[4] Thus, aware that class hierarchization affects all sectors of Bogotá's society and can never be understood in a vacuum, I consider in the next chapters some of the dominant workings, definitions, and ideologies of the most powerful and elite groups in society, particularly in relation to the continuous policing of boundaries of status in relation to consumption.

Finally, like other global middle classes, Bogotá's middle class is highly vulnerable and diverse to the point that it is not rare to see stratum differences within one family. José, another taxi driver from the south, explained, "I'm stratum 2. I have SISBEN [government-subsidized health services]. My brother is stratum 4. He is a professional. I live in stratum 3 because it's my father's home. But I consider myself stratum 2. This car I drive is owned by the company, not me." Or at the higher end of the spectrum, consider the case of Santiago, an engineer who migrated from Tunja (Boyacá) where he lived as stratum 5 but moved to stratum 3 in Bogotá while he attended Los Andes, one of the most elite private universities, with financial aid. He now lives in an apartment owned by his parents that is stratum 5 but identifies as stratum 3 because of his salary, 2 million pesos, which has him struggling to cover his costs. Notice how José identifies his stratum as lower class because he receives SISBEN and does not own his home or car, while he identifies his brother as middle class because of his profession. Santiago, for his part, identified his middle-classness purely in terms of his income, not his relatively better off background.

When I asked middle-class informants what defines the middle classes, the responses were just as varied. While most people identified middle classes with strata 3–4, definitions ranged from those who owned a home or a car, both widely recognized aspirational goals of many middle classes achieved by a small percentage of bogotano families, or with groups who earned about 1.5 to 2 million pesos a month, or more popularly, with people who were professionals or had "titles," which implied some formal education. Younger respondents who are faced with highly inflated and prohibitive prices in real estate, in particular, placed less emphasis on owning a home. As Oscar, a resident of Ciudad Salitre in his early fifties, and one of my few informants who owned both a car and his home, explained, "It used to be that middle classes owned their home, and maybe a car. Now it's the other way around. Middle classes are more likely to purchase a car, and maybe a home." In 2014, Bogotá's Secretaría de Hacienda chronicled that the city's real estate valuation has more than doubled since 2008, from $121 billion to $235 billion, a rate that has made purchasing a home an impossibility for most middle-class bogotanos, which is evident in the decrease in the number of families purchasing their home, from 50.51 percent in 1997 to 37.9 percent in 2012, while car ownership showed only a slight rise, from 22.2 percent of homes with their private car in 2003 to 24 percent in 2012 (DANE 2007–12).[5]

Notwithstanding Bogotá's complex distribution of stratum groups throughout the city, as a general rule Bogotá remains quite segregated, particularly because of its history of violence, mega securitization, and self-enclaving. I met residents from the upscale north for whom the south started as high as Seventy-Second Street rather than in the official designation, South First Street, and at least one claimed to have never been to Plaza de Bolívar and had avoided the entire historic center of La Candelaria altogether. The relative inaccessibility of the San Victorino market provides a good example of the spatial politics affecting residents' mobility across symbolic boundaries of class and space. While often described as dangerous, inaccessible, and out of the way, San Victorino is in fact located in the center of the city's historic district, close to the tourist neighborhood La Candelaria and in walking distance to the Plaza de Bolívar and the Palace of Justice. The market's spatial "accessibility" hence has little to do with its location and everything to do with its social repute, which places it beyond the socially accessible boundaries of more upwardly mobile groups in the city.

## THE SPATIAL POLITICS OF SHOPPING AND SECURITY

Shopping centers follow this dominant division of class and space, with those in the south, such as Plaza de las Américas, Centro Mayor, and Tunal, catering to lower classes with lower prices and more popular stores. In the south, one is more likely to find mom-and-pop stores or more popular national brands, whereas the north is the premier domain for international brands. Franchises may also offer the same goods but differently priced, or sold at different levels of promotion, at malls directed to different strata. This spatial/class segregation of shopping malls is so widely recognized that it was summoned as one of the biggest arguments against Mayor Petro's proposal to develop low-income housing in stratum 6 areas. Then, in addition to classist fears about the rise of crime and disorder that would be brought about by these groups, critics raised the specter of a "class war" as the unavoidable product of having the poor live close to Centro Andino. As a critic put it in a Facebook thread, exposing the poor to "beautiful products they can't afford" was akin to "bringing the hungry close to a place where there's a lot of food without allowing them to eat." On and on, the idea is that the poor have "their own shopping malls" and nothing to look for in the north, while just as the two respondents quoted in the epigraphs noted, the upwardly mobile have no reason to shop in the south.

This spatial/class segregation through shopping malls challenges the facile view that the spread of shopping malls signals the social opening and democratization of society. Instead, the development of shopping malls in lower-income communities has also contributed to anchoring class segregation and to the self-enclaving of upper-class sectors that continues apace. The implicit message here is that lower-middle-class groups may have access to shopping malls and to the some of the same brands that were once the exclusive domain of the upper-middling groups but only if they stay in place/space without venturing to the exclusive malls and neighborhoods of more affluent groups.

Shopping centers in the north hone in their class exclusivity through a greater representation of international brands, including recently arrived luxury brands like Louis Vuitton and Swarovski. In the north, security (or the performance of security) is tighter and events and activities are limited or reduced to less crowd-attracting programs. In addition, parking is more expensive and exclusive in the north where there is also a greater variety of products that are often displayed more freely for people to touch and try.

Access to exclusive parking has become a key means of class differentiation. While most Bogotá shopping malls are accessible via public transportation, how one gets to the mall, whether driving one's car or on public transportation, also matters, especially to higher-income groups seeking to differentiate themselves from the shopping mall masses. This explains the popularity of parking clubs and other exclusive parking offers by the most upscale shopping malls, which help set selected customers apart, not only from those who may arrive on public transportation, but also from the growing groups who are accessing cars and claiming the same parking slots when they drive to the mall. A good example is Andino's by-invitation-only Andino Pass, offered to its most loyal customers, where the first and most popular membership benefit listed is access to an exclusive parking area.

In contrast, shopping malls in the south and southwest (Titán, for instance) incentivize visitors with a greater presence of green and public leisure areas, as well as fountains and benches where people can linger. These serve as a magnet for families who make visiting a shopping mall a weekend trip, sometimes traveling for over an hour to reach a mall. Accessing "public areas" at a mall, however, always comes with the price of being exposed to brands and stores that remain largely inaccessible as public areas are always strategically located in the interior of the mall, ensuring that even the most humble visitors get exposed to all its commercial offerings, as is the case with Centro Mayor's interior plaza or Titán's water fountain.

Public events, concerts, exhibitions, and other cultural programming at shopping malls are also class-stratified and directed at different types of visitors and constituencies. Consider the contrasting cultural/entertainment events held in April 2014 at Centro Mayor, the largest mall in the south, and El Andino, the premier shopping mall in the north. True to its populist image, Centro Mayor hosted the exhibition *Tesoros, Mitos y Misterios de las Américas,* for which replicas of the Chichen Itza pyramids, the *moai* of Easter Island, and other Latin American archaeological landmarks were spread throughout the mall as a draw for families and visitors. For its part, Andino launched a more exclusive children-oriented game, the fairy tale adventure of "Pascual Andino," a North American–style "Easter bunny" celebration complete with egg hunts and giant replicas of Easter bunnies. Not only did Andino's event draw on a more "global" (North American) theme, but it also followed a pattern that is common among exclusive malls: targeting public events mainly at children, not the general public, to avoid attracting the "wrong" type of crowds, namely, those visiting for entertainment rather than shopping. Andino honed in its "children-only" program by enclosing the activity areas, a very different approach from the exhibition at Centro Mayor, which was located throughout the mall and accessible to any of its visitors. More popular malls are also more likely to feature crowd-gathering events, even filming TV contest shows like *Si te ven, ganaste* (Gran Estación, May

2012) or placing large screens for sports events and concerts that invite crowds to visit and linger.

In fact, when I asked visitors of Centro Mayor why they preferred this shopping mall over others, some of which were in closer proximity to their barrios, the answer was often because there was a lot more for their families to do. People pointed to the affordable entertainment alternatives, like kiddie rides that cost only 5,000 pesos for fifteen minutes, sketch stations where children can paint and keep their portraits for 5,000 pesos, and even the giant temporary ice-skating rink that customers could access with hefty pro-rated discounts with proof of purchase.[6] But even more often, visitors mentioned the number of promotion and marketing exhibits that could be used as play stations or as a background for pictures, the likes of which were entirely absent in shopping malls in the north. Indeed, most shopping malls' entertainment offerings involve marketing promotions that are spaced throughout the mall as family and crowd attractions. These were the most accessible entertainment options for the poorest families, not only because they were free, but also because they often involved a freer social context. For instance, some of these ads were freestanding and available to anyone to interact with and use as backgrounds for family pictures or were part of games in which crowds were actively encouraged to participate.

In the north background music is indiscernible or limited to classical music or a jazzy live pianist, while in the south recorded merengue and popular rhythms hit your ear at the moment of entrance. Hallway stands sell popular products like toys and trinkets and *obleas* (wafers filled with dulce de leche or other sweets) that you're likely to find for sale on the street, whereas northern malls lack hallway stands altogether or rent them only to upscale products like design custom jewelry or the sale of services like telecommunications. Bathrooms never run out of toilet paper in the north, while in the south toilet paper is a rarity and an amenity people must purchase for 200 pesos, or 20 cents.

Earlier, I pointed to the performance of security that characterizes most malls because while some upscale malls make the pretense of checking your bag with a magnetic strip (Unicentro) or having a dog sniff your car for explosives when entering the parking area (Andino), security seemed more like something the mall was assumed to have and embody than something that I saw enforced and acted upon. In fact, security and policing in Bogotá follow trends similar to many global cities: it is everywhere but increasingly invisible (Gilliom and Monahan 2012; Molotch 2014). I was told by most of the shopping mall managers I interviewed that security is their largest expense, roughly 30 to 35 percent of their budget. Guards are visible everywhere. Many ride two-wheeled electric vehicles around the mall, while some stand in strategic locations carrying threatening-looking rifles and security gear. Still, most security at the mall remains invisible in the form of hidden cameras and undercover officers dressed as civilians.

In fact, many malls equip their cleaning staff with the same monitoring devices and radios that their security staff has, doubling their role as both cleaning and security workers, which explained the ubiquitous presence of cleaning crews in areas that seemed spotlessly clean. Not surprisingly, the cleaning staff is neither recognized nor paid for the additional surveillance work that they are being asked to perform, particularly in areas that are off-limits to regular security, like public bathrooms. It is noteworthy that the cleaning and security workforce is hired from the same lower-class groups in society and are paid minimum wage despite working onerous hours and under difficult conditions. It is not uncommon for shopping mall security guards to have shifts of twelve hours, standing the entire time, with only a forty-minute lunch and two ten-minute breaks during their shifts.

Publicly, most security act almost as information and welcoming staff, hinting at O'Dougherty's (2006) perceptive observation that shopping mall security is itself a form of PR, a public relations mechanism to convey that security is a positive presence and that it is there ready to act upon and regulate social difference as needed. This was especially true at the point of entrance. Titán Plaza is perhaps the best example of this. While I was told that Titán has at least three different companies in charge of security and there are guards patroling the food court warning people to safeguard their bags and belongings, the busiest entrance is directly connected to the Transmileneo public transit exit and hence almost impossible to monitor. In fact, the security guard at the door confirmed that his job was counting visitors, not stopping them. His hand-clicker had counted two hundred visitors in the past five minutes, a slow day, given that he had counted as many as five thousand visitors in twenty minutes.

We could argue that shopping malls have contributed to the internationalization of security and to self-imposed ideas about who belongs to these spaces and *quien no tiene nada que buscar ahí* (who has nothing to look for there). We have already seen the relative weight of the spatial/class divide between the north and the south and how it affects who does or does not feel welcome to shop and linger in different types of shopping malls. Indeed, consumption scholars have long shown that intimidation, fear, and the shame of being exposed as a "nonconsuming" out-of-place subject can function as powerful deterrents for marginalized groups, which contribute to their exclusion from spaces of consumption alongside their historical pathologization as aberrant and unworthy consumers (Chin 2001; Zukin 2005). To this, we must add consideration of the "threshold fears" (Gurian 2006) and the "aesthetics of intimidation" (Ganti 2012) projected by most spaces of consumption, the ideological and cultural power of consumer landscapes, and what these spaces *do* to the bodies and affectivities of visitors (Miller 2013: 845; Goss 1993; Thrift 2007). In other words, it is important to acknowledge that many times a security officer may be less relevant to the surveillance and policing of a shopping mall than the look and feel of its extravagant corridors, or the flashy and illuminated product displays, or even the intimidating model-like sales clerks or the stares of other visitors, as I discuss later in greater detail.

The result is that, despite their class and spatial stratification, shopping malls in Bogotá are frequented by a considerably homogeneous visiting public of emerging and upwardly mobile groups, even if of low stratum. Visitor's studies by Titán Plaza confirm this pattern, showing that 81 percent of its visitors are stratum 3 (47 percent) and stratum 4 (34 percent), while groups of higher strata are scarce, despite the mall administration's efforts to court them.[7] In other words, shopping mall visitors are overall quite different from the popular crowds one would find at the city's center, or even at the outskirts of the mall. That's where you will see more marginal groups and informal vendors of all types: the woman selling *tinto* (black coffee) or arepas, or cell phone minutes, or trinkets, and even beggars at different proximities to the mall: at greater distance in the north and in new centers like Titán Plaza but ubiquitous in the south's Plaza las Américas, reflecting different degrees of surveillance and policing. Crowds outside the malls are also more racially and ethnically diverse than inside it, though there is greater diversity in malls in the south than in the north, where indigenous and Afro-Colombians are a rarity, unless they are hired as staff. Cleaning staff and security guards, in particular, have a strong representation of Afro-Colombians who, I was told, were especially sought after as security staff because of ingrained racist ideas about their supposedly stronger "build."

Still, my expectation that shopping malls would be exclusive and oversecuritized spaces, informed by many scholarly discussions of contemporary malls as highly policed spaces, was challenged. Instead, with the exception of higher-end malls in the north, most malls seemed to be open to anyone who "performs" the role of a shopper, as well as quite accessible via public transportation. This accessibility is one of the reasons some scholarship on Latin American malls has suggested that they are far more accessible and democratic than shopping malls in the United States, places that consumers can and do treat like "parks, streets, homes and offices" by transposing daily activities from public life onto the mall (Stillerman and Salcedo 2012). My observations, however, caution me from such rosy conclusions drawn from comparisons with malls in the United States and Europe. For decades generations of North American scholars wrongly argued, based on similar comparisons, that Latin America was a haven of racial democracies, mainly because of the scholars' own projections and failure to read and assess racism critically and as expressed in particularized locations. Similarly, I question some of these more optimistic studies' ability to read and assess how class and social inequalities are expressed, as well as actively reinforced, through shopping malls.

For instance, I noticed that use of the mall by different groups remains highly stratified. First, street vendors and the "indigent" are forbidden to enter by guards who are instructed to restrict admission to these groups, even if they only seek to use the restroom facilities. As explained by Carlos, a twenty-one-year-old Afro-Colombian guard from Valle Dupar whom I met at Salitre Plaza: "*ñeros* [lowlifes], indigents, and street vendors" are three groups management most seeks to target, admitting that it breaks his heart to turn away street vendors even after they request permission to come into the mall just to use the bathroom facilities. There is also a temporality at play in the class makeup of shopping mall visitors. On weekends, the food court, stores selling ice cream, the "free" architectural or design attractions like fountains and gardens, and freestanding seating areas are filled with *"familias Miranda"* (a pun drawing from the common family name Miranda, which loosely translates as "onlookers," used for groups who gather around the mall's public/entertainment areas and ice cream stores primarily), while most stores remain deserted and empty. The familias Miranda phenomenon is a key terrain of middle-class differentiation, denoting families whose use of the mall is limited to strolling and visiting and whose presence is highly visible because they gather in the public areas to eat ice cream and socialize, or walk in groups, or limit their strolls to the hallway areas, hardly ever entering the stores. Arguably, the very presence of these families is a testament to the use of the mall by the lower middle classes, though it is important not to lose sight that their visits are restricted to public areas while their presence remains socially stigmatized as familias Miranda. In fact, solidly middle-class informants were quick to point out and deride these groups, commenting on their lack of purchasing power and even ridiculing them for being so poor that "the whole family has to share an ice cream." Other monikers for these families teemed with social prejudice. Among these are "familia Peláez" and "familia Robollo," slang terms drawing on popular last names and the root words *pelao* (broke) and *robo* (theft) to underscore these groups' poor and morally suspect status.

I found that many so-called familias Miranda seemed well aware of these stereotypes, which affected their use of and how they went about the mall, particularly their preference for areas that conveyed greater degrees of accessibility. For instance, Titán's water fountain was especially popular among my informants. Here I asked women with children what sections of the mall they preferred and which shopping malls they liked visiting with their families, and the response almost always followed a similar pattern: malls where families are more visible, where there are more places to rest, where there are more activities and attractions, and where there is a variety of stores with affordable prices. Angela, a single mother who works two jobs, as an attendant in a bakery and as a tailor, was very straightforward: "I want to feel comfortable, and this is one place where I know there are always families present, and where you are left alone." She described being a regular visitor at Titán mall since it opened, even though she had only visited the fountain, the food court, and the kiddie rides, all of which were in close proximity, another convenience that signaled to her the mall's greater accessibility for families like hers.

Titán mall is especially interesting for examining intraclass dynamics because it purposely targets strata 4–5 and above but is located near neighborhoods that are primarily of strata 3 and 4, and because it features stores never before seen in Colombia, like Victoria's Secret or Forever 21, that even stratum 6 covets, making it a rare space for class intermingling and class performance. In fact, differences in class/stratum among visitors was a recurrent topic in my interviews with visitors, who were prone to comment on these differences or used them to describe their own class statuses and positions. Certainly, middle classes are never homogeneous, and it is the very processes of social differentiation among middling groups and vis-à-vis other groups that constitute the most important aspect of any class and identity formation. And defining oneself as upwardly mobile in opposition to familias Miranda was a key element of self-differentiation.

It is important to appreciate that shopping malls are a relatively new development for most residents of Bogotá and Colombia at large, and that until recently, shopping malls were either not accessible or largely out of reach to most of my emerging middle-class informants. Even for frequent visitors, shopping for clothing and other goods in a shopping mall was a relatively recent experience. In fact, even my youngest informants, in their early to mid-twenties, recalled the San Andresitos or stores in the center or outskirts of the city as the venues for their first shopping experiences with their families, not shopping malls. Margarita, a self-identified mall rat in her early twenties who visits her nearby mall Gran Estación on a weekly basis, recalled, "I remember when I was between six and eight years old, the place we would always go to shop for new clothes was the San Andresito of San José, because it had all the shoes and brands at very low prices. And the stores were not like now. There was a vitrine, and you'd go in and the merchandise was not displayed, you had to ask for it. And they had a small area with a curtain to try on clothes where everyone could see you." She went on to explain that the activity of shopping was very different then than today, how it was a task-oriented trip to secure whatever was needed but never about lingering: "It's not like today where you go and spend the day and get an ice cream on the way." Sebastian, another student who lives in proximity to Gran Estación and is also in his twenties, could not even remember where his family shopped when he was kid because the stores and bags were not marked and had no visible brands like today. Similarly, I met many people during their first visits to some of the newest malls or who had only begun to visit modern malls in the past few years, often prompted by friends, family members, or even their children. For instance, Winston, the stratum 2 taxi driver mentioned earlier, was introduced to Titán by his fifteen-year-old daughter who insisted they go there to purchase her Christmas gifts. He claimed to have spent 1,300 million pesos, or about $750, in the traditional once-a-year Christmas splurge purchase of new clothes for his family, following the traditional custom where people save year-round to buy most of their clothes at Christmas or midyear. This is the time when many workers receive their *primas,* biannual bonuses given to full-time employees with benefits, a time that still determines the shopping season for all workers, though this practice is increasingly challenged by the greater frequency of sales and promotions that are pushing people to shop year-round. In 2013 Colombian malls inaugurated Black Friday sales, adding to the abundance of confusing ads about the best time for cost-conscious families to shop.

Finally, the few respondents who were familiar with malls from their inception pointed to changes in their use of and consumption at the mall. Jennifer, a young lawyer whose family visited Plaza las Américas in the southwest, recalled how visiting the mall was the family plan itself, one that never involved purchasing products, just like the many familias Miranda who continue to make up the largest group of shopping mall visitors: "It was never the place where we would go shopping. Instead we would go get an ice cream or maybe eat lunch. It's not like today when you go to the mall to look for stores or a particular brand and to shop." Beatriz, a professional architect in her thirties, remembered visiting Unicentro with her family, but for them the mall was the spot to get *perros calientes* (hot dogs) on weekend outings, never the place to go shopping for products, much less for fashion. In this way, my informants anchored their class mobility by describing these early shopping memories as part of their "past," even though similar experiences are an everyday reality for many others who still rely on popular markets.

As the first modern, large shopping mall in Bogotá, Unicentro surfaced repeatedly in my informants' recollections of their shopping histories. It was the main example of the once aspirational shopping mall that for generations served as the reference for modernity and that people either coveted visiting or visited rarely, in contrast to the current popularization of shopping malls that places them in much closer proximity to communities.

While shopping malls are more accessible today, shopping at a mall is still the source of considerable status for many of my informants. For instance, when interviewing the well put together office workers around the area of Chapinero, most of whom hailed from the south and were stratum 3, about where they had purchased their work clothes and accessories most recalled the name of the shopping mall—Centro Mayor, Tintal Plaza, Plaza de las Américas, Gran Estación—and seldom the name of any actual store. Consistently the shopping mall became "the brand" that was flashed. In contrast, the same exercise around Unicentro, the premier upper-middle-class mall in the north, yielded names of shopping malls but also the names of local and international brands and stores, such as Mussi, Zara, Mercedes Campuzano, and Stradivarius, among others.

Indeed, until the early 2000s shopping malls in Bogotá were largely segregated in the most upscale areas of the city toward the north (Unicentro and Andino) and not as accessible as they became a decade later when the number of shopping malls tripled throughout the country, surfacing all over Bogotá, including in marginal barrios in the south and in emerging neighborhoods such as Occidente in the west. Notable examples are the development of Salitre Plaza (1996) and of Gran Estación (2006) in the west and Centro Mayor (2010) in the south. These developments brought shopping malls to groups that previously had to travel beyond their immediate communities to visit a mall, providing a level of accessibility to stores, brands, amenities, and experiences of "modernity" that were previously out of their reach, while helping to validate the coming-of-age of the region and its residents. The opening of Salitre Plaza, the first modern shopping mall in Occidente, was attended by then-Mayor Antanas Mockus and by business leaders from throughout the city and blessed by an auxiliary bishop, making for an event that was touted as momentous and a sign of optimism for Colombia (El Tiempo 1996). Eight years later, the success of Salitre Plaza led to the development of La Gran Estación, a megamall with 160,000 square feet, less than a mile from Salitre Plaza, helping to consolidate the area's commercial identity and attracting even more development, including an expansion of the mall into a second, even more luxurious phase and a string of corporate office buildings in its proximity. La Gran Estación's webpage video captures the ethos of upward mobility at the heart of its marketing efforts: "We were born for those who decided they could be more and they achieved it; for those who are not afraid to get ahead without leaving behind where they came from. We were born to provide a place for those who believe that they can do, that they can achieve. For those who do not want to pretend, because they simply are."

Gran Estación's marketing video addresses its visitors as those who have "made it," though the fact is that most of its visitors are best described as in the process of becoming. The level of class differentiation among visitors is well recognized among shopping mall managers, who regularly issue press releases announcing their visitors are strata 3, 4, and 5 but are the first to admit that weekends belong the strata 3 and 4 visitors and even lower, particularly residents from the nearby area. The manager of Gran Estación explained that during the week its visitor profile is boosted by the corporate types who work in the nearby towers built following the construction of the mall. On weekends, however, when the mall is most crowded, the rate of average purchases falls, pointing to visitors with less purchasing power.[8] The manager of Titán shopping mall agreed about the importance of lower stratum groups to its survival: "My bosses ask me to bring more people from strata 5 and 6, but I can't focus on them because they go shopping in Miami. I focus on strata 3 and 4, who are the ones who make their purchases here." Like other shopping mall managers, he emphasized the importance of never underestimating the purchasing power of lower- and middle-class consumers because they can ultimately surprise you: "Today, no one knows who has money anymore. It used to be that you could tell who was rich and was a potential customer, but today even someone who looks disheveled may carry enough money to make a purchase. And most likely they'll even pay you in cash."

Later I have more to say about how classist and racist ideas about who has legitimate spending power and who doesn't come to bear on the shop floor. For now, I want to remind readers that the middle-class status of residents living near the new malls is not uncontested. In fact, it is actively threatened by the rapid valorization of real estate spurred by the coming of megamalls. A vivid example is a couple I met at Titán Plaza who in the two years since the mall was built had witnessed the neighborhood's rapid valorization and even an increase in the costs of their services from stratum 3 to stratum 4. "Only the phone bill still comes as stratum 3," complained the young wife and mother of a two-year-old girl with whom she was sharing an ice cream while sitting in the common area of the mall. The working couple had administrative posts in multinational companies, she as a credit analyst for Citibank, he as an IT supervisor for Hewlet Packard, which assured them a solid upper middle-class salary by Colombian standards but were nevertheless finding their purchasing power diminished with the rising cost of living in the area. They paid $1,300.000 COL (about $650) in rent for an apartment on the twentieth floor but had learned that the same apartment on the first floor, supposedly of lesser value, was renting for $1,950.000. They were thinking of leaving the area altogether but were dissuaded by the possibility of a longer commute. She confessed, "Our purchases will be limited to ice cream." This is one of the many examples of the immediate effects of shopping malls on the valorization of real estate and ultimately on the pocketbooks of all bogotanos.

In this way, more than a de facto middle-class space, the shopping mall is best seen as a space of class encounter and differentiation, not only in terms of its visitors, which range from those who may have disposable income to shop to those who come primarily to *vitrinear* (window-shop), such as the familias Miranda, but also in terms of workers, the many clerks and attendants who travel hours to earn a minimum income and can't even afford a luncheon at the mall. The disparities between the retail workers' income and regular mall prices sustains an entire informal luncheon economy, bringing 6,500-peso homemade meals to retail workers, who are mostly young, work long hours, and can't take breaks, and whose daily base salary is almost the same as lunch at the mall. Viviana, a twenty-year-old clerk at a high-end shoe store in Salitre Plaza, movingly described the tedium of her daily routine and the difficulty of being enclosed in a small store with no one to talk to. She had grown up in the countryside with open spaces and was now living with her extended family, whom her daily two-hour commute, ten hours of work, and no weekends off made it impossible for her to see. Like other retail workers, Viviana never shopped at the mall, only at the Jumbo supermarket. However, many retail workers described visiting other malls for leisure or as a point of encounter; and a few had even purchased luxury goods that cost more than their entire month's salary as a treat. In summary, most people I spoke to could name and describe in detail at least one other megamall they had visited in the past year and could point to weekly movie specials and establishments offering two-for-one drinks as popular draws. In fact, for three years in a row the most popularly visited shopping center by all bogotanos was the newly opened Centro Mayor, a lower/mid-stratum mall located in the south.[9]

In this way, while lower-class groups make up the majority of most shopping malls' workforce, they also increasingly make up many of its visitors. On the one hand, the growing spatial accessibility of malls, alongside the lowering of prices following the growth of cheaper imported products, is increasingly transforming the overall image of the mall as a space that is still expensive and upscale but not entirely out of reach. This is so even if people's visits are limited to browsing. In fact, recent citywide statistics on culture, leisure, and recreation put visiting shopping malls as the number one activity and venue for bogotano families, second only to meeting with friends and family, activities that also often take place at a mall (Observatorio de Culturas 2011).

Likewise, some of the most common activities in the everyday lives of middle-class groups, from shopping for food to going to the movies to making banking transactions to paying for credit cards and services and taking kids to rides and playgrounds, are all attached to or found within the confines of a mall, almost ensuring their standing as the place for encounters or the weekend plan in and of itself. As described by a security guard who claimed to have visited all of Bogotá's shopping malls with his family "The idea is to get out of the house and not stay watching TV. Here, people go to a shopping mall as they would go to the park. If you go to Simón Bolívar Park at the minimum you take a little bit of money for an ice cream. It's the same thing for a shopping mall." I was surprised at how easily he equated shopping malls with a public park, spaces that we tend to think of as opposites and in fact not comparable in level of accessibility. For instance, the park is not protected by guards at all of its entrances while the popular practice of setting up a family picnic at the park is not an option at the mall. However, if we compare the park and the mall in terms of consumption, as did this informant, we can see how comparable they may seem as an entertainment choice for many bogotano families. In fact, this informant echoed the response of others who, seemingly blinded to shopping malls' offerings they could never afford, listed *ir de paseo* (strolling), meeting family and friends, and eating an ice cream as the main reasons to visit a mall, in other words, the same activities they would do in a park.

For all these groups, shopping malls are becoming a new reference and a popular spatial backdrop for defining and debating "authentic" class statuses through consumption. In the background, however, stands a larger context of social differentiation that remains in place and is arguably fortified by the expansion of consumers. The next two chapters elaborate on these issues to suggest that assessing the social role of shopping malls and their expansion in the city demands a consideration of Bogotá's dominant classist structure and appreciation of what remains a society marked by social inequality. Certainly there are more and new consumers, and many are even confounding ideas of who has money to make a purchase. But as we have seen, shopping malls are far from democratic spaces exempt from the dynamics of class anchoring and differentiation. Intraclass mingling does occur at malls, but not in all malls at all times. In other words, differentiation is central to the business of shopping malls. This is a process that is marked, produced, and even actively marketed not only through the development of class-stratified malls targeting diverse constituencies but also by the everyday practices of visitors and users staking a claim to the mall.

---

# FIVE

# *Cachacos* and *Levantados*

## ON THE POLITICS OF "MEASURING UP"

In this city 70 percent live off appearances, pretending to be what they are not. And I say 70 percent because I'm an optimist.

**OSCAR**, *taxi driver, stratum 2*

The sign of a *bogotano* is that we're always measuring each other.

**CLAUDIA**, *business owner, stratum 3*

The way you dress is the way you will be treated.

**POPULAR SAYING**

Over and above any other local definitions of class, upon asking people who make up the bogotano middle class, it was the idea that *la clase se nota,* or an individual's class status is noticeable, that was mentioned. How one looked was paramount, from what kind of clothing was worn to how one was "put together" and carried oneself, as well as how one sounded, what vocabulary, intonation, and speech mannerisms one used, among other specific yet highly subjective signs of class, that seemed to trump actual social and economic indicators. At stake, then, is the extent to which one's economic status can be "masked" by *apariencia,* or appearances, and the degree to which "middle-classness" and upwardly mobile identities are affected by processes of performance and construction.

This is a key question to consider when assessing consumption and shopping malls as spaces where both emerging and established middling groups learn, rehearse, and perform middle-classness as these identities are tested and validated in everyday life. It follows ongoing debates documenting the intensification of consumption as an axis of differentiation among new middle classes and the centrality of consumerists' middle classes within contemporary neoliberal states (O'Dougherty 2002; Ariztía 2012). In particular, a growing literature has shown the limitations of any easy equation between class, consumption, and identity by documenting the rising anxieties over the appropriateness of people's consumption as suitable, tasteful, and moral that often follow the intensification of consumption across newer sectors of society (Heiman et al. 2012; Liechty 2003; Rofel 2007). In other words, greater accessibility to shopping malls and to cheaper consumer goods does increase the realm of social maneuvering through consumption. What remains more unyielding, however, is the larger field of social and cultural inequalities in which this consumption is evaluated and judged. Here we must turn to Bourdieu's (1984) warning about the economy of practices of consumption and how they always operate against a larger social space of power and distinction that continues to strive and endure, even after it has been altered. Assessing the social significance of malls and their use for bogotano families thus requires a larger consideration of the field of cultural production in which people's use of shopping malls and their new practices of consumption operate.

This chapter examines these issues by looking at the larger social context that frames both the growth of new shopping malls and the growth of "new" middle classes in Bogotá. I focus on some of the ways in which the status and social position of new middle classes with access to shopping malls remain circumscribed in a larger context of social differentiation that continues to reproduce the cultural hegemony of a living and imagined traditional bogotano elite. My goal is to account for the continuous reproduction of social hierarchies in what remains a highly unequal and segregated society as a first and necessary step to appropriately evaluate the politics of consumption among any emergent society.

But first I should clarify that this chapter and the next, which looks at fast fashion, draws primarily on conversations with female university students and professionals women in their twenties, thirties, and forties. In the context of shopping malls, women have been found to bear a disproportionate share of the burden of establishing and reinforcing class identities; and because my focus was shopping malls and fashion, I was unable to gauge more information about how men fashion middle-class identities and what may be some key performative spaces where these identities are shaped. In other words, I am unable to make generalizations about the gendering of class distinctions, nor do I seek to make them. There is also the key issue of how sexual identities intersect with class identities—and the pivotal role that consumption plays in fashioning gay, queer, and other non-normative sexual identities, especially among the youth—that my work did not consider. I clarify the scope of my research to ensure that my discussion is not interpreted as a generalized argument about women becoming the only or the primary agents affecting class differentiation through consumption. In other words, inside shopping malls we could also look at men, especially younger men, and how they relate to leisure and fashion, or at families for interesting clues about class identity and consumption. It is also important to note that both inside and outside shopping malls I met people who sought to challenge the social pressure to shape and communicate class through consumption or dress, even when they were often caught up in other types of culturally motivated consumption, from artisanal furniture to instruments to cappuccino makers to crafts and more. Most important, my focus on younger women is also the expected result of the great impact that fast fashion and the advent of retail brands like Zara and Forever 21 are having on everyday popular culture, concerns that drive the next chapter's discussion on the growing impact fast fashion is having on young and professional women's self-styling. But first, I turn to some dominant ideas framing the representation and styling of class that circulated quite widely and beyond my primary informants, shaping a highly stratified context for analyzing the intersection of class and consumption.

## *CACHACOS* AND *LEVANTADOS:* ON THE LANGUAGE AND STYLING OF CLASS

Like other Latin American cities, Bogotá has been the center of traditional classist distinctions and culture hierarchies in what is a highly stratified and classist society. One of its expressions is the dominance of Western-centric and colonial-based hierarchies of race, class, and region, whereby the interior regions of Bogotá and other highland regions are considered more cultured, more urban, whiter, and more modern than populations on the coast and in the Amazon, associated with blackness and indigeneity, respectively (Wade 1995; Escobar 2008). Another is the dominant legacy of the so-called *cachaco* traditional culture. A regional term associated with residents born and raised in the interior and Andean sections of Colombia of which Bogotá is a part—as opposed to those from other regions, whether coastal or from other provinces—*cachaco*'s use and definition have been extended into a cultural reference to identify the most traditional and old-fashioned components of Bogotá's society as formal, family oriented, protocol and socially conscious, as well as sober in consumption patterns, speech, and demeanor; in sum, a class-based referent for people who are *gente de bien y de cuna,* or well-to-do from the cradle.

This equation of *gente de bien* or *gente bien* as stemming from the "cradle" is obviously not new but has roots in colonial and historically ingrained notions of middle classes as the outcome of "cultural immersion" in proper and suitable families, social backgrounds, and cultural environments, all of which are part and parcel of racist-based colonial formulations of *gente de bien* at play throughout the Americas.[1] The prevalence of these ideas brings to light the racist foundations of definitions of class and status that render these socially constructed groupings into more inherited and ingrained categories than is commonly recognized. In particular, they hone in on the well-documented dominant association of middle classes with respectability, which links them to "respectable behaviors" such as in the realm of sexuality, and in the contemporary neoliberal context, also undergird ideas of who is more or less likely to be "entrepreneurial" (Mosse 1997; Freeman 2014).

The term *cachaco* is not as popularly used today, when Bogotá's population has become more diverse and many regional elites can also claim status based on well-off backgrounds. Outside Bogotá, particularly among costeños, many use *cachaco* as a derogatory term for pretentiousness, while in Bogotá many terms, like *rolo* and *bogotano,* are used to distinguish those with deeper roots to the city and hence more legitimate urban belonging and standing. What remains, however, is the continued association of old Bogotá's cultural traditions as the entrenched reference for buena presencia involving people who are imagined to have a cultivated manner of speech, to live in good neighborhoods, to have "good" family origins, and to have proper modes of behaving and consumption against which the newly rich, new middle classes, and groups from rural backgrounds and the coast are often differentially positioned. Not for nothing is the most prestigious, expensive, and luxury-branded shopping mall in the north named Andino, the only shopping mall in Bogotá whose name is a widely recognized regional reference.[2]

Indeed, the growth of shopping malls and of emerging groups has been accompanied by an exponential growth in Bogotá's population and consequently by the number of stakeholders who seek to claim belonging, legitimacy, and recognition in a growing city that clings to its racist and classist origins. On the one hand, the past decades have seen a rise in the number of displaced populations fleeing the violence of war, poverty, and paramilitary activity, groups that still make up the majority of Bogotá's poor. Many of these displaced persons come from rural and provincial places with different class imaginaries, adding another dimension to Bogotá's newly arrived and emerging groups and to the meaning of upward mobility as literally tied to urban lifestyles, of which frequenting shopping malls is a key component. Then there is the growth of the "new rich" and new middle classes, whether emerging from the city or from nearby cities and provinces, with contrasting manners of speech and customs as well as imaginaries of class. Many bogotanos with roots in the provinces pride themselves on their supposedly looser and less deterministic notions of class, versus the stringent value systems they encounter when moving to Bogotá, yet I learned to be very skeptical of the "class democracy" that these informants told me prevailed in their home provinces, finding that many of them were from landowning backgrounds or had a level of education and resources that translated into better positions in Bogotá than their counterparts migrating with less resources. Moreover, positions of class-blindnessness and class democracy do little to challenge the suspect position allotted to those that remain outsiders to dominant notions of middle-class respectability, similar to how color-blind positions fail to account for the pervasive reproduction of racial inequalities, whether it in the United States or in Latin America (Telles 2006; Seigel 2005).

Further, many of Bogotá's new rich are stereotyped as having attained their wealth from narco-traffic and the paramilitary, feeding the stereotype of the *traqueto,* or the *mágico,* and among women, the *prepagos,* the ostentatious rich whose wealth comes from suspect and illicit activities, be it narco-traffic or prostitution. The popular put-down *"como traqueto mostrando la marca"* (like a narco showing off the brand) points to the penchant of the new rich for displaying their wealth through consumption, a sign of bad taste and overall tackiness, but also to their popular association with narco-traffic. The influence of narco-culture and narco-aesthetics in assessments of class, consumption, and taste are determinant in contemporary society because profits from drug trafficking are at the heart of public displays of wealth and consumption that percolate through all levels of society, from the most humble communities where cars and expensive goods may suddenly appear to the most fantastic stories of conspicuous consumption of narcos portrayed by the press or mythologized in the media. Most middle-class Colombians adopt the official posture of distancing themselves from these expressions and berating them as low-class, excessive, and tacky, yet the wide reach of narco-culture in all aspects of popular culture (consumption, language, music, fashion, telenovelas, etc.) has made it indiscernible from urban modern culture to the point that it is practically impossible to draw strict aesthetic distinctions between "narco" culture and "proper" middle-class taste (Rincón and Martínez 2013; Suárez 2010). In particular, writers have focused on the use of plastic surgery to mold bodies to narco-aesthetic ideals that have redefined beauty standards across many sectors of society (Forero-Peña 2015; Taussig 2012). Many have thus concurred that bad taste is not the monopoly of the narcos; narco-culture has simply exposed the bad taste of the Colombian bourgeoisie, which has always wanted the same things as the narcos, except narcos had the money to actually expose Colombians' popular national taste, a far cry from the cultivated European aesthetics professed by the traditional bourgeoisie (Abad Faciolince 1995). It figures that *que no sea traqueto* (that it is not and does not look too ostentatious and revealing) would stand as the most concise explanation offered about what the essential prerequisites are for good taste and buena presencia.

Most perniciously, there is the category of the *levantado*—a term that literally means "pushed up" by a sudden external force—used to define someone whose status is believed not to "belong" to him or her—which was described as the worst insult anyone can make. This is a term that evokes the most traditionalist and static notions of class as inherited and embodied, rendering the upward mobility of anyone who is not socially regarded to have the inherited right to "belong" to an illegitimate, ill-gained, and ultimately transparently fake status. Mónica, a professional woman residing in the upscale section of Los Nogales, explained this over a three-course sit-down luncheon served by her maid on a dining table with a fine tablecloth, a luncheon that included a flambé dessert. "What I am comes from many generations," she said, pointing to the ingrained legacy that had shaped her good taste and standing in opposition to the new rich who could never fake it. The one exception she made was the wealthy Venezuelans who were fleeing Chávez and settling in Colombia, many of whom were "gente decente" and could be rightfully accepted in social clubs. Her views thus echoed dominant associations of the middle classes with notions of "respectability," this time with Venezuelan exiles' conservative and hence more "appropriate" political orientations.

Arguably, most of Bogotá's urban middle class and the new rich could be described as levantados insofar as their origins contest dominant notions of class mobility through purported inheritance, with some hailing from poor rural backgrounds, others from riches gained from narco-traffic, and still others from new middle classes with no ties to traditional middle classes. The category of the levantado, however, is mostly used in relation to the new rich and always with the connotation of improper modes of consumption and behavior. Once again Diego explained: "These are the new rich who don't originate from birth. No matter if they have money, they continue to behave like poor people. They are loud, show-offy, they are into brands, they play music too loud, and they think they are better than everyone else." In sum, levantados counter the sobriety and propriety that is supposed to characterize gente decente and speak to the ultimate fear of being exposed as lesser and poorer than one pretends.

In all, Bogotá is riddled with telltale signs of class and demeanor sustaining the primacy of old, idealized visions of cachaco and rightfully bogotano culture, and primary among them is language. The idea is that how one speaks, the words one uses, one's expressions and intonations, are key signs of class, over and beyond one's appearance. Thus while class can be seen—in how one dressed, the quality of one's clothes, the look of one's teeth and hair, among other variables that can be manipulated through consumption— above anything else, class can always be heard.

In this way, language was revealed as the surefire means of class differentiation. Words like *cabello, bolso,* and *labial* and verbs like *colocar* and *comer* were linked to the higher classes and educated groups, whereas *cartera y colorete* and verbs like *poner* and *cenar* were regarded as terms used by lower groups, or costeños. Similarly, "proper" and educated language was associated with a greater degree of protocol, etiquette, and distance, for instance, the tendency to apologize before any request is made or any opinion is offered (*"Ay, qué pena,"* "How sorry I am") and the preference for *usted* over *tús* in most interpersonal relations, especially among superiors. Greetings are especially hierarchically marked, and in shopping malls clients can greet attendants with diminutive forms of their names, "¿Cómo está Johancita?," but attendants are always expected to address to clients by their full names: "Muy bien Señora María Fernanda," or even more appropriately, "Doctora María Fernanda," to refer to any professional or anyone of higher status. As Juan, a teacher and art photographer, explained, "We like to embellish language and use words to seem extra educated, to the point that people develop idioms that make no sense, like when people say, 'Me regala' (Can you gift me?), to ask for anything." He went on to explain: "Because they think the verb *dar* sounds too abrupt and low-class. And there are people who would say, *'Me coloqué nervioso'* (I positioned myself nervous) instead of *'Me puse nervioso'* (I got nervous), because *poner* (to put) sounds low-class." I was told that a proper bogotano man never *"tutea"* another man, unless they are related, even if they are young and friends, lest they risk being considered homosexuals. Foremost, regionalisms and phrases associated with narco-culture were considered low-class and linked with lower-class and uneducated groups, even though they were commonly used across classes, with different degrees of social implications for their users. *"Uy sí, parce, re aspero,"* a popular phrase that some of my informants associated with the region of Antioquía, that conveys, "Yes, friend, you're right," or "Yes, dude, incredible!," and anything that started with *"Mami . . ."* or references to *parche* or *parcero* (friend), were offered by some of my middle-class informants as examples of the type of "vulgar" regional expressions that indexed stigma, despite their widespread use and popularization.[3]

The differential valorization and racialization of regional dialects in Colombia is well known and documented by linguists, who point to the existence of a dominant linguistic ideology that is inflected by race and regional hierarchies, whereby the Spanish spoken in the capital is considered a "purer" and more "standard" variety of the language that is more exact, prestigious, and the sign of propriety for all educated Colombians (Garrido 2007). Institutions like the church, the government, and the school system held up these views by promoting the image of Colombia as the "South American Athens," the stronghold of educated proper culture and language. In recent decades, however, this view has been forcefully challenged by the moniker "the South American *tenaz*" or "the tenacious of South America," a phrase that comes from famous graffiti in the early 1990s to shed light on the city's state of violence, where it is tenacity, not "nobility," that is most demanded from city residents (Ospina 2012). Still, ideas about bogotanos' more "proper" language and manners endure and are particularly summoned in opposition to coastal and regional expressions and manners of speech that are seen as vulgar and too abrupt and lacking in the protocol and appropriate degree of salutations that are believed to characterize proper manners.

These associations of linguistic purity had spatial connotations among my informants, many of whom associated sophisticated ways of speech with the northern part of Bogotá and a greater degree of *popularismos* and more abrupt language with the south. In this way, the linguistic ideal was midpoint between two stereotyped ways of speaking, one associated with a highly pretentious *gomelo* (*hijo de papi*) style,[4] which some described as "speaking as if you had a potato in your mouth," with a more nasal affectation of language, and another that sounded ñero, or ugly, that was described as more abrupt, popular, and faulty, with ñero serving as the catchall term for lower-class, debased, urban popular culture that was most shunned. Similarly, more educated and middle-class demeanors were associated with more formal uses of language, as, for instance, formally greeting someone before speaking or addressing them, as opposed to just addressing them outright. I myself was corrected multiple times when I approached people directly without having "properly" addressed them with a greeting or some other pleasantry. This somewhat muted my New York directness while sensitizing me to linkages between popular ways of class indexing and the most "appropriate" ways to start a conversation. This last issue also surfaced during my discussions with store clerks, who I found to be expert in deciphering the class and linguistic codes of anyone who stepped into their stores.

As a general rule, and with the exception of higher-brand international stores, retail work is considered a low-status occupation that higher-status groups avoid and devalue. Many stores have only one retail worker in charge of all tasks, from the most low-ranked tasks of cleaning and mopping the store to dealing with sales, with no differentiation between the two in ways that veil and devalue the affective aspects of retail work, from communicating the intangibles that make a product "valuable" (quality, material, design, etc.) to dealing with customers from different strata and learning to manage their class codes. Thus, many clerks are stratum 3 and of backgrounds similar to their consumers; yet clerks felt mistreated by both higher-stratum visitors and those like them. Both acted ill-mannered, they felt, failing to greet them and acknowledge their presence upon entering their stores. Still, language served as a decisive guide for these workers. Thus, Ricardo, a twenty-one-year-old stratum 3 from the south who had been working for three years in a leather goods store in Avenida Chile shopping mall, explained that higher-stratum consumers sounded softer and more polite: "They think they are better than you, but they also seem very 'attentive and kind' as opposed to harsh, like when they greet you with 'Good afternoon,' as opposed to *¿Usted qué hace?* [What are you up to?]." Tellingly, when asked what he had most learned from working in a store, he mentioned how to talk to different people and how to ask for things in ways that could not be read as signs of a lack of status and purchasing power, for instance, with directness and lack of hesitation. Ricardo was going to school to become an engineer and saw his three years of retail work as a break in his larger plans to leave shopping mall work and become a professional, though I very much doubt that the language codes learned at the mall will do him much good. For as many people pointed to the importance of language as claimed the ability to determine when language sounded more affected and intentional, rather than a natural and truly inherent component of the speaker's speech.

The preeminence of language as a class-defining register also surfaced during my discussions with middle-class informants about their chosen mates. It is not common for people from different strata to date or engage in formal heterosexual romantic relationships because of the spatial segregation that characterizes the work, residential, and leisure spaces of different strata—one of the things that adds to the interest of multistratum malls as spaces where lower and higher classes may encounter one another publicly. Stratum 3 may date stratum 4 and stratum 5 may date stratum 6, and vice versa, but it is very rare for stratum 3 to date stratum 6, and so forth, unless these relationships are purely sexual or casual. The sociologist Uribe-Mallarino (2008) found that stratum definitions were often included in personal ads, even though my informants had never seen such ads but admitted to the use of euphemisms, like identifying oneself by title (connoting educational and/or professional rank), neighborhood, or specifying that the preferred mate should be educated, or of "buena presencia." This tendency belies the intraclass romantic archetype of most Latin American telenovelas—which rely on intraclass love and social mobility through marriage, though it is not unique to the case at hand. Historians and sociologists have provided ample evidence of the ways in which class permeates marriage markets in the United States as well as in Latin America, contributing to social inequalities.[5] In this way, while intraclass relationships exist, they can often be qualified and explained in classed ways. Consider the example provided by Andrea, an opinionated journalist I met at a movie theater who described herself as a "proud *cachaca del centro,*" someone unconcerned with stratum and status (as demonstrated by her pride in living in *el centro,* downtown) and whose tale turned out to be not much of an exception: "Our friend who is really into appearances and who works in the advertising company Burson-Marsteller is stratum 3, and she dated someone like stratum 0. But let me clarify: he lived in a stratum 0, but he kind of was not stratum 0. He was a math student, about to graduate, even a math teacher; in other words, he was not entirely disposable or indigent. On the contrary, he was very ambitious and a great dancer." Andrea could not keep from laughing when she added that the "indigent" boyfriend (described as belonging to stratum 0 to emphasize his lesser status) had actually broken up with her friend, aware of the reversal in class hierarchies represented by the breakup.

Yet the preference for intrastatum/class dating was euphemistically explained in relation to people's intimate preferences for how and what others talked about, ways of speaking, and use of language rather than in terms of stratum or class differences. After all, class is seldom directly inquired about but always informally summoned. For instance, most of my middle-class informants claimed they could measure other people's class belonging based on where they went to school or lived, or even based on their names: Yesenia, Jésica, Lady, Yulitza, Albeiro, and any other name too obviously drawn from TV or from English-sounding idioms, like Usnavy, were offered as examples of lower-class names, and Castilian-sounding names like Santiago and Sebastián or Ana María, Patricia, and María Fernanda as their opposite.[6] Meanwhile, race was never mentioned as a variable affecting people's socioeconomic status.

Wrapped in the common Latin American ideology of mestizaje, Colombians are taught early on that they live in a racially homogeneous society, with a predominant mestizo identity. While historically challenged and succeeded by the 1991 constitutional recognition of Colombia as a multiethnic and multicultural country, the ideology of mestizaje, and its whitening logics, is very much alive. Contemporary society is characterized by the ongoing denial of racism and by the continued valorization of whiteness. In fact, the official recognition of multiethnic diversity has done less to challenge the dominant association of whiteness with modernity and progress and more to anchor "race" and "ethnicity" as the exclusive concern of Afro-Colombians or indigenous groups (Urrea et al. 2014). Consequently, Colombians, especially the urbanites that comprise most of my informants, are extremely reticent about discussing racism as a variable of social inequality that affects everyone, irrespective of self-identification. Still, and notwithstanding the silence and misrecognition that surrounds it, race is determinant in everyday society. It is overt in the rise of hate crimes targeting Afro-Colombians, as well as in proposals to outlaw "champeta" and other Afro-Colombian musical rhythms, as well as in subtler ways (Rodríguez Garavito 2015). Think here of the tendency to call higher-class people *monos* or *monitos* (blondes) irrespective of the color of their hair. Recently, a group of researchers described Colombia as a pigmentocracy, finding that beyond racial self-identification, lighter-skinned people consistently have more education and higher occupational status than darker-skinned people. The researchers conclude that in Colombia, "social classes have skin colors" (Urrea et al. 2014: 125). This finding is confirmed by reports that skin color is the number one factor determining whether an applicant is called back for a job interview after filling out an application, a process that regularly requires applicants to submit a picture (Arjona 2015).

Yet it was language—how people talked and what they talked about—that was often the most important reason given for why people hit economic ceilings and for why people from different strata would not make a good match. As one person said, "I could never date someone who spoke ñero or talked only about telenovelas," even though few people could offer examples of "faulty speech" more concrete than regional phrases like *"¿Qué hubo mami?,"* among other popular phrases that everyone agreed a stratum 6 person was free to utter without stigma. How people talked in telenovelas became a common reference of class, pointing to a trend in Colombian television to represent popular classes and regional differences in soap operas like *Nuevo rico, Nuevo pobre,* featuring the culture clash of two men, one rich and one poor, who switch worlds; or *Los Reyes,* in which poor fruit vendors become rich and move to an upscale barrio, causing mayhem in their neighborhood. Finally, the use of English was also a key index of upward mobility. Most of my middle-class informants had low to medium levels of proficiency in English; they could understand it to some extent or speak from having learned it in school. However, ease and familiarity with English, and its use in casual conversation, was pointed as the reservoir of elite groups, not so common among regular middle classes.[7]

Arguably, the preeminence of language as a class-defining sign stems from its power as a racial and status marker that remains more lasting and reliable, especially as a sign of education and upbringing.[8] In particular, I began to appreciate language as a primary code for managing and maneuvering through the growing diversification of the population as well as of styles and tastes, such as those allowed by the advent of fast fashion. In this regard, I was repeatedly told that dress criteria for gente bien remain formal and sober. My stratum 3 interviewees in focus groups held at malls all came fashionably well dressed, and when I asked if they had dressed up to come to the mall or to meet with me they all maintained, "Bogotanos dress formally" or "This is just how we dress." Many were quick to respond with descriptions of how different class groups dress, similar to those shared by Ana, a student in her twenties I met at Gran Estación: *"Clase media y alta* [The middle and upper class] wears more neutral colors, more real jewelry, rather than *bisutería* [costume jewelry], and their colors will be coordinated. Lower class will be fatter, will wear less makeup, and will be more informally dressed. And they dress in colors that clash."

The color one wore was often explained in relation to regional differences: neutral and dark colors were associated with Bogotá, bright colors with the provinces and the coast; synchronicity in tasteful color combinations was seen as a skill that came more easily to those with higher class and connections to Bogotá culture and the city. Some informants described learning the proper ways to combine colors from their families, others from etiquette courses that are common in private universities; but others relied mostly on television, whether it be local shows like Caracol TV's *De tu lado con Alex,* which dispenses fashion, makeup, and hair advice, or imported shows like "Tim Gunn's Guide to Style" or on fashion blogs and social media, which I discuss later in greater detail.

However, certainties about what makes for appropriate fashion are increasingly up for grabs as the advent of pronta moda and shopping malls are influencing popular ways of communicating, reading, and determining class. For instance, I was told that traditionally it was customary to match shoes, belt, and bag in the same color or tone, a practice that is still quite common, especially among lower-middle-class groups. I recall the styling lesson shared by a female vendor at a leather fair: she pointed to a lean, tall, blonde wearing white jeans and a blue belt that matched her blue leather moccasins as a good example to follow. "See how she's dressed? You can tell she's stratum 6. My clients are all office workers, and they know about the importance of matching shoes and bags to communicate who they want to be." I jokingly picked a bag to match the color of my boots, and she immediately approved. I began to perceive attention to shoes and matching bags and belts among office workers around Avenida Chile shopping mall, a popular lunchtime destination, and that the color schemes of leather goods in Colombian stores were produced in a far greater variety than were leather goods at the American chains Payless and Steve Madden that were showing up in Colombian malls. One would see products in hues of blue, pink, nectarine, green, and honeycomb whose proper combination communicated consumers' purchasing power to acquire the necessary accessories to most appropriately combine color in their outfits. This color synchronicity, however, was bemoaned by others, who stressed the importance of combining colors but were especially concerned to not look too *uniformada,* or overly matched, as they were wearing a uniform—a telltale sign of lower-class mimicry but also of being a low-wage worker who had to wear a uniform.

The number of uniformadas has grown in recent years as result of the rise in the number of transnational companies that require workers to wear uniforms and the threat to office decorum represented by the rise of pronta moda. Even retail workers and office receptionists, who could previously style themselves and thus dress in a manner that was indistinguishable from that of professionals, have been required to wear uniforms, a result of the growing availability of fashion trends and women's penchant for them. As a bank teller explained, "They were afraid that women would wear leggings to work." This trend, in turn, has contributed to female workers' consumption practices as they seek to differentiate their looks from their uniforms. The fear of looking too uniformada has also been intensified by the rise of fast fashion and the "massified" look that some felt makes it seem as if women are in fact wearing "uniforms."

In contrast, on the few occasions I met with more elite groups, their color sobriety was apparent. Thus my luncheon hostess and her friend at Los Nogales were both dressed in hues of beige, camel, and white. One was carefully coordinated in an expensive-looking layered outfit that included an open cardigan and a smooth leather chaleco of honey color that matched her shoes. Her hair was also neatly held in place by a barrette. Similarly, on a Sunday visit to the exclusive Los Largartos country club, the crowds leaving Sunday Mass struck me as similarly conservative in their choice of color. I asked about this tendency and was told, "This is how we dress in *tierra fría*" (colder Bogotá weather), but then my anthropologist-tango friend Oriana reminded me of the European aesthetic and look of upscale sports—golf, tennis, waterskiing—that are regular mainstays of elite clubs. Overall, dark blues, grays, blacks, and pale colors were identified as signs of good taste, while color combinations—traditionally favored as a sign of good taste and purchasing power by those not limited to neutral colors, which are more easily matched and hence more economical—were identified as tricky terrain that could easily become a sign of bad taste if not "properly" done.

Styling with color is also loaded with racial and social significance, often associated with costeños. In fact, the disciplining of Afro-Colombian children for wearing bright hair adornments and "disheveled hair" is a common concern in the Afro-Colombian community because it is widely recognized as an ingrained expression of racism (El Tiempo 2014). I also found that the examples of inappropriate color combinations were often so exaggerated and outlandish (for instance, combining flower prints with stripes or vivid colors that clash, like red and emerald green) that they were more appropriately seen as powerful mechanisms of social differentiation than a representation of any type of color combination one would see people wearing out and about. In fact, my interviews yielded nothing close to a universally approved color scheme, though patterns were obvious. Among them is the practice of matching shoes to the color of blouses or shirts worn under jackets, or matching accessories (bags, belts, shoes) of the same color, or in the same color spectrum. In this way, discussions of taste and color surfaced not as a given but as a revealing space communicating dominant beliefs about the nature of class/status differentiation. Key among them is the cachaco/costeño symbolic divide, implicating the race and regional distinctions at the heart of the differential associations and evaluations of "culture" with color, and the fear of appearing too close to narco, or tranqueto, culture, by being too "colorful."[9]

Regional hierarchies around culture are also stereotypically displayed in popular culture such as in the Colombian soap opera *La Costeña y el Cachaco* (2002), which I first heard mentioned by a customer at a shoe store in Avenida Chile shopping mall. A well-to-do visitor from the coast wanted to exchange her open-toe shoes for more "conventional" closed bogotano shoes, tired of the stares her shoes elicited from onlookers, a culture clash she described as being typical of *La Costeña y el Cachaco*. In this soap opera, the male protagonist is a wealthy businessman from Bogotá who is transferred to Santa Marta, on the Atlantic coast, where his white skin, uptight demeanor, elitism, shyness, and penchant for somber, neutral, and dark suits, and his tendency to overdress for the tropical weather place him at odds with the local costeño culture, embodied by his love interest, the Costeña. The Costeña is represented as his direct opposite: carefree, lively, and dressed in colorful, breezy, and revealing clothes and totally immersed in Afro-Colombian music and culture, even though—not uncommon for telenovelas—she is played by a blonde actress whose long curls stand as the only physical "sign" of costeño culture. The popular soap opera revolved around the culture clash between the two characters as they fall in love; and while it is the cachaco who, as the outsider, is the subject of local jokes by costeños, it is he who—through his open assessments of the region's lack of civilization and winning the costeña's love over her costeño suitor—asserts the greater value of cachaco culture.

In all, the need to project buena presencia through self-styling and consumption was a widespread concern. This was especially so among the working professional women I met around Avenida Chile shopping mall in Chapinero. Most of these professional women were between twenty-five and forty, had some years of higher education, and had worked full-time as office workers and administrators, lawyers, accountants, bank tellers, and journalists. Most were stratum 3 and a few were stratum 4, and all represented the first generation of educated professionals in their families. Some of them lived with husbands and partners who also worked, but most still lived with their parents or extended families, which contributed to the pooling of resources and to their ability to consume. Most were regular visitors to malls and were self-described fashionistas; at least one had a side job in addition to her full-time job just to cover the "necessary" costs involved in looking her part at the office.

These professional women echoed the aforementioned concerns over speech and color, even though—like practically everyone I talked to—they also showed great diversity in what counted as appropriate color combinations in their clothes. However, they added two more key requirements and telltale signs of class: *pelo arreglado y cepillado* (straightened and blow-dried hair) and manicured nails. I myself became very self-conscious about wearing a *moñito* (ponytail), as moñitos are read as a sign that you're lower-class or saving up for a *cepillada,* as opposed to the loose, straight hair that is the ultimate complement to any proper look for the office or to go out. Most women I talked to considered a visit to the hairstylist a non-negotiable expense, and one that was considerably more expensive for my costeña informants, whose hair was naturally wavy. A wavy-haired woman from Cali said she paid 19,000 pesos, a lot more than the 6,000 pesos that her friend with straight hair paid. This practice explains the ubiquity of *peluquerías* (hair salons) in the urban landscape that offer a wash and blow-dry for as little as 5,000 pesos, to ensure that anyone can "solve" any image problem. This style preference has affected consumption, with styling irons among the most popular beauty accessories owned by my informants, which allowed them to save on cepilladas. The racial connotations of this hairstyle preference are especially relevant in light of the already noted disregard and devaluation of any sign of costeño culture (in this case, curls). At the same time, the need to straighten hair is not only about taming any possible signs of blackness. In a highly racialized context no one is ever exempt from the politics of hairstyling and race, given that straight hair can also signal race through assessments of texture and consistency (Candelario 2007). In this way, a cepillada is also about signaling whiteness by marking one's hair as wavy, in opposition to the straightened hair that is often associated with Indians.

Similarly, I was told that nails could not be too long or painted in too loud a color but should be nevertheless "dressed." "It's the first thing that a client sees, because you're always in front of a keyboard," explained a young lawyer, adding that she could never date a man without clean and well-buffed nails. In all, nails were offered as signs of taste that also signaled people's purchasing power, because, like cepilladas, manicures could be found for as little as 5,000 pesos, although the cost can mount up. Nail styling, however, has also changed. Johana, a manicurist recommended by Diego, described how color and designs have become more acceptable over the classical and muted "French"-style manicure that was favored in office settings and how there is a greater degree of acceptable nail styles to choose from. Further, the importance of nails is also changing. As Mabel, a licensed technician with degrees from private universities locally and abroad, who works at a Korean multinational company, explained, "Even if your clothes were not perfect, if you had your hair and nails done you'd look great." She herself described spending thousands of pesos on hair straightening and nails. But now, as people are getting better at doing their own hair and fashion is more accessible, she noted that nails are still important, though increasingly it is fashion that reigns supreme.

Obviously, there were enormous differences in taste, style, and consumption. I met many middle-class professional women who do their own hair, or placed less emphasis on manicured nails, or paid more attention to other style items for differentiation. Some key ones are wearing the right shoes for the appropriate occasion (long boots, ankle boots, narrow heels or chunky ones, pumps, leather or synthetic shoes, and millions of other differences) or knowing how to walk elegantly in heels, as well as the ability to combine accessories or wear the right makeup, among myriad other ways they mentioned for reading "good taste" in themselves and others. What remained constant, however, is the overt preoccupation with one's style and the ongoing transformations in the ways in which class is communicated, read, and determined through consumption.

In this regard, upwardly mobile groups with more opportunities and resources could afford to subscribe to different conventions than those of shopping malls and brands, and many purposefully took pride in doing so. Recall my earlier discussion of the general disregard of shopping malls and consumption culture among key sectors of Bogotá's society (intellectuals, elites who can travel). But this stance of differentiation from the culture of brands and shopping malls was not available to most people. Thus, echoing what other young women discovered upon entering the professional world, Diana, an office administrator, explained:

> My friends have other possibilities because they work on their own, or in
> academia, but I work in an office. And in this context, you can't go without

sleeves. I used to wear T-shirts and jeans. My secretary would dress better than I did, and this was OK with me until everyone began to call her "Doctora Diana" and not me. Because here there's an ingrained issue of respect where they treat you according to how you're dressed. And if you're not dressed the part you're not going to get the treatment. So you end up assuming these types of behaviors and ways of dress even if you don't want to.

This concern with "dressing the part" even translated to the most intimate facets in the lives of my working female informants. Rocío, a lawyer at the government pension company Colpensiones, talked about being especially concerned with how she looks for her husband, who works with professional women like her, making it important to look equally good in her home. The professional women I met in Avenida Chile could not agree more with the pressure to look the part and offered similar stories of *como te ven te tratan,* or they treat you the way they see you, linking their professional identity to their outfits, which they recognized as the sure tell for others that they are, in fact, professional women.

Their comments evidenced the preference for projecting some sense of buena presencia, which came easily to some of the women but with a great deal of effort for others. This issue echoes Méndez's (2008) discussion of the Chilean middle class and the growing preoccupation with "authenticity" and "artificiality," where some middle classes distinguish themselves by their authenticity and the naturalness of their tastes, as opposed to other middle classes, especially "newer" ones, who can't cultivate such authentic postures and are in need of guidance. Similarly, many of my middle-class Colombian informants described themselves as dressing more "informally," or as being more *descomplicada* or *relajadita,* uncomplicated or relaxed, in their dress, to distance themselves from those they felt were ostentatious or trying too hard. This was so even when their own "uncomplicated" looks were the product of many shopping trips and of purposeful self-styling. Valeria, a graduate student pursuing tourism administration in El Externado whom I met at Unicentro, is a case in point. When probed, she revealed how her self-described "relaxed" look was in fact carefully contrived with local and international brand clothes, including Mussi leather shoes, a "simple black romper" from Forever 21, and a worn-out, yet authentic, Michael Kors bag that a friend had purchased for her in an outlet in Miami.

Finally, the view that not everyone has a natural or "innate" ability to style themselves appropriately is also at play in the spread of office dress manuals, describing the basic and usually unspoken rules of buena presencia. One example that was discussed frequently, mainly because it was exposed and circulated by the press, is the workers' manual produced by the Fondo Nacional de Garantias. It urged women to avoid plunging necklines and shiny fabrics and recommended conservative colors, such as navy blue, beige, and gray and avoid bright hair dyes and visible roots, red lipstick, and too much eyeliner. Men were told to get regular manicures, among other recommendations. Interestingly, public opinion was pretty much in agreement about the need for these types of manuals, with many readers acknowledging that one's manner of dress is connected to the good and positive values one is imparted at home and in schools and that "any medium decent family already imparts ways of dress that are appropriate to the place and the occasion" (El Espectador 2013d). In sum, a manual like this was deemed a necessity for those who had not learned from their families or received the "proper" education and hence had to be "civilized" into buena presencia by being taught appropriate forms of consumption. In fact, how-to-dress manuals and tips were regularly shared among corporate office workers on a more confidential basis. One informant shared emails circulated by her employer with the subject heading, "You are what you reflect," detailing how even "Jeans Day" or casual Friday is regulated by her company. In the email, workers are specifically warned against wearing torn, spoiled, or *descaderados* (low-waisted) jeans, tennis shoes, sweatshirts, sleeveless shirts, or plunging necklines, lest this benefit be removed.

Like the dress manual, the media are filled with examples of tensions and debates around matters of class and appropriate and inappropriate consumption, and I will end this section with one that was especially prescient during my fieldwork. This is the case of Fabio Salamanca, a twenty-three-year-old drunk driver responsible for the death of two young female workers and the paralysis of the surviving taxi driver who was sentenced to five years of house arrest. This case is especially revealing because it put on display the widely accepted biases that the Colombian justice system is *para los de ruana*,[10] or for people with money who can compensate their victims and are given special consideration because of their status. Most important, the case exposed the range of anxieties unleashed when levantados are believed to engage in improper and excessive modes of consumption.

Early reports presented Salamanca as a young, pale-skinned, and wide-eyed kid of high stratum, evidenced by his recent graduation from the Universidad de los Andes, the most elite private university, and by the luxury Audi wagon owned by his dad that he was driving when he crashed into the taxi. In sum, an "hijo de papi" with all the resources in the world. His victims, two young female systems engineers at BBMV bank who were on their way home after a late shift at work and the taxi driver, were lower-stratum individuals "who worked hard for every single thing they had."[11] Salamanca came from a family with economic resources: his father runs a successful shoe factory plant and owned multiple shoestores. However, he was far from a distinguished business entrepreneur: his stores were not located in shopping malls or in the Zona Rosa but in popular barrios and sites such as the San Andresito of the 38 and San Victorino (Quevedo 2013). Most of all, Salamanca was raised and still lived in Barrio Kennedy, not the traditional barrio we would associate with someone driving an expensive luxury car but instead a barrio of the popular classes, or *nuevos ricos*. In other words, as I was repeatedly told, Salamanca turned out to be the son of a levantado and a levantado himself, someone with money to purchase an Audi but "no class." As evidence of his lack of class, people pointed to his poor upbringing, evidenced in his parents having given their son free access to a luxury vehicle, and to his own inability to control his drinking or driving speed.

Responses to the accident were highly polarized around class. The popular sentiment predicted that Salamanca's victims would not get justice, that they would be paid, and that Salamanca would ultimately go free, which is exactly what happened. Salamanca's five years of house arrest was accompanied by financial remuneration to his victims, who complained that Colombia's justice was "classified according to stratum" (Noticias Caracol 2014). But I could not help wondering if the notoriety of the case, which received daily coverage in the media during the seven months that transpired from incident to sentencing, was not linked to the perpetrator's suspect levantado status. Unfortunately, cases like this are an everyday occurrence in Colombia, with the rich paying their victims or not having to pay them at all and the media hardly covering the stories. Salamanca, on the other hand, had the money but not the status to keep things quiet. He was a longtime resident of Barrio Kennedy driving an Audi SUV, one of the flashiest vehicles available in Colombia. The "shouldn't have owned," "shouldn't have been driving" motif lingered, suggesting that while no justice was ever to be expected for the lower-class victims, a driver with a more authentic class pedigree than Salamanca would have acted more "appropriately" and certainly would not have been subjected to such public scrutiny, much less a public uproar.

Hence I end with a vivid example of the rising anxieties over consumption unleashed by its expansion among middling groups who remain at the margin of dominant definitions of middle class and buena presencia. At the least, this discussion should alert us to the continued and steep reproduction of class distinctions alongside the growth of consumer culture, as well as the limited ability of consumption to affect upwardly mobile identities of unquestionable recognition and repute.

# SIX

# Shopping Mall Fashionistas

## FAST FASHION AND THE WORK OF SHOPPING

In Colombia, the history of fashion is divided in two: before and after the arrival of Zara.

**PILAR CASTAÑO**, *Colombian fashion expert, cited in Rolón 2013*

The point is to be looked at. If I'm dressed divinely and no one looks at me, I know there's something wrong with my outfit.

**ROSA PAULA**, *thirty-two, accountant*

*La mona aunque se vista de seda, mona se queda.* (A monkey may dress in silk, but it's still a monkey.)

**YURI**, *twenty-six, lawyer, repeating a popular saying*

In light of the discussion so far it is not surprising that visiting a mall is a class-charged experience. This has been documented at all malls where visitors are confronted with the social pressure to perform or "look like a consumer" as the price of entry.[1] Specific contexts call for different types of negotiations, however, and what is especially pertinent to the case at hand is how people are actively learning and negotiating changing norms for taste and buena presencia amid rapid societal transformations. Central to this development is the advent of global fast fashion, or pronta moda. If shopping malls are a relatively new phenomenon for many Colombians, even more novel is the advent of international brands and stores that are bringing to locals the possibility of wearing the same brands and styles "as people in the United States and Europe."[2]

The dominance of pronta moda through the arrival of brands like Inditex's Zara and Bershka in 2007 and 2008, respectively, and Forever 21 in 2012 was a recurrent topic among shopping mall visitors, designers, shop owners, and everyone else I talked to when I introduced shopping malls as the topic of my research. Even TV shows and radio programs like Dario Arizmendi's Caracol morning show pondered the possible effects of the sudden availability of "high-style" but low-quality clothes to Colombians and the best ways to purchase such clothes. And almost always the arrival of these brands was celebrated as a sign of the coming-of-age of Colombia, a revolutionary development that divides the history of fashion (before and after Zara), at the same time that people were counseled to choose classic styles over trendy ones and to purchase Colombian products whenever possible, an option that few consumers can actually afford. This chapter considers how many middle-class female professionals and self-described fashionistas used shopping malls as premier sites to learn and perform class identities and to reassert value systems that while in flux remain largely unchallenged. In particular, I focus on their engagement with fast fashion, a relatively new development tied to the growth of shopping malls that are introducing new brands and cheaper clothes while raising the stakes involved in the process of defining identities through self-styling and consumption.

Critiques of fast fashion—the more intensified model of commoditized production and consumption that is dominating global retail, involving a faster turnaround from production to consumption and faster obsolescence of the fashion value of different trends—are numerous and growing (e.g., Briggs 2013). Writers have pointed to the high costs of production both for the environment and for the fate of safe, fair, and well-paid jobs. Writers have also probed fast fashion's role in launching an addiction to trends (Cline 2013; Collins 2003) as well as the way it is helping to reorganize global chains of production and the way design is developed (Benzecry 2014).

In contexts like Bogotá, however, where global fast fashion is often regarded as an aspirational product, questions also emerge about its significance in the everyday self-styling of class. Here I follow Daniel Miller's (2010) warning that clothes are not superficial but actually make us what we think we are and his urging that we consider "fashion" not only as a particular trend, but rather as "the individual construction of an aesthetic based not just on what you wear, but on how you wear it" (15). There has been a great deal of research on fashion, consumption, and class in developing societies, most of it focusing on contexts where ideas of traditional or ethnic dress are represented as threatened by the advent of Western fashion—always equated with "global" brands. Seldom do we consider developing societies that are bombarded by multinational brands and fashion as "fashion capitals" of their own or question the hierarchies of value in fashion and taste that are reproduced when fast fashion brands become the means to reproduce geopolitical distinctions that continue to link fashion with global fashion centers in the United States and Europe, and even with a limited number of cities (Gilbert 2013; Skov 2011).[3]

These questions are essential when considering the case of Bogotá's shopping malls fashionistas, urbanites in a metropolitan city that is not only recognized for the quality of its fashion products in Latin America, particularly in the area of luxury leather goods, but has also long been exposed to "Western" fashions and historically conditioned to covet international brands. In places like this, it is important to account for the particular classed context that frames shopping and people's use of the mall (Conroy 1998), as well as for the ways in which fast fashion affects local fashion. One way is by helping to strengthen the role that fashion plays in social differentiation while reproducing differential systems of value where only "global brands" become coded as conduits of global fashion and modernity. In addition, local concerns about fast fashion are extremely political and can lead us to larger considerations about the work involved in all types of shopping, including the affective work of self-styling. In sum, I suggest that engaging the fickleness of fast fashion can sharpen a consideration of the larger spatial and political economy of contemporary malls.

### ON BEING MEASURED UP WHILE SHOPPING

As we have seen, accessing the mall has become a common paseo for many families and middling groups in Colombia. However, for many middle-class fashionistas, most of whom are educated and working women, accessing the mall was not gauged in relation to gaining entrance to its common areas or supermarkets, among other spaces associated with familias Miranda—that is, onlookers stereotyped as lacking purchasing power who are increasingly populating malls. Neither was it defined in terms of going to the bank or paying your cell phone bill, among other activities that regularly attract visitors to shopping malls. Instead, for these informants, the standard was accessing branded stores and, most important, successfully performing their ability to consume.

In this regard, how one appeared at the mall was a common concern, even among relatively frequent shopping mall users and visitors. For instance, many of my informants shared tales about feeling measured and evaluated at the mall, though not necessarily by guards and the private police but most surprisingly by retail workers, the people with whom they interacted most closely upon entering a store. In particular, some felt judged and surveyed by retail workers who are incentivized to be attentive to clients and to approach them with questions and offers immediately upon their entering a store. They also felt pressured to shop or to appear as if they legitimately belonged there, even though they often had backgrounds similar to those of the retail workers. Claudia, a thirty-year-old professional woman and recent graduate from La Nacional discussed the pressure she feels upon entering a mall and how it informs concerns over self-styling.

> When you go to a shopping mall and you're not dressed appropriately, everyone's eyes, especially the guards', are focused on you. And you feel the pressure, even if you're only going to the movies or waiting for someone. If you're not well dressed, people around you will get the impression of insecurity. Right now we're all dressed appropriately for a mall [pointing to her friends who are in their late thirties, one an academic, the other a pharmacist, and me, all of us dressed to go dancing], but if you go with a worn-out shirt or dirty jeans or sport clothes that are not brand-name, it's noticeable. That's when the retail worker mistreats you and looks at you like, "Why are you here if you can't shop?"

Similar fears of being "discovered" as a nonshopper were palpable in interviews and observations of shopping behavior. I recall a woman at a Juan Valdez coffee shop in the north whom I overhead confessing to a friend that she had purchased a fruit salad because *"le daba pena ordernar solo una aromática,"* that is, she was embarrassed to order only a tea. Whether this admission of concern was informed by anxieties over how she came across to the waitress or to other customers, her embarrassment ended up costing her an extra purchase.

In particular, asking a question about a product was recognized as an especially class-loaded activity that could expose and immediately put on display one's knowledge, or lack thereof, of fashion, materials, or consumer goods more generally or one's hesitation (and lack of resources) at the point of purchase. Higher-class groups were constructed as ideal consumers who are always confident and knowledgeable, informed about whether a product is leather or synthetic, for instance, as well as discriminating and confident. *Gente de alta* were described as highly discriminating with regard to quality but never with regard to price, as a cosmetologist at Centro Mayor put it, echoing what I was told by other fashionistas: "You can tell when people have class and money because they never ask for a price. They just pick out what they want, and that's it. But lower-class people ask a million questions, but they never purchase a thing." With these considerations, some of my informants described arming themselves with as much information about what they needed as they could before going to the mall to ensure they were directed in their shopping excursions and did not come across as hesitant and "unknowing." Cathe, a super-stylish and color-coordinated young lawyer I met at Avenida Chile shopping center, described keeping a diligently studied wish list on her smart phone of the items she needed to complete different *pintas* (outfits). Her carefully studied list comprised forty-eight items, some of which she planned to buy and some of which she hoped would be given to her as gifts, that included jackets in black, blue, mint, and pink; handbags in black, white, and green; high heels in purple, green, and yellow; Puma socks; Besame lingerie, Victoria's Secret bronzer; Jessica Simpson perfume, Ralph Lauren perfume; Lacoste tennis clothing, Nike tennis shoes in mandarin, V-neck Tommy Hilfiger sweaters, Studio F sandals, and Careta makeup—the one used by beauty queens, she explained. These and other items were identified not only by type but also and most important by brand name, underscoring her preference for the very best. As she put it, she was as diligent and disciplined about shopping for the necessary items to complete each of her outfits as she had been about achieving her academic and career goals.

The reluctance to browse when one could not shop explains why so many stores remain mostly empty, especially the more expensive and exclusive ones. High-end stores like MAC and L'Occitane in Gran Estación were free of visitors most of the time I observed them, their tester counters free of passersby unwilling to try or ask the price of a product they could not afford. In contrast, more accessible local brands like the local shoestores Aquiles and Kalifa and supermarkets and big-box stores like Exito and Jumbo were always brimming with people. In particular, big-box supermarkets like Exito and La 14, which in addition to groceries sell every imaginable product, from beauty supplies to home appliances to underwear to religious candles and more, are the heart of most low- and middle-rung malls, almost self-contained because of their promotional credit card offers that make it possible for shoppers to purchase everything they could possibly want inside their walls. These are the stores where I observed the most shopping activity, as well as the most lingering. Teresa, whom I met at Pan y Queso, the cafeteria at the store La 14 in Centro Colima, waiting for a friend with her two children, is a good example of how people use these very popular stores. She said she does her grocery shopping in barrio stores nearby, but she came to socialize in the cafeteria inside La 14 because it offered the cheapest luncheon choices inside the mall. The more popular feel and the popular music in the background clashed with the restraint that characterized most other areas of the mall, with the exception of the movie theaters and the play ride areas. The sales clerk at MAC confirmed the more intimidating feel that dominated branded stores by noting that her clientele consisted only of people who came to shop, never to linger or play with products. "Lingering" was openly discouraged by the presence of a guard near the entrance and by the solicitous sales clerk.

The impetus to look like a consumer was even felt by higher-stratum respondents who had greater purchasing power and access to stores. Thus Angie, a stratum 4 lawyer, described her routine to prepare to go shopping at Gran Estación's MAC: "My hair has to be flawless, and my makeup also has to be perfect. Because the first thing they are going to do is look at your face, and there's going to be a judgment by the clerk, assessing what you are wearing and what type of products you regularly purchase. So I go well made-up and always dressed up: impeccable." Angie described how the clerk would spend up to an hour with her, even doing her makeup, a treatment she attributed to her presentation, fully aware that this was not how informally dressed clients were treated. As an example, she offered the case of another shopper who arrived in sweatpants and was immediately asked for specific information about the type of makeup she used (which she did not have). For Angie, this question was the same as essentially pushing the woman out of the store and asking her to come back with "proof" of purchasing power. In Angie's view, the customer would have been treated differently if, like her, she had come "looking the part" and already made-up.

This pressure to look respectable and appropriate when visiting a mall was echoed by most respondents, from the solidly middle-class women I met in Salitre Plaza and Gran Estación to the more aspirational informants from strata 2 and 3 I met in Centro Mayor, even though they subscribed to different definitions of what was appropriate to wear at a mall. Some, like Angie, felt that one had to purposefully dress up and look "impeccable," while others felt that it was appropriate to dress more casually, bemoaning any type of *dediparado* look (someone with a pinky pointing up, too eager to look refined). What everyone shared was little tolerance for ways of dress that were associated with ñero or traqueto culture and demeanor, which though different—ñero referring to lower-class urban groups and traqueto implying narco-traffic connections and ostentatious dress—were often described in similar ways. Both were associated with the tendency to wear too many colors with no care for their "proper" combination or outfits that were too tight and revealing, for example, clothing made of Lycra or showing one's midriff especially if one was overweight and out of shape, or wearing too much makeup. Wearing sneakers meant for sports, not fashion, or clothes that were disheveled, torn, or dirty were also among the many varied definitions that were regularly offered of what made a ñero look. In contrast, a traqueto would be more likely at fault for wearing luxury goods in ways that would be considered too flashy or vulgar. The specter of these two symbolic references fed into the imaginary that *gente normal,* or normal people, would dress more soberly, to avoid coming across as either poor or illegitimately rich.

I also noticed that whenever I met friends and acquaintances casually at shopping malls they always looked very well put together and that when I prompted them about their pintas they always had something special to flash or to point to: silver earrings worn only on special occasions, shoes with a fashionable stacked heel, or a classic jacket that was bought years ago at a special boutique in Unicentro, and so forth. Likewise, more informally dressed informants made a point of excusing their manner of dress during the course of the interview when the conversation turned to their clothing preferences. In sum, people's responses were often more aspirational than represented by the outfits they were currently wearing, and they would point this out by excusing whatever they were wearing as "not representative" of what they would normally prefer to wear at a mall.

Returning to the social pressure to look like consumers, the tendency among my fashionistas to avoid embarrassment at the mall often limited their ability to try on products and their engagement with stores to window-shopping. Many described their preference for purchasing in department stores (which are also a new addition to shopping malls, primarily introduced by Chilean developers) because these spaces provide them with a freer space to look at products without having to interact with a sales clerk and risk having their purchasing ability gauged. Another common class-charged use of the mall was window-shopping to learn about trends and fashion, only to use this knowledge when shopping at San Victorino and more popular stores in the city's center, which were both cheaper and more socially accessible. Margarita, a graduate student, who lives near Gran Estación, explained:

> Part of window-shopping is learning how to discern trends. Because you can see pants well put together on a mannequin at the shopping mall and realize they are part of a trend, but if you see the same pants on a mannequin that is

not well put together you ignore them. So the great thing about coming to a mall is that you always see clothes that are well styled as part of an image, which makes it easier to identify what to buy when you see the same or a similar piece in San Victorino.

In this way, the mall was valued not necessarily for the items it sold but rather for the *styling* involved when showing such items, in other words, for staging and exhibiting fashion. What Margarita and other fashionistas I spoke to tried to avoid was trying on items they knew they could not afford to buy—once again part and parcel of their attempts to avoid the potential shame of appearing as a nonconsumer.

I have more to say about the use of shopping malls as styling and educational devices. For now, the issue is that asking any question about a product was recognized as an especially classed-loaded activity that could expose and immediately display one's knowledge or lack thereof. The "naturalness" of higher-income groups' "knowledges" and "ways of being" at the mall echo Bourdieu's (1984) perceptive discussion of the ways in which cultural capital can so easily translate into "natural dispositions" and taste. The latter is always constructed as being innately possessed by those "in the know," when, in fact, these "dispositions" have been carefully cultivated and are best seen as the product of people's class-based position, origins, and exposure to dominant symbolic economies and goods. In particular, the confidence exhibited by more affluent visitors to the mall was not only a product of their greater purchasing power. It was also undoubtedly linked to their greater exposure to consumer products and the practices of shopping at malls. This is in sharp contrast to the hesitation that is common among groups who have had less exposure to new practices and spaces of consumption.

Even the most lower-class interviewees recognized and spoke about the confidence associated with higher-income groups. On a busy Sunday afternoon, I met some stratum 2 single mothers overseeing their children at the kiddie rides at Titán Plaza. They were sitting in lounge chairs in the hallway, an area popular with families. I approached them about my project, and soon the discussion turned to whether it was possible to recognize the "look of class," an exercise we tried by guessing the strata of passersby. Like my other informants, they insisted it was possible to discern people's economic standing based solely on their appearance and consistently pointed to women or groups who dressed fashionably and carried shopping bags as "high class." However, they similarly identified people who they perceived to be walking and acting confidently, or as one put it, "like they belonged at the mall and could shop here." Mostly, they pointed to women who moved freely and happily, as if they were advertising their presence and taking up space with their bags, a sharp contrast to their own staying-in-placeness. It seemed as if, in pointing to others' confidence, they were expressing their own out-of-placeness.

Earlier I discussed the role that shame and intimidation play as tactics of security that help communicate who is acceptable and who *no tiene nada que buscar ahi* (has nothing to look for there). What this concern with feeling confident at spaces of consumption points to is a general awareness of the public enforcement of security, not by security guards, but by how one is seen by other visitors at the mall and the potential shame of being considered out of place.

Most of my informants could point to moments when they recognized themselves as being out of place because of the stares they felt others directed at them. Many also recalled witnessing how guards and clerks treated people who "didn't belong" at the mall, which pointed to their own fears that they too could be similarly read or considered. Indeed, people's social fears are informed by the "public correction" that is a common occurrence in shopping malls. During my research, I witnessed security guards chasing people (for shoplifting, I was told, though I could not confirm it), kicking people out for being "indigents," or redirecting people away from "private areas" (i.e., areas reserved for particular restaurants or establishments) and even imparting lessons in civility and fear. Especially in the food courts, security staff would go up and down the aisles urging people to hide their valuables, not to take pictures, and to keep their voices low so publicly and visibly that it magnified the "correction" and policing. One instance of a "public correction" involved a group of youths hanging out in the food court at Centro Mayor, dressed in what locals would term ñero: baggy jackets, caps, wide-legged jeans, and carrying backpacks. Immediately upon their entering the court, many stared at them with obvious signs of fear and judgment, prompting two security officers to come forward and add force to the public's stares. Within minutes the kids left the area, forced out as much by the guards as by the food court patrons. Groups of kids are a common sight around shopping mall food courts, where the self-serve organization of fast-food restaurants and tables offer a more socially tolerant context for lingering. But this was a weekend, when food courts are filled with families and a greater degree of surveillance, so there was little tolerance for the youths.

Another humiliating correction involved a modestly dressed grandmother with indigenous features who wanted to treat her granddaughter to a kiddie ride but was turned away because she lacked the necessary "proof of purchase." The grandmother had stayed behind, trying to figure out the instructions for entry, but the child had rushed to the kiddie ride entrance, waiting eagerly, when she was turned away. I tried to plead with the young woman guarding the entrance but to no avail. The embarrassing drama had significantly shrunk the crowd of onlookers and deterred others from going on the kiddie rides. Witnessing or hearing about shopping mall dramas like these informs people's internalized ideas and self-disciplining to claim "belonging." Most important, even when these fears and attitudes may have little relation to any specific action, they speak to a wider history of class stigma that is very much alive, reflecting and reinforcing social inequalities.

The irony is that both being looked at and looking at others are common practices of social assessment and differentiation at the mall that many of my fashionista informants purposefully sought. As noted by Rosa Paula in one of this chapter's epigraphs, outfits are meant to be looked at. As we have seen, however, people are just as sensitive about receiving approving and admiring stares from strangers or pleasantries and positive comments from friends about their outfits as they are about not receiving a *mala mirada,* or a bad look, from strangers. I found that concerns over how one is stared at, whether approvingly or disprovingly, were always more revealing of people's levels of comfort at being "seen" at shopping malls than about the meaning of a stare, whether imagined or real.

Even informants who lived in close proximity to shopping malls hesitated about fully accessing them. This was the case for a group of women in their twenties who were recent graduates of El Rosario, a private university that afforded them considerable cultural capital and, one would assume, greater comfort with accessing malls. Yet they too felt intimidated by different stores and spaces in the mall. One said she hung out only in the main wing of the mall, considering the newer section with fancier stores as a "dead" zone. Another woman felt especially uncomfortable in stores that sell perfume because, she said, "one can't always identify their smells, whether they are sweet or musky, and the clerk knows, and then you appear as if you know nothing." She described shoestores as "safe zones" because it is easier to come up with an excuse not to buy a certain pair of shoes without implicating her purchasing ability; for instance, she can say the shoes don't fit property or the color isn't exactly what she needs. The third woman described being profiled at a jewelry store, with the clerk following her as though she was there to shoplift rather than browse. Another recalled the embarrassing moment when a clerk expressed doubt that she could afford an item after she had asked its price. All four spoke about areas in their own neighborhood mall that were off-limits, stores they have never entered, not even to browse, as well as shopping malls in greater Bogotá, most of them in the north, that were entirely out of their reach.

The fear of being exposed as a nonshopper affects the store choices of Bogotá's new middle classes, particularly their preference for international fast-fashion brands and department stores over local Colombian stores and brands. We tend to associate the preference for international brands with the globalizing consumer capitalism that overtakes modernizing societies, but this perspective misses the democratization aspects that international brands may also represent to locals, not unlike what Williams (1991) described in relation to the role played by nineteenth-century department stores in exposing the masses to "dream worlds" of mass consumption that had previously been out of their reach. Let us consider that a traditional Colombian brand and retail store, whether in a shopping mall or elsewhere, differs from an international brand store in at least two important ways. First, Colombian stores are smaller, which means that less merchandise can be shown at a given time, so customers usually have to rely on sales clerks to get different size or styles. Smaller stores also mean that a customer is always noticed when she enters the store and that within seconds a sales clerk will greet her. Local stores in popular venues like San Andresitos and San Victorino avoid this intimate setting by displaying racks of merchandise in hallways and by having a more casual atmosphere and more open access to the common areas. In a shopping mall, however, stores are enclosed, and visitors are immediately in the spotlight when entering a standalone store. Second, brand-name Colombian stores put a higher price and value on exclusivity and customization. They also sell more one-of–a-kind merchandise, which is considered a sign of status by many consumers but which few people are able to afford. In addition, these stores require interaction with sales clerks to find out about a product's availability and whether it comes in other styles or colors. My informants found such interactions a source of great anxiety; they felt obligated to make a purchase and less able to make an excuse for not doing so. In contrast, international brand stores carry bulk and generic mass-produced merchandise, accessibly displayed so that customers can shop on their own and browse more freely. And this is exactly what consumers were doing when flocking to new stores like Forever 21 that not only offer cheaper goods but also considerably freer and less scrutinized modes of shopping and new types of relationships to goods, where looking at clothes and trying them on entail less social pressure and obligation to buy. Two accountants in their late twenties whom I met shopping at Forever 21 described why they liked the store in these terms. They especially liked the option of "feeling lost" in the store and asking for help only if they needed it, as opposed to being bombarded by clerks who pressure them by asking, "So, what are you getting?" (¿Qué te llevas?), the moment they start looking at merchandise, or else they look at them as potential shoplifters.

At the same time, international brands, considered low- to mid-end by U.S. standards, are becoming the coveted standard in Colombia, especially among new middle classes, who lack the familiarity with these brands that upwardly mobile groups have cultivated through travel. This symbolic identity also made these stores unapproachable for many of my informants. For instance, the sales clerks were described as "looking like models." In fact, the way they looked was described in exaggerated ways that acknowledged some of my informants' feelings of inadequacy. "I'm intimidated by how they dress. The sales clerks are super tall and super skinny. They look like models and are all spectacular, and their bodies and faces are divine, and they wear these high heels, and the first thing they do is look you up and down to see if you're a potential customer."

In other words, the seemingly more "democratizing" context of shopping was simultaneously tied to new forms of subjection. In particular, the latter informant is reacting to the upscaling of retail workers, which is another component of the internationalization of retail. As noted in chapter 3, working in retail has traditionally been considered a lower-class service occupation that is avoided by middle-class and upwardly mobile groups. In contrast, working in an international brand store like Zara or Forever 21 has become fashionable among university students in some of the most elite universities, as a shortcut to getting discounted prices. These chain stores are transforming retail work by hiring part-time rather than full-time staff and making style and "look" prerequisites for being hired. Colombian brands also discriminate in terms of "look" when hiring sales clerks, but this is done based on the type of shopping mall and its location. Retail workers at the middle-rung malls I studied came primarily from the south, whereas the flagship stores of the same brands located in Zona Rosa or in shopping malls in the north were tended primarily by young, model-type white Colombians, many of them students. Retail workers at international brand stores were always distinguishable, especially because their peers working at Colombian stores in the same shopping mall were markedly less dressed up and less made-up while being more racially diverse and from popular backgrounds.

Many Colombian merchants have reacted to the advent of international brands by emphasizing the distinctiveness and better quality of their products, even appealing to Colombian nationalism by urging consumers to buy locally made products. A good example is a sign posted on the window of the women's fashion store California Inn. Like other national brands, California Inn features a North American–sounding name, a common trend to index cosmopolitanism and modernity among national retailers such as Crepes and Waffles, Studio F, and Tennis. The sign greeting customers at the door, however, points to the store's Colombian origin: "IMAGINA SER ÚNICA!! EN UN MUNDO DE RÉPLICAS . . . Sin miedos experimenta entre telas y formas. UNA COLECCIÓN HECHA CON TALENTO COLOMBIANO!!" (Imagine being unique in a world of copies. Without fear, experiment with fabrics and forms. A collection made with Colombian talent.") Another example is the clothing line named "Not Made in China," which was developed by the independent designer Juana Rojas for Industrial Glam, which markets itself as unique, "not for the masses," and, "above all, Made in Colombia."

Rojas is one of the few independent designers still standing in Zona Rosa, a hub for independent designers where few remained after major international brands such as Zara began to open their flagship stores in the area. In fact, she immediately described herself as part of a resistance movement against the attack of international retail that had displaced most other designers from the coveted Zona Rosa. "My prices were actually higher seven years ago than they are today," she noted, adding that the arrival of international stores had pushed her to lower prices not only to compete, but to survive. At the same time, as one of the last remaining independent designers in the Zona Rosa, right next to the new Forever 21 that opened in 2014, her store had benefited from the greater foot traffic in the area and a growing interest in alternative design amid a limited number of choices. She was especially happy about the growing interest of selected customers who were looking for clothes that would set them apart from those wearing mass-marketed products. Her clients were "women who don't want to look uniformada or disfrazada," she explained, using the metaphor of the standardized uniform to characterize the massified look of pronta moda as akin to wearing a costume.

In this regard, pronta moda is recognized as a key impetus for many independent designers seeking to capture the market of exclusivity while challenging a dominant view about Colombian products whenever these are compared to imported goods. This is the view that Colombian goods are durable and of good quality but not necessarily novel in design like pronta moda. This view was echoed by Pilar Castaño during an interview about fast fashion's influence on Colombian designers. She specifically praised Zara and similar stores for "rejuvenating" Colombian design: "For me, the arrival of these new stores is giving new air to the stodgy and boring collections presented by our Colombian brands. Now we have new options that help us feel like we're part of the world, where we don't have anything to envy, in terms of urban fashion, about global capitals of the world like Washington and Paris" (Rolón 2013). While equating Washington with Paris as a global capital of fashion should be concerning, the opinions of this "fashion" expert are quite revealing for placing Colombia squarely behind any recognized hierarchy of global fashion capitals and for identifying "global brands" as the only medium for being fashionable. Still, not all fashion experts and designers subscribe to such narrow views. Juana, from Industrial Glam, agreed that the arrival of international brands was indeed turning more people toward fashion, even playing what she described as "a pedagogical" role for consumers by exposing them to more choices and designs. Akin to what I heard from other designers, she felt that global fast fashion brands had helped popularize Colombian designers among those who prized, and could afford, more selective designs. At the same time, she totally rejected the view that Colombian designers were behind the times, that their designs were stodgy and lacking in style and innovation. In her view, Colombian designers are as global and innovative as the next, and in fact, many designers I spoke to had been educated abroad and traveled regularly. Most were well versed in international fashion blogs and Instagram and were very familiar with global trends, which they regularly scrutinized for ideas. The difficulty was the quick turnaround of fast fashion against which Colombian designs will always seem less exciting and novel. Most important, pronta moda is introducing the concept of disposability to a consumer culture in which clothes were traditionally most valued for their quality and durability. So said Paula, a lawyer turned fashion promoter and the founder of La Percha (The Rack), one of the few local hubs for independent design in Bogotá: "We have the custom of inheriting clothes and recycling clothes, like passing that dress you love on to your daughter being the maximum." Yet this tradition is being quickly eliminated, she added, because it is practically impossible to produce clothes that are durable when the fickle taste of fast fashion makes trends quickly redundant.

The result is that fashion is emerging as another medium for reasserting hierarchies of cultural evaluation, in which local designers are slated to lose. Specifically, in fashion we see a reversal of the aesthetic hierarchies that dominate discussions of Latin American shopping malls, where Latin American shopping mall designers are posited as more artful but less technical than their North American counterparts (see chap. 2). In the case of fashion, the opposite view holds: local designers are seen as dull and stodgy in comparison to the edginess and supposed inventiveness of pronta moda. According to this view, it is only stores like Forever 21 that are introducing "real" global fashion to Colombia and expanding access to the same clothes that global citizens would wear, as if Colombia had no fashion history or no indigenous creative production that could be worthy of recognition and global repute.

Notwithstanding the starkly opposing aesthetic binaries at play in regard to shopping mall design and fashion, in both cases allotments of Colombians' aesthetic ability or lack thereof are deployed in ways that position them as lacking vis-à-vis the "true" innovators, the North American shopping mall professionals and international fashion designers. It is the latter who are positioned as international tastemakers, whether it be in the shopping mall industry or in international brands. These assessments point to the local and international geopolitics that are always involved in determinations of quality in the aesthetic realm; in particular, to how design and aesthetics are continuously marked by racial and imperial social hierarchies that subordinate the aesthetic potential of marginal groups however defined (Tu 2010; Londoño 2012). This situation can also be found in the United States, where designers of color remain a minority and where blacks and Latinos are not only underrepresented on the runway as models, but also as designers and even as art and design students, sustaining the racial divide in fashion (Friedman 2015).

Yet the view that local design is always inferior vis-à-vis "international" design has not remained unchallenged. This is true in Colombia but also throughout Latin America, where fashion is slowly being recognized as a key creative industry and a must-have in any national repertoire of cultural offerings deserving of recognition and promotion by ministers of culture as well as by government and tourism proponents. The rise of international fashion fairs like Colombiamoda and Perú Moda, which are promoted internationally, illustrates the trend. At the same time, fashion remains a tricky terrain for asserting national differentiation, as Lisa Skov's (2011) important piece on the dreams of small nations in a polycentric fashion world notes. As she writes, regional fashion centers may receive some partial international attention once in a while, but the fashion circuit remains dominated by the same limited number of fashion capitals. Peripheral countries and cities face added suspicion about whether their collections can have international appeal and follow "international standards" in ways that further hinder their dreams of global recognition as fashion producers (Skov 2011). These dynamics were evident during Colombiamoda 2015, Colombia's annual fashion festival held in Medellín, where visitors were exposed not only to a large display of pride and buoyancy among national designers but also to a circuit of professional development conferences flaunting the primacy of global trends, of fashion as a "universal" language, with New York and European cities as the named and unnamed reference for taste.[4] International media coverage of Colombiamoda 2014 also evidences the steep challenges that confront a peripheral Latin American city seeking to be recognized as a global fashion capital. The event was mostly ignored by the international press, and when it was covered, the exotification and stereotyping of "Latin" culture tended to trump any serious consideration of the fashion. It was as if Medellín's narco-traffic history had taken center stage, with fashion blogs pointing to "the crimes against denim, butt enhancing undies, half-naked Latin models (of both sexes), knife-proof hoodies" as major draws rather than the work of any specific designer or product.[5] One year later, the fair did no better since the mainstream press seemed to reduce the exhibits and runway shows to a spectacle of bright colors and patterns and "hot looks" (Reuters 2015).

Hierarchies of value are also at play whenever Latin American fashion becomes coded as "ethnic," and when "culture" becomes the key authenticating element for international recognition, as when designers are mentioned for their "Latin flavor" and vivacious colors or for their pre-Columbian motifs. These are all common ways in which Latin American designers are described by the fashion press—when they are discussed at all. Many Latin American countries, in turn, have contributed to this "ethnicization" of fashion by linking it to their tourism industries. This is the case with the government- and business-sponsored Peru Fashion Show featuring designs in alpaca and vicuña that was celebrated in Washington, DC (2013), and New York (2014). This raised the question of whether Peru is more interested in promoting nationally produced fibers like alpaca than in the promotion of fashion in and of itself.

Unfortunately, often coded as "cultural," the aesthetic dimensions of many Latin American creative designs become easy targets for cultural appropriation by "real" designers, as a "bohemian" or "ethnic" addition. A good example is the Colombian Wayuu crochet style, now found in all types of accessories beyond the *mochilas* that originally popularized it. Hence the plagiarism scandal unleashed when the Spanish designer Stella Rittwagen included several Wayuu-style bags in her Spring 2014 collection, which circulated in the press as a product solely of her creation. This case is especially revealing, considering that the Wayuu style is internationally known, as well as one of the few artistic expressions protected as intellectual property by the Colombian state.[6] This protection, however, was ultimately irrelevant against the muscle of international appropriation, which more often than not occurs without much fanfare. Another example is Tori Burch's calf-hair saddlebag (2014), advertised as drawing on "traditional Colombian handicrafts." Selling for US$995, the bag is a direct copy of the Colombian carriel, a leather satchel one would find in any artisanal shop in Colombia, at a much lower cost, yet it is only described as "drawing on" or "inspired by," erasing the work, design, and originality of the original bag. This is just one instance when we see the problems involved in the appropriation of Latin American designs: it erases the innovation in the design of anything that is slated as "inspiration" for Western designers while reifying differences between Euro-American designers and everyone else. The fashion scholar Min-Ha T. Pham (2014) has discussed this in relation to the appropriation of Asian culture by Euro-American fashion design, where she finds how charges of cultural appropriation tend to reproduce and reify a high/low cultural binary. Accordingly, high culture is always identified with Euro-American fashion design and low culture with Asian and "ethnic" cultures as raw material, which obscures the complex aesthetic and social histories of whatever is being appropriated by Euro-American designers, reinstating them as the only possible innovators (Pham 2014).

Back to the challenges faced by local designers, the mall-ification of retail has also hindered their ability to access distribution spaces to reach customers. This was noted by Paula when she described the demand for alternative shopping spaces catering to independent designers. Her call for independent designers to sell at La Percha was answered by over a thousand designers seeking to rent a rack to exhibit and sell their creations—an indication of the growing interest in independent design as local resistance to fast fashion. In her words, the project was about providing a space where designers could "keep their production small without looking small," reasserting one of her main goals: challenging the massification of retail that limits fashion and design solely to mass-produced items.

I found local brands and designers who presented "buying Colombian" as "added values": authenticity, quality, and exclusivity. These values were assumed to be coveted by any discriminating customer above *productos chinos*—the catchall phrase for anything imported, cheap, and, hence, immediately considered of lesser quality than nationally produced products. Unfortunately, the constant emphasis on self-styling and *el que dirán,* or appearances and concerns for what people will say, work against the marketing efforts of many Colombian brands and designers. Even "uniformadas," referring here to the uniformed workers who presumably have less need to purchase clothes on a regular basis, face similar pressures. Consider the case of Yurany, a Davivienda Bank teller who was very proud that his uniform was designed by the stylish and popular store Armi, which allowed her to save, reuse, and restyle it. As she explained, wearing uniforms did not preclude her and her colleagues from engaging with consumption; they chose their own perfumes, bags, shoes, and accessories, and they were allowed to wear their own clothes when they attended meetings, special events, and seminars. Yet for Yurany, wearing local brands was not an option: "With the salaries we earn, I have no option but to purchase *ropa china.* I know it's no good and that it affects the Colombian economy, but I have to. I can't afford to purchase brand-new clothes all the time." In particular, she stressed the need to wear a brand-new outfit on those rare occasions when she was allowed to dress in her regular clothes, something she was not willing to compromise for the sake of purchasing higher-priced locally produced goods.

The fact is that most female professionals are purchasing ropa china even if they are not aware of it. Ropa china was associated with cheap clothes one would purchase in San Andresitos or at outlets, but the fact is that imported clothes had become commonplace in the seemingly more high-end establishments my fashionista informants coveted as symbols of "good fashion." This is true of stores such as Studio F and Armi, regular fixtures in most shopping malls, whose prices have significantly dropped in recent years because of their increased reliance on imports, as evident in the ubiquitous "Made in Bangladesh" or Morocco or China labels on their clothes. Most had noticed the cheaper prices and the sudden rise in promotions that allowed them to shop in stores that until recently had been out of their reach. But not everyone had made the connection that ropa china was responsible for the cheaper prices at their coveted stores.

Even more threatening than the cheaper prices of fast fashion, local designers face the challenge of having to compete with the "democratized" space that modern stores represent to Colombian consumers. Paula from La Percha acknowledged this was one of her biggest problems: the invisible barriers that a store that markets itself as high style, exclusive, and alternative, like hers, may represent to the very customers she needs. As she recognized, many people are too intimidated to enter her store, even though she sells merchandise in all price ranges and she frequently offers promotions and sales. She had to fire a classist sales clerk who was rude and insulting to some gay patrons, who were among her most faithful consumers. As she acknowledged, given the threat posed by shopping malls and pronta moda, "exclusive" stores could no longer afford to adopt traditional and classist attitudes of the past. Instead, all stores were being pushed to strike a delicate balance between the need to project exclusivity and the need to communicate openness and accessibility in order to expand their customer base, which now more than ever before represented the key to their survival. We might recall here the shopping mall manager's comments about the growing difficulty of assessing who might be a customer based solely on their appearance. He too described efforts to train store managers to be accommodating to everyone, lest they miss out on a sale if they misjudge a potential consumer.

Finally, another particularity of Colombian and most Latin American malls is the historically slower turnover of merchandise and collections, with fashion being mostly unaffected by seasonal changes. New collections take longer to arrive, clothes remain on sale for months at a time, and the lack of seasons makes many purchases appropriate to wear year-round. For instance, before Zara arrived in Colombia, my informants reported that the slow turnaround in collections made it much easier for them to learn about clothes and fashion and purchase coveted items. They said they were able to save for an item without the risk that it would no longer be available or no longer in fashion when they were finally able to purchase it. It was also easier for them to attain a level of expertise on favorite brands, products, fabrics, and styles, which was the source of great pride among many of my informants. Rocio explained, "I can always identify the brand because I go to so many shopping malls all the time. I know what is from what store or another."

The arrival of more international stores and brands, however, has raised the stakes of acquiring fashion know-how, not only by introducing rapid turnaround in merchandise but also the concept of seasons in a country where sales have traditionally been driven by holidays (e.g., Mother's Day,

Christmas) rather than seasons (Rolón 2013). The fact that fast fashion's "seasons" do not coincide with changes in climate in most regions in Colombia and most Latin American cities, which are either tropical, dry, or cold year-round, also adds to the irony of the new shopping regime, which only makes sense in relation to the "newness" of new seasons, not fit with local weather conditions. In this context, "season" becomes another word for modernity, or what gives locals the ability to wear the same clothes at the same time of year as global fashionistas, which is always equated with Europeans and North Americans. During a shopping mall tour for Latin American industry visitors, the manager of Andino repeatedly stressed that the merchandise sold at her mall "is the same as the collections that are being sold concurrently in Europe and the United States, and made with exactly the same care and materials." She took pride in achieving a new level of parity with other countries, given that before the advent of international chain stores, Colombians could only purchase branded goods locally that were out of season, dumped by retailers, or fakes or contraband.

People were also proud of their ability to identify knockoffs, or *chimbo* or *chiveado* goods, which signified their knowledge of and access to international brands. Andrea, the cachaca journalist introduced earlier, explained, "We play a lot with images, and if you have Gucci boots or Tommy Hilfiger or Nike, I'm going to think that you're stratum 7, until I discover that your Nikes have a double *k,* then I realize where you've really purchased them." It is not only the forged item that is exposed by the misspelled brand name but also the "fake" place of purchase, an informal market somewhere rather than the appropriate branded store, which would most likely be located in a shopping mall. This comment confirms Cecilia Rivas's (2014) observation about the interrelationship of informal markets and shopping malls in creating imaginaries of value and hierarchies of distinctions and differentiation. As her research on shopping malls in El Salvador shows, while informal markets and shopping malls are posited as starkly different spaces, both are directly involved in maintaining imaginary landscapes and ideas of inequality between their visitors and consumers by helping to generalize ideas and meanings about the differential value of the commodities and the spaces in which they are sold.[7]

It is also important to note that informality and fake goods (chiveados) are not uncontested categories; an informal market may contain different sectors and sell a variety of products that may be recognized as more or less legitimate or informal, or upscale or popular, just like the category "fake" may include some versions that are more legitimate or convey higher status than others. Thus, while the upper classes may disdain all types of "fakery," the middle classes are more ambivalent about brands. In Bogotá's San Andresito de San José, for instance, fake Louis Vuitton and Michael Kors bags carry different prices if they are identified as "imitations" or "replicas." Imitation products are often made locally and do not have as many identifying brand details, whereas replicas are primarily imported and were described as featuring "better detailing" and materials. The inequalities of value in the world of fake goods and how they both sustain and are sustained by a hierarchy in the markets where they are sold deserve more attention than I can give here. The point is that in a context like Bogotá, where almost every international brand is copied and forged, it is not only purchasing or wearing a chiveado product that communicates status but also the type of copy, where it was purchased, and even which brand is copied. A woman in her thirties who met me for an interview carrying a fake Michael Kors bag readily admitted that it was a copy purchased through a friend, but she was nevertheless quick to disparage informal markets and San Andresitos for the ubiquity of chiveado products. She noted that Michael Kors bags, which she knew were in a popular upswing internationally, were just beginning to be copied in Colombia and that the style she had purchased was newer and rarer than what a San Andresito vendor would sell. In sum, her bag was a better and more authentic version than the fakes sold at this market.

In this way, talk about shopping led me to appreciate the real work involved and the importance of reframing dominant notions of consumption that see it as a leisure or purely distracting activity; instead it should be theorized in relation to the labor, time, effort, and stamina that are required. This perspective jibes with Miller's (1998) argument about the relationship between shopping and sacrifice, where shopping is seen to be ultimately about social relations, obligations, and sacrifices, providing a perspective that stretches dominant explanations of shopping as an activity involving only the subjectivity and desires of an individual shopper. Whether these social relations or desires are real or imagined, shoppers' efforts are almost always directed by imaginaries beyond their individual positions, as well as fueled by a constant desire to transform and impart social meaning to an activity that we have tended to deride as mundane and insignificant. In other words, shopping is decisively a lot of work, exactly because it is loaded with social significance and meanings that, as we have seen, often transcend an individual's immediate friends and community to encompass concerns about how one is "seen," assessed, and regarded by social others. Most significantly, the work of shopping is visible when we broaden our consideration of consumption as an active process of production and imagination and appreciate the affective labor and "entrepreneurial" practices involved in fashion and self-styling (Freeman 2014).

Writers have recognized the labor involved in the activity of shopping among European and U.S. middle classes: they work to reach outlets and hunt for the best prices and in general invest time and effort in achieving thrift (Conroy 1998; Miller 1998). Certainly these investments were also at play among my Bogotá fashionista informants. Yet they also faced the additional work of learning the ins and outs of new products and finding out about what was worth spending money on and what was ultimately a waste. These activities were especially taxing, not to mention quite costly, because this knowledge could often only be obtained through experience.

For instance, that pronta moda can fall apart after a few washings, that a fashionable boot with a thin sole will make your feet hurt after a few blocks, that a brand-name shoe may turn out to be of low quality, or that a knockoff was easily recognizable because of a misspelling in the brand and bad design were some of the lessons that my informants learned only after they had purchased items that ended up hurting or embarrassing them. I bring to mind a taxi driver who had saved up to buy a pair of Diesel jeans in Unicentro but no longer wore after a friend publicly pointed out the logo on them was the same as the logo on jeans he bought in San Victorino; or the university student who refused to wear a Coach bag her mother purchased for her at a Miami outlet because the logo was too flashy and she feared could be read as a fake. Increasingly available to locals at retail franchises or at informal markets, brand-name goods were highly coveted but also the objects of concern, hence the preference among many fashionistas to avoid brand-name products so as to eliminate the possibility of misreading or miscommunication.

Similarly, concerns about what to wear with which outfits are bound to result not only in detailed lists like Cathe's but also a preoccupation with the hows and why of style. Yuri, the twenty-six-year-old Colpensiones lawyer, confessed, "I wake up in the morning, and I'm already thinking about my outfit for the day. I go to bed, and I'm thinking about the next day's outfit. Fashion is always on my mind."

Moreover, using shopping malls as resources or style guides was especially frustrating because it helped launch dreams of consumption that could never be fully realized. My assistant Natalia expressed very lucidly the frustration that is structurally inherent to the world of retail during one of my first focus groups in Gran Estación. She, like her two friends, who are also university students, is a fan of Naf Naf, a French brand that is produced locally and touts itself as offering bold and affordable looks. This was causing a furor among Bogotá youth but also much frustration. In Natalia's words: "It's frustrating that things are so expensive and that there are so many beautiful things you want but don't have the money to buy. It's really frustrating being able to make purchases only when there are promotions, then finding out when you're finally ready that the store is launching a new collection with even better and more beautiful clothes but super pricey. And you feel maddened because you want those clothes, but they are not on sale." Indeed, because of the rapid turnaround of clothing it was not possible for her to purchase clothes at the rate that satisfied her craving for Naf Naf, which confronted her with the cruel realization that her purchases (on sale) would always appear less shiny and new than the store's coveted new collection. Natalia described taking revenge at the madrugón, where she can purchase a ton of clothes with 100,000 pesos ($50), but she acknowledged that it was never quite the same: "You always know that these are the clothes at the madrugón and not exactly what you saw at the mall, so it's frustrating."

The built-in disappointment of shopping and self-styling was heightened by social media whose use was ubiquitous among younger fashionistas, who seemed to be as freed by fashion-oriented sites such as Instagram as they were confined by them. From Instagram they learned ways to refresh their outfits and save money. A common strategy was to browse at the shopping mall but refine their ideas through Instagram, then purchase the same or similar styles at the cheaper San Victorino or at cheaper stores in the Centro. This constitutes an important resistance strategy when one considers the stigma that markets like San Victorino and the Centro still hold in the imaginaries of many upwardly mobile groups. Another common strategy was to have a local seamstress make the same or a similar outfit at a significantly lower price. This was a common tactic to address the disconnect between how beautiful an outfit may look online, or on a shopping mall's mannequin, and how flimsy and ill-fitting it was in real life, which was a common complaint about pronta moda.

Fit and a garment's *orma,* the way it is cut in order to emphasize or deemphasize certain parts of the body, were regular references among all the fashionistas. Many of them had grown up in families where at least one member knew how to sew or had had at least one special outfit made specifically for them, giving them firsthand experience with the type of fit that can only come from an individually tailored piece, against which pronta moda could only seem flimsy and ill-fitting. This is an area where generational differences were especially evident. Sandra, a thirty-four-year-old educational consultant, was one of the many professional women who criticized pronta moda as flimsy and ill-fitting. However, she also admitted liking the variety and taking pictures of designs she had seen on the Internet or in shopping malls and having them custom-made for her whenever possible. But this practice was becoming too time consuming and costly compared to pronta moda, so more often than not she was left to pick and choose from the badly designed pronta moda offerings. Her strategy was to draw on her previous experience with handmade outfits to make the most informed selection: "You have to look at the materials and their texture. One piece can look more or less elegant than another just based on the materials. So I look for things that don't wrinkle too much and that are better made. I make sure that if I look at myself in a mirror one side isn't longer than the other." She also made informed distinctions about what was worth buying and what was a pass: "If I'm committed to something, but it's flimsy, I buy it and reinforce the stitching before wearing it." Younger women, who lack Sandra's experience with "good-fitting ormas" and do not have direct knowledge of the benefits of tailoring, however, are left to contend primarily with the allure of looks. And once again, social media was an important resource for self-styling.

As Cathe explained, "I follow nails and fashion on Instagram, and it's great because if I purchase a yellow jacket and want to learn how to accessorize it, I simply go to the site and write down 'yellow jacket,' and I can access and learn a million ways to wear it." Cathe and her Colpensiones friends documented everything about their outings at the movies, at restaurants, and at shopping malls on Facebook, especially what they wore, from head to toe, so that all their Facebook friends could appreciate their attention to style. Shopping malls were a frequent background in Cathe's Facebook pictures, as were restaurants and other places of consumption. Similarly, it was not uncommon for my informants to follow the Instagram accounts of fashionistas around the world in search of ideas about how to look modern and global. Instagram, Pinterest, and blogs like thestylechick, fashionaddictxo, chicperks y stylishoutfits, studiooficial, modaparameninas, and nuevamoda 94, among others too numerous to mention, were common resources where global and mass market brands were a dominant reference and where trends in North America and Europe, and the styling of fast-fashion alongside high-end designers confounded fashion hierarchies. TV fashion shows were also popular, with one informant claiming that Tim Gunn had changed her life by teaching her what a good wardrobe's essentials should be. At the same time, the social media fashionistas were also aware that photographing and documenting their wonderfully put together outfits on Facebook and Instagram "devalued" the wow factor if they wore them again. It also demanded more knowledge of how to restyle the same clothes to look different, and ultimately more consumption.

### CONSUMING IDENTITIES AND THE PERILS OF CREDIT

At the heart of all my informants' preoccupation with their looks, fashion and shopping remains the "cruel optimism" of capitalist consumption where the promises of consumption can never fully deliver the imaginaries one seeks with every purchase (Berlant 2011). One of the reasons for this is the overwhelming classist beliefs that frame new forms of consumption; people are constantly measuring up their own and others' consumption in a larger context where canons of buena presencia may be in flux but nevertheless remain a dominant reference in assessments of proper consumption. Another is the hierarchies that continue to rule the world of retail and shopping malls; this practically guarantees that most consumers can never fully catch up with the latest trend or learn everything that is necessary to gauge new products and their "proper" styling. This point was brought home by one last research exercise, in which I took pictures of some of my interviewees modeling their pintas from the neck down to avoid identification and randomly showed them to others to elicit their views. I found that the spiffy outfits that people proudly showed off were often derided by the others as "low-class," and few outfits met with universal approval for being tasteful or classy. In all, the common disposition was one of critique, as few outfits were deemed "just right." The lesson that emerged was the reality of people's constant public and social evaluation of themselves and others, exposing the general fear that "one's best" could easily be rendered inadequate by someone else.

To conclude, the growth in imports and the availability of low-priced goods have opened up the possibility of consumption for many but also raised the stakes and criteria of good taste whereby the winners were those who were most "in the know." These were the most frequent visitors to and consumers at the mall; whether they came to shop or to browse, these visits afforded them knowledge about fashion and products. This knowledge came from their access to and from their consumption and use of the mall as an educational and styling tool that cultivated their ability to discern the most coveted product (newest collection, best materials, etc.), in themselves and others. In this way, the greatest consumption among my young female informants was of the shopping mall itself as a socializing tool. In this context, the biggest fear was looking like a levantado, someone who purchased expensive and fashionable clothes but did not know how to style them because they had not developed the proper *ambiente* (social skills). As Rocio pointed out: "There are people who purchase the most expensive styles but look terrible in them. And the word is *levantado,* a terrible word, but people know when someone is a levantado." In fact, there is a popular saying that captures this dynamic: a monkey dressed in silk is still a monkey. This saying is well known throughout Latin America, and I heard it frequently from my own mother when I was growing up in Puerto Rico. It speaks to the limits of performativity where class and status are concerned by reminding us that clothes and outfits are never enough; it all comes down to who has the *buena presencia para lucirlos,* or the appropriate presence to style them and make them look good, and who does not.

Finally, it is important to note that concerns over fashion and self-styling are not limited to the Bogotá fashionistas who inform this chapter, but are increasingly common among people across the globe, even if they are more intense at certain points in their lives. In other words, there is a temporality in what I have described that varies according to age, gender, lifestyles, resources, and life stages. For instance, at least one of my informants became a mother during my research, shifting her consumption to her first child and becoming far more relaxed about her own self-styling. What I want to call attention to, however, is the hyperconcern about fashion and styling that has been unleashed by fast fashion, where there will always be women who resist its allure but also many others who will want to be "Forever 21."[8]

Not one of my informants talked about being in debt because of fashion. Most had credit cards but were skeptical of them, limiting their use to necessities or large purchases such as appliances. Those who used credit cards to buy fashion items or clothes were in a minority and were from higher-stratum groups (strata 4 and 5) or students living with their families and who had credit cards cosigned by them. Their stories countered what retail workers in shoestores and fashion stores said about their sales, which is that up to 80 percent were paid for with credit cards, often at cuotas, which involve five or more payments at as much as 36 percent interest. My own observations revealed the widespread use of credit cards for both small and large purchases and the common practice of dividing the amount into installments based on the commonly held belief that dividing payments lessens its impact in ways one won't feel. The result, of course, is just the opposite: one pays far more than the original cost because of accrued interest.

Still, while my fashionista informants were careful with their credit cards, few could imagine a future that included long-term financial security or owning a car or a home, even on credit. For now, fashion was the goal, and I began to appreciate the sense of making clothes their number one choice for short-term investments. When clothes function as *the* status marker, over and above traditional markers of class, when how you are seen and treated is intimately tied to how you look, and when opportunities to move up and get ahead professionally are so connected to one's look and image, my informants were betting on the "surest" investment for long-term gain. Let us not forget that the TLC and the rise in imports are making fashion one of the cheapest purchases in a neoliberal city where land prices have increased 309 percent in a mere six years (Redacción Bogotá 2014). Let us recall also that clothing, home furnishings, and home electronics are three of the most significant categories in which locals accrue credit card debt.

Unfortunately, class performances through shopping and fashion are tied to a hierarchical system that fuels more comparisons, more evaluation, and more consumption. In sum, this is a system that points to a bubble, similar to what looms over real estate, though it is one that is not felt or experienced as oppressively but, on the contrary, where it is agency, aesthetic self-styling, and invention that seem to prevail. This is exactly what makes fashion and shopping so powerful, especially among emerging consumers. This alone is a key reason for taking seriously the rise in immaterial and seemingly intangible realms like fashion and consumption as the most important factors in the neoliberalization and privatization of our contemporary cities and economies.

# Shopping Malls and the Fight for Public Space

> In general, the heterotopic site is not freely accessible like a public place. Either the entry is compulsory, as in the case of entering a barracks or a prison, or else the individual has to submit to rites and purifications. To get in one must have a certain permission and make certain gestures.
>
> **FOUCAULT,** *"Of Other Spaces, Heterotopias"*

> Access to the centers is public, but all private property's norms and laws apply. Visitors do not always understand this, though, and they are often surprised to be reminded that they are not in a public park.
>
> **CARLOS BETANCOURT,** *president of Acecolombia,*
> *cited in Bird Picó 2014a*

As shopping malls continue to dominate the physical landscape of so many Latin American cities, they are becoming the space where equity and citizenship rights are consistently contested. And central to these debates is a growing demand for their use as public space. Brazil's rolezinhos, the organized mass takeovers of shopping malls by working-class dark-skinned youth that made front-page news in the international press throughout 2014, are a relevant example. Most commentators agreed that whether it was simply the search for entertainment or the need for access to public space that guided the youths' action, their mere presence in Brazil's upscale shopping malls represented a public confrontation of its own, not only because the scandalous reaction by security and management exposed ongoing racism and the racial profiling of dark-skinned youths. It was also because of the boisterous, collective, and festive manner in which the strolls were organized and conducted. Not even the fanciest malls were spared by the youth, whose takeovers conveyed a sense of entitlement and a challenge to prevailing social stigma insisting that the poor and dark-skinned do not belong and should be kept away from these spaces.

Concurrently, Bogotá saw similar demonstrations confronting the sexism and homophobia that exists in shopping malls and in society at large. One instance was the groundbreaking *plantón de minifaldas* in 2013, a mobilization of miniskirt-clad women challenging statements by the owner of Andrés Carne de Res restaurant, a well-known tourist destination, who dismissed a woman's accusation that she had been sexually assaulted upon leaving the restaurant. The owner said the woman had asked for it by wearing a miniskirt, a not uncommon view that victims of sexual attacks are themselves to blame because they were wearing provocative clothing. The plantón confronted and challenged the owner's sexist view, upholding women's right to wear whatever they wish in restaurants while exposing the deep-seated sexism and classism of many people who responded to the incident by suggesting the victim "shouldn't have worn such-and-such," or "shouldn't have been partying," or that someone with the "right" upbringing would have known what to wear and where not to linger. Ultimately, the demonstrations led to apologies, and although the restaurant's owner downplayed the incident, everyone I spoke to agreed that it had been a precedent-setting mobilization, the first to actively expose sexism and assert feminist ideals through demands of consumer citizenship.

Months later, in 2014, Avenida Chile shopping mall became the target of a *besatón,* a public kissathon, to challenge the expulsion of a young gay couple from the shopping center. Two security guards had confronted the couple, claiming their behavior was indecent and brought shame on the shopping center. The couple, however, was defiant. They demanded to know if the guard would dare to kick out heterosexual couples who were kissing at the mall and insisted on their right to stay, accusing the mall of discrimination. Additional security staff were called, and the couple ended up leaving, only to return a week or so later with supporters and signs reading "Kisses are affection, not a crime," in a social-media-organized kissathon in front of and inside the shopping center. The event received a lot of media attention, accompanied by revealing pictures of gay and lesbian couples kissing passionately all over the mall and onlookers cheering. And while the manager of the shopping center claimed that more investigation was in order, he was quick to issue a public statement clarifying that his shopping mall does not discriminate or restrict entrance to people on the basis of their sexual, political, or religious orientation.

Shopping malls want to symbolize modernity, and part of this image involves projecting inclusivity and political correctness. However, when malls celebrate Catholic masses and cater mostly to heteronormative families, there is a fine line between inclusion and accommodation, in their case obviously in favor of sanitized versions of difference. In this case, gay couples were welcome to shop and linger, but kissing was neither welcome nor tolerated.

The irony is that Avenida Chile shopping mall is notorious for being a cruising place for gays and a well-known place for pickups and hookups. My friend Diego had pointed this out to me during my first trip when he gave me the novel *Al diablo la maldita primavera,* by Alonso Sánchez Baute, in which the mall serves as a backdrop for the story about the escapades of a drag queen in the neighborhood of Chapinero, referred to as Gay Hills. The reputation of this mall had to be known by its administration, raising the question of what differences are accepted and tolerated and on what grounds but also pointing to the multiple imaginaries that a shopping mall may sustain for different users at the margins of management's dominant script for its visitors.

I met with Alejandro, the student at the center of the kissathon at the scene of the crime. His memories of the event were as vivid as his discomfort at returning to the mall. Further, his comments were insightful in terms of the larger issues of shopping malls and people's right to access public space. It turns out that Alejandro is an anthropology student at La Nacional, a self-described expert on public space. As a gay youth he was once kicked out of a public park, and this experience had heightened his sensitivity and pushed him to study the regulations that protect his rights. He had developed a mental map of "safe" spaces, which included the university, most public parks, Plaza de Bolívar, and shopping malls.

A key reason why shopping malls were so identified by Alejandro is because of his solidly middle-class background. Alejandro grew up in San Cipriano, a stratum 3 barrio. His parents, who worked at nearby social clubs, as an accounting assistant and a swimming instructor, moved to Los Cedritos, an aspirational neighborhood that was strata 4 and 5. He also attended private school. As he admitted, it is not common for private school kids to attend the public university, but this was what he and his family could afford.[1] Still, shopping malls were very familiar to Alejandro, a place that he felt comfortable in. He dresses in stylish clothes purchased mostly at Falabella, the Chilean department store that is a common fixture in most middle- to upper-class Colombian malls and that is well known for its sales and promotions. He told me he was "dressed all in Falabella," with a wool jacket and nice suede shoes, when the incident happened. His boyfriend, however, is a different story. Of costeño background and a lower stratum than Alejandro, he was hesitant about meeting him at Avenida Chile shopping mall because he was coming out of a dance rehearsal and was not dressed appropriately to meet and socialize "in the north," echoing the internal check and self-awareness I found so common among informants about visiting a place that would be considered above their station. It should be noted, however, that Avenida Chile's location in the north is more symbolic than real, since it is considered at the low end range of "northern" malls.

As we spoke, it was obvious that Alejandro's outrage at being kicked out was compounded by the class injury entailed in having a guard of a lower stratum question his purchasing power. For it was not only their "amoral behavior" that had gotten them kicked out but also the offense of being found "lingering" rather than shopping. Alejandro was livid; he is not used to having his purchasing ability questioned. The event was therefore very embarrassing on many fronts; it involved an assault on his class identity, his sexuality, and his right to a space he had considered "public," all at once and in front of his boyfriend.

Assuming that the guard was from a lower stratum is not a difficult stretch. Guards are often drawn from the poorest sectors of society and from the south, and many are costeños and Afro-Colombians. In sum, guards represent the same groups that are most discriminated against but are ironically placed in the position of having to discriminate against other marginal groups. I was unable to interview the guard involved in the incident, but other guards shared with me the trials of occupying this difficult position. Carlos, the Afro-Colombian guard who hated to remove vendors who wanted to use his mall's public bathrooms, is a good example. Originally from Valledupar, he now lives in a stratum 1 neighborhood in the south and commutes to work at the middle-class Salitre Plaza shopping mall. There, he and another guard who is also Afro-Colombian had not only experienced racism and name-calling from visitors, which they had not reported for fear of losing their jobs, but also witnessed the classism and disdain toward lower-class groups expressed by middle-class visitors in the mall. "You can hear what people say about people of low stratum when they come to the mall. Like, what are they doing here? They make fun of them, you overhear people say that these people should stay in the south." Carlos had heard about the kissathon at Avenida Chile because it had prompted the management of the mall where he worked to instruct guards not to bother gay couples who were kissing. Still, he went on matter-of-factly about how his work entailed profiling people based on their look and dress. As he described it, he had been trained to target people wearing baggy or dirty clothes, people looking ñero, people who seemed to be on drugs, and indigents. Although race and color were not mentioned, he seemed fully aware that if he was not wearing his uniform, he himself would be deemed suspect inside the very mall where he worked. In fact, not unlike other shopping mall workers I interviewed, he told me that he dresses "in his best" whenever he visits his local mall (Centro Mayor) during the one day off from his six-day workweek, a practice likely reinforced by the levels of racism and social stigma that he experienced while on the job.

It is especially telling that it was Alejandro who took the initiative to organize the protest and not his boyfriend, whose class identity and background vested him with less social entitlement to claim his right to the mall as openly as Alejandro. In this regard, an interesting trend I observed during my research is how claims of discrimination on the basis of sexuality seemed to be more publicly acknowledged, as well as given far more consideration by shopping mall managers, than any claim of discrimination on the basis of class or race.

For instance, most shopping mall managers admitted having had to rethink their treatment of the LGBT community, because *ellos se quejan*— they complain if they are mistreated. The poor, the disheveled, and the popular classes, however, seemed open targets for harassment and intimidation; no one expects these groups to complain or to demand respect in places where they are viewed as not belonging. And in fact, security staff did not seem to have to do much to keep "suspect people" at bay. As I noted earlier, there is a class order to the mall, whereby people generally visit malls according to region and class, staying away from shopping malls and other spaces in which they are considered out of place. Alternatively, visitors used the mall in class-marked ways that were more socially accepted, such as visiting malls on weekends and remaining mostly around the entertainment areas or the food court. For its part, management described a range of tactics of dissuasion that they were ready to use against suspect groups' "misuse" of the mall. Assigning security staff to follow suspect people until they felt uncomfortable and decided to leave on their own (*ponerle escolta*) was one common strategy. Another was to remove benches and seating areas from spots that had become popular among unwanted visitors. In other words, shopping mall managers seemed to be far more worried about coming across, or being seen, as sexist, homophobic, and, to a lesser degree, racist than classist; and in fact, most were quite open about the need to keep "the wrong crowds" out of their malls. They seemed to have adopted the work of classism and reproducing distinctions between who is welcome and who is not as "what shopping malls do" and were required to do by their visitors. The fact that Alejandro's boyfriend was initially apprehensive to meet him at the mall because he was not "dressed appropriately" and his reticence to initiate the protest speaks to these larger biases at work.

In addition, it is not uncommon for acts of discrimination on the basis of race or sexual orientation to be couched in "classist" terms, for instance, as a breach of some unspecified dress code, among other racial euphemisms that have been well documented throughout Latin America (Dulitzsky 2005; Williams Castro 2013). Bars and private restaurants are well known to recur to these tactics by upholding the right to admission and to particular dress codes, allowing for wiggle room to engage in acts of discrimination. Specifically, while private venues cannot state that gays or black Colombians are not allowed, they can claim that these people are not "appropriately" dressed or that an invitation-only event is being held or some other "socially" accepted excuse for engaging in social exclusion. In other words, it is important not to lose sight of the ways in which race and class interact to reinforce intersecting types of social exclusion and marginalization, especially of the ways in which classism can function as a veil that renders racism difficult to be named, identified, and redressed.

Ultimately the besatón was a huge success. It exposed the shopping mall's homophobic treatment of the couple broadly and publicly and took place without any incidents and without the permission or containment of the shopping mall. As private space, public activities in malls require permits from their management, which explains why it is mainly Catholic masses, cultural events, and major sporting events transmitted via giant screens that are the most common events taking place in Colombian malls. Social protests, however, are very rare. And, not surprisingly, when they do occur, they tend to follow more "sanitized" formats than the type of public and open demonstration one would find, for instance, in Bogotá's Plaza de Bolívar.

Demonstrations at Plaza de Bolívar are characterized by their diversity and populist character, with people hailing from all over the city, including the outskirts and the most marginal barrios. People sometimes camp out or erect temporary public displays with protest signs and even light fires, while flags wave liberally. Of course, protests can also vary in their makeup, depending on the cause and whether it is galvanized by students, workers, or marginal groups. Still, Plaza de Bolívar is never silent; chants and speeches can be heard everywhere via loudspeakers and microphones. It was there that masses of people demonstrated against the politically motivated removal of Gustavo Petro; where residents of Ciudad Bolívar, which contains Bogotá's largest slum, met with scores of university students, activists, and people from all over the city to express outrage at what was largely recognized to be an undemocratic decision. Plaza de Bolívar is where people go to expose urgent claims of rights, inequity, violence, and more. It is open twenty-four hours a day seven days a week and welcomes everyone. And, of course, protests here are also the most subject to surveillance and repression, especially from Colombia's infamous Escuadrón Móvil Anti-Disturbios de la Policía Nacional (ESMAD).

In contrast, most of the protests that take place in shopping malls in Bogotá and elsewhere in Latin America follow a very different script. First, the protests are primarily made up of middle-class groups demanding a larger imaginary of the middle classes. Second, like the besatón, these protests tend to be more purposefully performative—a choreographed kissathon, an invasion of women in miniskirts, or, as in Puerto Rico, the reproduction of an *asalto navideño,* a traditional Christmas takeover of song and dance to challenge university tuition hikes (Dávila 2012). In all, it is important to acknowledge that many of these protests are made up primarily of middle-class students and youth demonstrating in socially palatable ways: through music and entertainment or through public performances of affection, however stigmatized these may be. Not to downplay the political significance of these demonstrations or the risk involved in taking over malls without permits, or to question their effectiveness, it is necessary to point out that these demonstrations were not the type of spontaneous and even heated and confrontational protests one is likely to see in a Plaza de Bolívar. In other words, at least for now, many contemporary protests at malls seem to revolve around issues of cultural citizenship, sexual rights, or matters affecting particular constituencies such as students, led by primarily middle-class groups. These are not the type of radical consumer politics directed at transforming structural inequality but rather politics that exert the rights of "purchasers" that are common to many contemporary consumer movements (Cohen 2003). More challenging demands of economic inequality and more widespread protests by popular classes have yet to find voice in most Latin American shopping malls. It is precisely because they are so rare that the protests by poor, dark-skinned rolezinhos became so threatening and so compelling to the press. Third, unlike the overt repression of street protests, mall demonstrations tend to be met with targeted and careful responses by mall managment, which is wary of escalating the situation and attracting bad press.

The point here is that we must be very careful to avoid romanticizing social activism in shopping malls without first assessing the extent to which the very space of the mall conditions what kind of protests can be conducted and by whom. Shopping malls have been a leading force in the privatization of space and the creation of "no politics" spaces, where rights to free speech, assembly, and privacy are subordinate to people's "right" to shop without interference and stores' rights to make a sale (Farrell 2010). This is especially the case in Latin America. Whereas in the United States a few states have upheld the right to use shopping malls for limited political uses, in Latin America these issues have only begun to get notice and to date industry professionals have by and large protected their standing as private space (Bird Picó 2014a). It is also important to remember that racial and sexual discrimination is rampant in most shopping malls and across society at large. However, it is only when incidents inconvenience the middle classes or take place in upscale shopping malls that they are the subject of a major outcry, as if these incidents were not everyday occurrences that affect people unequally and as if people were not allowed differing rates of legitimacy to claim their rights.

These issues take on added significance as shopping malls continue to attract new middle classes, becoming the laboratory for new identities and the venue for families' weekly paseos and entertainment. Recall that according to governmental statistics, shopping malls are the number one entertainment choice for Colombian families, over and above any other cultural offering. What this shows is that many families are claiming shopping malls as public space, which is not surprising considering that decades of pro-shopping mall urban planning have made shopping malls one of the most accessible urban fixtures for most Colombians. They are accessible by most major highways, and there is direct access to them from the Transmilenio, which assures that they are one of the most convenient venues to meet friends and family. The problem, however, as I hope to have argued convincingly, is that shopping malls are not public space but space that is commercially conditioned. Far from neutral spaces, shopping malls demand particular performances, attitudes, and behaviors from visitors if they are to "fit" in them. For some, this includes performing the role of a shopper, by dressing the part, for instance; for others, it is all about avoiding stores and gathering in "safer" areas of the mall, such as seating areas or areas with "public" amenities like fountains or benches. Thus questions remain about the ways in which shopping malls are conditioning particular subjectivities in its visitors, marking and exacerbating social distinctions in the process. I recall a shopping mall manager who proudly described his shopping mall as a "producer of citizens." In his view shopping malls were key socializing institutions that taught people "citizenship skills," pointing to the civilized behavior the mall had managed to elicit from visitors on its one-year anniversary. As part of the celebration the mall gave out cake to anyone who waited in line for a piece. And to his surprise, people lined up and waited calmly to get a piece of cake served by waiters dressed in elegant black-and-white outfits. This scene would be unimaginable on a public street, he noted, insisting on his shopping mall's social and citizenship-making mission. Shopping malls are indeed forging citizens and citizenship norms while remaking cities before our eyes. But I hope to have shown that definitions of citizenship are far too restrictive when they involve one's ability to wait in line for a piece of cake, not unlike the definition of cities when based on the standards of a sanitized, commercial space.

Finally, the case of Colombia is especially interesting considering that the right of public space is enshrined in the constitution and some of its major cities have governmental offices charged with its defense. If shopping malls and private developers are having such overwhelming influence here, one can only speculate on the privatization of space in other contexts where there is less awareness about matters of public space. In particular, Bogotá's Administrative Department for the Defense of Public Space (DADEP) is charged with the regulation of public space, which it defines as any area required for circulation; areas for public recreation, like parks, plazas, and green zones; and areas needed for the installation of public works; and so forth. But what about shopping malls? "Private in their interior, but the exterior and its surroundings are public," explained Blanca Inés Durán, DADEP's director. However, she was the quick to admit that these determinations were not so easily recognized or enforced. By law, Colombian shopping malls are required to provide some public space to the city in exchange for construction permits –requirements that the last POT sought to increase to make them more commensurate with shopping malls' demands on public infrastructure. However, shopping malls often designate "public space" in its proximity, which eases its treatment as private property, making it almost impossible for people to distinguish it as public space. This is a common problem with the spread of privately owned public space as a solution for the creation and management of public space documented in cities across the world. One example is the great plaza in front of Gran Estación, which DADEP had discovered the mall had been renting and commercializing when in fact the area is designated as public space. Unfortunately, DADEPs strategy to reclaim the space—holding government-sponsored events in the plaza—was largely ineffective, because any event that attracted a crowd around the perimeter of the shopping mall would likely benefit it, especially when the shopping mall is not paying for or sponsoring the event. At the same time, Blanca acknowledged that when events are organized by the shopping mall it is not possible for just "anyone" to attend: "We want people to understand that this is public space, to stop associating it with the shopping mall. We want to ensure that anyone who strolls around the area can use this space, that it is not only for their clients, but for everyone." The perimeter around Titán is another public area that has been appropriated by the mall. Most of the time the boulevard is empty, free of street vendors and passersby, the result of overzealous guards protecting the area as if it were, in fact, the mall's private property.

Unfortunately, cities like Bogotá are likely to face greater difficulty reclaiming public space for its citizens amid the ongoing boom in construction and development. And the stakes are extremely high. The boom in Latin American shopping malls has coincided with an emphasis on public space as the driver of urban prosperity, where "gains" and achievements in the development of "public space" seem to overshadow any serious engagement with the privatization of space that has been expedited, often as a result of seemingly pro–public space policies. For instance, the development of bike routes and consumption-geared "public areas" in Colombia has been central to key public relations campaigns to promote the country's "brand" in ways that have incentivized shopping mall investors and other types of developments. We see the same dynamics in Peru, one of the Latin American countries with the most well developed *marca país* campaigns, linking tourism and business promotion strategies as central to the reinvention and refurbishing of its image as it seeks new investments and closer integration with the world economy.[2] Ultimately the issue is that we are likely to see more linkages between urban planning and international public relations to ensure, in the perceptive words of an artist, "that when people think of Latin American cities, they no longer think of narco and violence but instead think of bike routes and shopping malls."

However, if we think of public space not solely in terms of leisure and consumption, but instead in the broader and more challenging terms advanced by scholars of public space, we can see the limits of these urban policies/public relations strategies and why they should be questioned for facilitating the spread of shopping malls throughout the area. Here I point to the narrow definitions of public space that are commonly advanced by many neoliberal urban policies, which tend to link public space with the creation and expansion of zones of leisure and consumption while making architects, designers, and urban planners the lead in defining what is an attractive and successful public space. Missing from these definitions is how easily "public space" becomes restricted and surveilled, especially when it is cared for by private entities and commercial interests like shopping malls or even by private residents. In particular, a common outcome of this top-down emphasis on public space is a general upscaling of public space along with its expansion. The bike routes in Bogotá are a good example: we see an expansion of public space and greater transportation accessibility but also a narrowing of the uses of public space as it is reconditioned for the single and specific needs of bikers, whether for transportation or leisure. The Parque Tercer Mileneo, built as part of Peñalosa's plan to clean up the city, is another example of an urban project that transformed a bustling urban zone into a bare and empty park while displacing its original residents. Similar examples abound across the Americas.

But what if we defined public space beyond leisure and consumption, as space where there is also freedom to make a living, freedom to linger and congregate, and, most important, freedom to make social and political demands?[3] As proposed by Margaret Crawford (2014), the answer may lie in placing less emphasis on "feel good" public spaces, or its quality and number of visitors, and more on the rights of people to access public space for social and political uses or to ensure their economic well-being. In fact, these are exactly the types of access to and uses of public space that are most contentious, most policed, and most surveilled in most neoliberal cities across the Americas and that have also historically affected people of color disproportionately, as well as the undocumented, especially amid the militarization of the police and the rise of punitive policing.[4]

In sum, public space is less a question of design than of politics, and it demands the type of social legislation and contexts geared not only to protecting or promoting public space as an empty goal but rather to its access and uses by all people. Under these broader criteria, it is evident that cities like Bogotá have seen a narrowing of public space alongside a spread of retail real estate square footage and that shopping malls fall short of any definition of truly accessible public space. At the least, then, it is time that we stop equating shopping malls with "public plazas" and that we are fully aware of the stakes involved when we naively associate the spread of shopping malls with urban openness, diversity, and progress. What is certain is that the "new middle classes" of the world are likely to be at the center of these debates and that shopping mall politics are never enough, and should never be. Shopping malls display and exacerbate social inequalities, but these are not solely of their making. Today's class-stratified mall is the product of larger policies, politics, and ideologies that profit from economic inequality and of its many outcomes, and it will take more than shopping mall politics to challenge them.

I want to conclude with a sobering warning against the uncritical celebration of shopping malls and of new middle classes. More Latin Americans are accessing the world of consumption and shopping malls, but their power to consume is not limitless. These groups' long-term sustainability is far from certain. Their survival is actively challenged by the rise of debt and credit cards, by the attack on informal work, and by the general upscaling of space, a direct outcome of the boom in shopping mall construction that is making everyday life more expensive and challenging for city residents. Bogotanos now spend more for rent than for any other expense. The lack of affordable housing in Bogotá echoes the housing crisis in New York and other neoliberal global cities throughout the world. These are realities that the dream world of brands and shopping cannot hide in the long term because their seductions do not last. Instead, they trigger more consumption and more types of differentiation, processes that may very well be the impetus for people to stop coming to malls.

What we may not be able to stop as easily is the mallification of our cities and the spread of the logics of security, surveillance, commodification, and precarity into more aspects of everyday life. These are the logics that make it seem normal that a city already saturated with shopping malls would build even more and bigger malls while its public infrastructure crumbles. This is exactly what is at stake in Bogotá and many cities across the Americas. Thus, after the announcement of the soon to be developed 320,000-square-meter El Eden, said to be Bogotá's largest shopping mall to date, critics wondered, Why can't we be known as the city that builds the country's biggest university, educational center, hospital, subway system, or public park instead?

Others insisted, however, that this is just a dream: private investors have the "right" to do whatever they wish with their investments.[5] These divergent opinions point to a larger rethinking of shopping malls and the role they play, not only in privatizing our cities, but also in naturalizing the "rights" of capital, rather than the civil rights and entitlements of everyday people. Shopping mall pundits already see our cities as shopping malls in the making. They welcome and celebrate the kind of rent increases that make global brands, rather than people and local businesses, the only viable tenants in our contemporary cities, leaving us with urban landscapes that increasingly resemble shopping malls.

My hope is that we never get to this point and that these pages foster an appreciation of the material and political repercussions of shopping malls and point to the numerous local and global policies that sustain them. Even more, I hope these pages incite people to claim ownership of public space and engage critically with their larger societies, beyond el mall.

# NOTES

## INTRODUCTION

1. See Grupo de Inteligencia de Mercado del ICSC para América Latina 2015. This figure was announced at the annual conference of regional Latin American shopping centers in Cancún, Mexico. These new malls were developed in the span of five years, pointing to the rapid increase in construction. Just the six main markets of Brazil, Mexico, Colombia, Argentina, Peru, and Chile account for upwards of 1,555 shopping malls as of 2015, though this figure is conservative given that the industry only counts malls that fit its size specifications. I discuss these issues in greater detail in chapter 3.

2. Shopping centers and industrial parks have been recognized as key components of urban and suburban geographies; see, e.g., Feagin 1983. My point is that the spatial effects of shopping malls have tended to be overlooked in relation to shopping malls' symbolic roles, their architectural design, or the social and cultural practices of visitors, among other issues that have received a lot more attention from writers and scholars.

3. See, e.g., Beatriz Sarlo's (1994) important critique of shopping malls as embodiments of the rise of mass mediated and postmodern culture in Argentina. Sarlo acknowledges that malls have a different life and temporality for different classes, pointing out that they are used more heavily by poorer sectors on weekends when the upper classes flee from them, which belies her totalizing view of these institutions. See Ortiz 2013, on how users appropriate shopping malls in Puerto Rico, which provides a good counterpoint to this study.

4. I am aware that any strict distinction between the "developed" and "developing" world is always problematic, insofar as both geopolitical entities are culturally and historically co-created. When drawing distinctions between the shopping mall industry in the "developed" and "developing" world, I seek to differentiate patterns in the relatively earlier development of shopping malls in the United States and Europe from those in Latin America, which are more akin to other non-Western contexts such as China and India, while highlighting the developmentalist logics of

progress of modernity that have historically warped the rise of shopping malls in many of these contexts.

5. These findings, based on Stillerman et al.'s (2013) comparative research in Chile, Turkey, and India, jibe well with my observations of shopping malls in Latin America. While some important developments were built prior to the 1980s (especially in Chile, Brazil, Venezuela, and Colombia), the shopping mall boom in the region began in the early 1990s and follows patterns similar to those documented by the authors, particularly in regard to their location in some of the main urban centers. See also Dávila-Santiago 2005; Stillerman 2015; Salcedo and De Simone 2012.

6. As I write this book, the future of shopping malls in the United States and Europe is uncertain. While there has been a lot of attention to "death malls" and the failure and closing of shopping malls throughout the United States, observers document that the story is more complex. One interesting trend is the upscaling of shopping malls and the development of new luxury malls alongside the withering of shopping malls catering to working- and middle-class groups (Kolson-Hurley 2015). This trend points to the luxurification of retail, stemming from the rise of income inequality and the greater economic gains among the highest income groups across the globe. What this suggests is that shopping malls may continue to thrive in the United States but refashioned to attract primarily higher income groups. It is also important to note that while shopping malls are on the upswing in Latin America, ghost malls have begun to appear in some markets, particularly in Brazil, which saw the earliest shopping mall boom in the region, raising questions about the likely inevitability of the industry's economic downturn across the region (Dickinson and Jelmayer 2015). As the next chapter argues, such industry upswings and downswings are central to its global success.

7. David J. LaRue, "Global Perspective of the Shopping Center's Industry," presentation at RECon Latin America, Cartagena, April 4, 2014.

8. RECon Latin America, Cartagena, 2014, "General Overview of Latin American Shopping Centers," April 4, 2014.

9. The literature on consumption is extensive, but see Appadurai 1996; Miller 1995, 1998; J. Miller 2013; Rofel 2007.

10. See also De Simone 2015 for a discussion of the ideological deployment of shopping malls as part of the neoliberalization project in Chile.

11. See Ellin 2001 for a discussion of the history of fear in architecture; and Gurian 2006 for a more detailed examination of the many programmatic and physical barriers that affect people's access to public museums. Gurian's discussion is quite limited—she even suggests museums could learn accessibility lessons from shopping malls—though useful for the ways in which seemingly "open" spaces like museums and shopping malls can represent visible and invisible barriers to visitors.

12. I draw here on Beckford's (1999) discussion of the plantation as a settlement institution, which illuminates ways to think about shopping malls and their role in creating wealth while sustaining persistent underdevelopment and dependency in developing societies. The use of the plantation as a model and metaphor for other industries, from tourism to prisons to mining, has been advanced to highlight the

existing continuities between this early colonial institution and modern institutions of capitalist economic development responsible for the opening and transformation of societies economies that have fostered their continued underdevelopment and dependency. This metaphor also indexes the continued logics of racial dispossession, subjugation, and exploitation that continue to be reproduced by "modern" institutions of capitalist development (Best, Polany Levitt, and Girvan 2009; McKittrick 2013). However, while useful for thinking about the speculative nature of the shopping malls industry, this model is more limited for theorizing the "openness" and dream worldliness that these spaces foster, which as I note below set them apart from other land-intensive economic industries and the plantation model itself.

13. See Rivas 2014 for Guatemala. In Puerto Rico, Plaza las Americas (1968), which for years was one of the largest shopping malls in Latin America, was built on a former sugarcane estate turned into a dairy farm, Las Monjitas, also the name of the dairy farm owned by the Fonalledas family.

14. Draper (2012) also discusses the development of other incarceration sites into tourist sites and commercial centers in Argentina as part of a larger memory market. Peru's Larcomar shopping center in the upscale district of Miraflores was built on the same main street and within a ten-minute walk of the Shining Path's Tarata Street bombing of 1992 and was pivotal in transforming the zone into Lima's premier tourist district. In Bogotá, shopping malls and the tourist Zona Rosa were also targets of terrorist attacks and car bombs, a history that has been sanitized by its development as a tourist and consumption mecca.

15. Redacción El Tiempo 2015.

16. Michael Kercheval, president and CEO of ICSC, "Industry Overview," RECon Cartagena 2014. According to Kercheval, of the 56 malls under construction in Colombia, the majority are in medium-sized and small cities. Similar trends are described for Argentina, where 4 of 15 of the shopping malls currently in development are in cities with fewer than 100,000 people, while in Brazil, of the 41 shopping centers, only 17 are in the central cities of São Paulo and Rio de Janeiro.

### CHAPTER 1

1. Milton Cooper, executive chairman, Kimco Realty Corporation, New Hyde Park, NY, Industry Leaders Series, Research on Demand Videos, 2010, ICSC.

2. Richard Sokolov, Industry Leaders Series, Research On Demand Videos, 2010, ICSC.

3. ICSC 2011; Economic Impact of Shopping Centers 2011. www.icsc.org /uploads/press/ICSC-PressKit-2011.pdf.

4. See ICSC 2014 for a rosy picture of the shopping mall industry distributed during the 2015 New York City RECon conference, whose main goal was to defend the long-term viability of shopping centers. A key point concerns their changing formats and their growing use of technologies to increase synergies between online

and brick-and-mortar retail. See also Schwartz 2015 for a discussion of the rising threat of dead malls to the industry's future.

5. "Consumers Prefer the Mall to the Internet," *Shopping Centers Today*, May 23, 2013, ICSC, http://general.icsc.org/apps/news_item.php?id = 2996.

6. "The Death of the Big Box," CNBC Video, Thursday, August 23, 2012. Available at http://video.cnbc.com/gallery/?video=3000111140&startTime=198&endTime = 636.

7. http://thelegaspi.com/la-gran-plaza/.

8. Consider McGuirck's (2014) discussion of Bogotá and Medellín as important examples of "radical cities," which treat Latin American politicians, activists, and architects as maverick innovators and problem solvers for most contemporary urban problems across the globe. The author praises the urban reforms instituted by Mayors Antanas Mockus and Enrique Peñalosa but never considers the neoliberal projects and investments that accompanied and were expedited by these reforms.

9. The group was able to delay Unicentro's plan by revoking a construction license that had been issued without complying with the requirements. The discovery also led to the suspension of the issuing governmental official.

10. See *Revista Centros Comerciales*, December 2012, March 2013, May 2013.

11. See Silva 2003 for documentation of Unicentro's key position in residents' popular perceptions of the city.

12. Ramon Pineda, presentation at RECon Latin America 2013, on March 19, based on Comisión Económica para América Latina y el Caribe (CEPAL), 2012, Santiago, Chile.

13. Brad Hutensky, presentation at RECon Latin America, March 20, 2013, based on Banco Interamericano de Desarrollo.

14. For instance, according to a regional study by the ICSC 86 percent of Brazil's population is urbanized, as is 79 percent of the population in Mexico, 80 percent in Colombia, 89 percent in Chile, and 94 percent in Argentina (Grupo de Inteligencia de Mercado del ICSC para América Latina 2015).

15. David LaRue, Global Perspective on Shopping Centers Industry, RECon Latin America, Cartagena, April 7, 2014.


CHAPTER 2

1. ICSC Historical Timeline, www.icsc.org/about/historical-timeline, and 2013 Annual Report. RECcon Middle East and North Africa celebrated its twentieth anniversary in 2014, making it one of the oldest regional conferences.

2. John T. Riordan and Michael P. Kercheval, "A Discussion on the Past, Present and Future of ICSC," Industry Leaders Series, www.icsc.org/research /research-on-demand-videos/b-industry-leaders-series.

3. Sergio Andrade de Carvalho and Family, Founder, Ancar, Rio de Janeiro, Brazil, Industry Leaders Series, www.icsc.org/research/research-on-demand-videos /b-industry-leaders-series/sergio-andrade-de-carvalho-and-family.

4. See comments by John T. Riordan, ICSC's past president and lifetime trustee, in interview with Sergio Andrade de Carvalho and family, www.icsc.org/research /research-on-demand-videos/b-industry-leaders-series/sergio-andrade-de-carvalho-and-family.

5. Aníbal Quijano's (2011) notion of the coloniality of power insists that foundational hierarchies instituted through colonialism persist in present-day knowledge regimes and social structures, including notions of race, as well as in dominant definitions of modernity and development. See also Escobar 2012 for a discussion of development in Latin America and its role as a medium of social and cultural domination.

6. See, e.g., T. Mitchell's (2002) analysis of the rise of a "rule of experts" in the economy. See also Seabrooke 2014 for a discussion of the growing call for a "transnational sociology of the professions," examining the development of global professional regulations directly tied to the needs of neoliberal capitalism.

7. From 1957 to 1970 about a hundred students were trained who went on to transform the Chilean economy and influence privatization and neoliberal economic formulas throughout the region (Grandin 2006).

8. See Gill's (2004) analysis of some of the personal and political relations fostered by the School of the Americas among students and alumnae and their importance to the developing and functioning of counterinsurgency tactics across the region.

9. I attended the course by paying a student rate of $50. Otherwise the cost of conducting a project like this would have been prohibitive—one of the biggest obstacles that confront researchers seeking to study institutions of power.

10. I am not implying that "anchor" stores in the United States do not act similarly to those in Latin America, demanding rent giveaways and becoming too determinant to a project's success, simply that developers have greater choice of anchors.

11. This is akin to Bonnie Urciuoli's (2009) discussion of the type of "skill discourses" that consolidate "expertise" in the new economy, which Shalini Shankar (2015) brilliantly explores for the case of Asian American marketing. As Urciuoli's case study of higher education and Shankar's discussion of multicultural advertising show, shopping mall "professional" terminology is first and foremost about producing efficiencies within the new economy by communicating authority, expertise, and unity across their industry. See also Ho's (2009) discussion of the use of professional language on Wall Street.

12. According to the ICSC Latin American staff, there were 1,500 ICSC members throughout the region in 2013, representing a steep growth from 2006 when there were only 400 members. Their projection is to grow to 2,100 in 2017. While these numbers are small relative to the industry's growth, they point to the continued relevance of the "global" as a platform and reference for industry developments throughout the region.

## CHAPTER 3

1. Estimate from administrator. There is a notable lack of public information about ownership and real estate dealings around malls. The point here is the

difficulty this model of shopping mall ownership presents for global brands. The coming of Zara to Unicentro was achieved through dealings with six different owners, who I was told were members of the same family, which extended the lease of the traditional store Iserra to Zara.

2. The fastest growth is seen in cities like Cali, Manizales, and Barranquilla, led mostly by the Chilean developer of and investor in Mall Plaza (Fresneda 2013). As of 2013 there were only five shopping malls in Bogotá (of a total of forty-eight) built on the single-owner model (San Rafael, Atlantis, Diverplaza, San Martín, and Calima), though most were built recently, pointing to more of the same type of developments.

3. See Economist 2012; Samper Pizano 2013.

4. Sections of Chapinero were always solidly middle class and more upscale, but now most of the neighborhood has become subject to rapid hikes in price, placing it among the most highly valued barrios in the city.

5. The mayor was removed from his post and banned from office for fifteen years by the city inspector Alejandro Ordóñez, in 2004 over what was widely recognized to be an undemocratic and politically motivated move. The decision was based on the mayor's handling of the deprivatization of the city's trash collection, where Ordóñez accused him of interfering with the rights of free enterprise and risking the health of residents. The Inter American Commission on Human Rights and President Santos became involved in suspending the sanction and then upholding it, until Santos followed the Commission's recommendation to reinstate the mayor some months later. This incident became a social drama where citizens debated the ability of a former left militia member to enter formal politics and also the power of popular democratic processes and a popularly elected candidate over the political impositions of a politically appointed officer.

6. See debates in El Espectador 2013b; Redacción Bogotá 2013.

7. As of 2012 Colombia had ratified additional trade agreements with the United States, Chile, the Andean Community, the European Free Trade Association, Mexico, and Can-Mercosur and was negotiating agreements with South Korea, Panama, and Turkey (Invest in Bogotá).

8. Protesters received ample news coverage, yielding them an invitation to participate at the international exhibit for the first time under the trademark "Hecho en Restrepo." Their exhibit was placed in a remote space subsidized by the fair's organizers, far from the high traffic areas and luxury products and brands, representing a small step to counter their losses. Still, this important and primarily symbolic inclusion met just a fraction of Restrepo residents' demands.

9. See Portafolio 2013 for discussion of the issue of dumping, which is not limited to leather products. In 2015 the government passed an anticontraband law stiffening the penalties for the offense as a means of protecting the local industry and of limiting the use of contraband for money laundering. However, the effects of the law are yet to be determined. It is certain that informal vendors will be negatively affected and at risk of greater fines and penalties. What is also certain is that exportations of Colombian textiles and leather products are minimal compared to

imports in manufactured goods (Observatorio Económico de Moda RADDAR-Inexmoda 2015). Focused on neighboring countries, like Mexico, Ecuador and Peru, local entrepreneurs are far from reaching and competing with the global fashion markets to which they are increasingly exposed (Empresas 2014).

10. In 2014 some twenty-two local retailers organized as a group (the G40+) to bolster their negotiation power against the spread of shopping malls and exert more leverage in the lease rates and conditions. Consisting of some of the most powerful local brands, such as Velez, Spring Step, and Gef, the group evidences the growing vulnerability of local retailers in their struggle to gain presence and stability in shoping malls.

11. Mauricio Vaca of Cinépolis described the Mexican movie chain as one of the largest companies in the world, with 350 screens in Latin America and India, most of them located in shopping malls.

12. The growth of cinemaplexes in consuming spaces like shopping malls are leading to what Ganti (2012), looking at India, has termed the "gentrification" of the film industry and to its ongoing eliticization. Most of these new theaters are class marked, with many of them selling "luxury" and comfort, as for instance, allowing consumers to purchase preferential seats. Colombian theaters have discounted daytime movies, where consumers can purchase half-price tickets. However, even more affordable are the pirated movies that are sold in almost every corner of the city, including the same blockbusters shown in theaters, for about 2,000 to 3,000 pesos, or $1.50.

13. Distinctions between the formal and informal economy need to be measured against the reality that the so-called formal sector features different degrees of informality—such as in the very process for obtaining permits and funding from the government and private investors. Likewise, within the "informal" sector, vendors may operate under different degrees of formality. In San Victorino for instance, a merchant may pay rent and have a formal contract and permit to operate while at the same time carrying on with little scrutiny. For instance, while a purchase at a shopping mall includes taxes and is always documented with a receipt, which sometimes involves customers' personal identification, no receipts are given or expected at San Victorino, where merchants can also sell products in bulk or at retail. In addition, at malls prices are set, but bargaining is expected and heavily practiced at markets like San Victorino.

14. It is important to point out that the area of San Victorino has not been exempt from urban restructuring, gentrification, and the inroads of developers, particularly from the late 1990s on, after the administration of Enrique Peñalosa when there were numerous projects in the area geared to the area's formalization, which led to displacement of numerous informal vendors. For a succinct treatment of the area's historical transformation and ongoing contests over space and urban informality, see Carbonell Higuera 2011, 2013.

15. A recent study by Nielsen estimates that local barrio stores represent 53 percent of all grocery sales, while only 30 percent of shoppers go to supermarkets. The same study found these stores especially popular among the middle classes, who

were found to visit a barrio store every two days but a supermarket every ten days (El Tiempo 2014d).

16. Comments at Colombia Inside Out, September 16, at the New York Palace. Interestingly, these comments coincided with the announcement of Exito's takeover of Super Inter (another chain of retailers focusing on lower stratum communities) and a judgment forcing Exito to sell some of the stores it had acquired amid concerns over the company gaining too much dominance, including the possibility of price fixing in the grocery market (Arteaga 2014).

17. "Tarjetas de crédito," *Especiales Pirry,* September 30, 2013; www.youtube .com/watc h?v = ywHzo_o_Xlg

1. According to Bogotá's Planning Office, 67 percent of all bogotano families live in strata 2 and 3 and 34 percent of residences are cataloged as stratum 3, as opposed to 16 percent cataloged as stratum 4 and 5 percent and 4 percent classified as stratum 5 and stratum 6, respectively. (Secretaría de Planificación 2013).

2. My interviewees were mainly young professionals, whose starting salaries ranged widely, from 1,200.000 pesos a month to 3,000.000 pesos, depending on experience. Many pooled resources, however. The consumer marketing firm Raddar puts the median middle-class income at 3,378.395 for a family of four (Correa 2013).

3. Consider how a modest one-bedroom apartment in Chapinero where I lived (a gentrifying multistrata area that has sections of strata 2, 3, and 4) can cost 700,000 pesos or 900,000 pesos for a two-bedroom, amounts that exceed locals' minimum salary. Less centrally located areas can be cheaper, about 400,000 to 500,000 pesos but involve longer commutes to the center and north, where most jobs (both informal and formal) are concentrated.

4. For instance, statistics from the Ministry of Education show that 58 percent of all recent college graduates secured their jobs through family and social networks, versus the 15 percent who found employment through public advertisements contest. See Ministerio de Educación Superior 2012.

5. Bogotá is one of the most expensive Latin American cities (Ruiz Granados 2014), a city that observers note features "first world prices but third world salaries" (Hincapié 2013).

6. The fee at the ice rink at Centro Mayor was 27,000 pesos, but customers could get a 12,000-peso discount with proof of purchase of 30,000 pesos in small stores and 100,000 pesos in department stores, a recognition of customers' differential purchasing power.

7. Visitor Survey, representing average figures for August 2013 as shared by the Titán mall manager.

8. These frequentation patterns were observed qualitatively by me and corroborated by most shopping mall managers I spoke to. Unfortunately, even the most modern shopping malls, which have research personnel to study the flow of visitors,

don't segregate visitors in terms of stratum, income, or class. Figures shared by the managers of Titán and Gran Estación in 2013, however, do corroborate the largest number of visitors on weekends, the same times when there are fewer average purchases made.

9. Centro Mayor, Gran Estación, and Plaza de las Américas, all located in lower-middle-class neighborhoods, two of them in the south, have consistently occupied the position of the three most visited malls since 2011 (Gómez 2014).

### CHAPTER 5

1. See López 2012 for how these ideas were promoted among Bogotá's middle-class professionals in the 1950s; Lomnitz 2001 for early ideas of "gente sensata" and "gente buena" in opposition to the masses; and Stoler 2002 for an important work on how the centrality of moral and affective and civilizing regimes around hygiene and manners were constructed as key to the disciplining, education, and differentiation of colonial subjects.

2. Other Bogotá shopping malls have mainly aspirational names (Titán, Gran Estación, Centro Mayor) or are named after the neighborhood or region in which they are located (Salitre Plaza, Santa Fe, Portal 80).

3. On this point, see Omar Rincón's (2009) brief dictionary of popular narco-language phrases and Juana Suárez's (2010) discussion of the extent to which the discourse of violence percolates through all areas of Colombian cultural production.

4. I was told that the term *gomelo* originates from "Plástico" (plastic), which is more widely used throughout Latin America to evoke superficiality and materialism, as popularized by Rubén Blades's 1978 song "Plástico." Gomelo hints at *goma,* or rubber, which has qualities similar to Plástico. I thank Félix Manuel Burgos for the linguistic insights.

5. See Martinez Alier 1989 for a classic study focusing on the intersection of class, race, and marriage in nineteenth-century Cuba; and Carbone and Cahn 2014 for a recent study on how class affects marriage markets and contributes to the reproduction of social inequalities in the United States.

6. Naming children with made-up names from popular culture, primarily influenced by the United States, is a common practice across Latin America that evokes U.S. imperialism. State officials have tried to regulate this practice by banning names whose meanings or origins are unknown to parents. The novel *Usmail* by the Puerto Rican Pedro Juan Soto, originally published in 1959, is one of the best portrayals of the colonial foundations of this naming practice.

7. See Sánchez Voelkl 2011 for an interesting study of how bilingualism and English proficiency become a medium for the preselection of elite groups as workers in transnational companies who are in turn positioned at the apex of the corporate ladder.

8. Research by the linguistic anthropologist Jonathan Rosa (2010) is relevant here for showing the racial underpinnings of language ideologies, evident in the

tendency for language to trump race and appearance as the primary defining element of "latinidad."

9. See Londoño 2012 for a discussion of the racialization of color and how it communicates hierarchies of value in Latino/a culture in aesthetic realms like architecture and design and, in the case at hand, fashion. See also Taussig 2009 for a more general discussion of the colonial linkages between color and "the primitive."

10. This phrase has very interesting roots. *Ruanas* originally referred to indigenous wool outer garments or shawls worn along with a hats by the rural indigenous population. This outfit, along with indigenous culture, was the subject of much derision among urban elites, thus the use of *ruana* to refer to people with money is one example of the many cultural approprations and resignifications of indigenous culture in everyday Colombian society. I thank Oriana Prieto for this insight.

11. "Caso Salamanca," *Especiales Pirry,* www.youtube.com/watch?v=KLY h3R69_s.


CHAPTER 6

1. On this, see Zukin 2005; for Puerto Rico, see Dávila 2012.

2. In this chapter I use "fast fashion" to refer to the imported global fast fashion brands and clothier chains that are entering, and quickly dominating, the local fashion market. I make this distinction to highlight that Colombia has a strong textile and apparel industry of its own. However, since the passage of the TLC, the expectation of increased textile and apparel exports to the U.S. market has proven greatly misleading. Colombia finds itself unable to compete with the cheaper production costs of imported fabric and apparel, especially from Asian countries (Economía 2013). As this chapter notes, this deficit is also manifest in the realm of brands, with global fast fashion brands accruing a disproportionate competitive advantage against local products.

3. This discussion is currently being thickened by important work on aesthetic markets focusing on Asian countries that seeks to anchor the aesthetic histories and contributions of countries like China and Korea, repositioning their role as producers and innovators, not simply "recipients" of Western fashion. See, for instance, the recent symposium "Global Circuits of Fashion and Beauty," organized by Sharon Heijen Lee, Christina Moon and Thuy Linh Tu, Social and Cultural Analysis, New York University, February 20, 2015.

4. I attended Colombiamoda 2015 and found it heavily influenced by global trends, with most fashions indistinguishable from offerings in New York City stores and boutiques. Everywhere the talk was about global fashion and universal tendencies, though there was also a noticeable trend toward the inclusion of artisanal details and local patterns and materials, pointing to local designers' quest to establish a distinctive Colombian style. An interesting development was the stark difference between the official catwalks and the exhibit halls, dominated by more "high fashion" designers, where the design was defined in relation to European standards of fashion and beauty, and "Moda Para el Mundo," a subsection of the larger fair

focusing on mass market Colombian fast fashion. This section of the fair focused primarily on jeans. While often bemoaned by fashionistas because of their overdone and, to some, "trashy" decorations and design, Colombian jeans are among the fashion products that are most recognized and sought after in the local market as well as internationally. See *Vice* magazine's video on Colombiamoda, held in 2011, for an exposé of the class dynamics at play in these different sections of the fair. The video shows how high-end fashion is linked with European trends and European-looking models, in contrast to narco-fashion, which is linked to the mass-market and populist show, Moda para el Mundo. While simplistic and stereotypical in its emphasis on Medellín's narco-culture excess and plastic surgery, the video and its responses illustrate the classism surrounding definitions of "fashion" locally and the dominance of Eurocentric and elitist parameters in the local scene. Fashion Week Internationale—Colombia Fashion Week 2011, www.vice.com/video /colombia-art-1.

5. See, e.g., Catchpole 2014; Kliest 2014; and *Vice* magazine, cited in note 4 above.

6. Elle España 2014.

7. The irony is that many products coveted by local fashionistas can be found only in the popular stores that higher-stratum groups shun. A good example is Angel jeans, which are worn by Colombian women across strata and are sold at San Victorino and recently at their new store in the Centro Mayor shopping center in the south. Neither of these shopping venues is a place that higher stratum women would be likely to visit. Frequent shoppers in these spaces told me that it was not at all uncommon to see assistants fetching things for their employers, saving the latter from the "risk" of shopping in informal markets or the shame of being found "out of place."

8. I thank Marcel Salas for the important observation about the temporality involved in women's relationship with fast fashion and for the "Forever 21" metaphor that the store exploits to capture the attraction of fast fashion among young people and as the embodiment of trendiness and youth.

### CONCLUSION

1. Higher education is extremely classed and politicized in Colombia, not unlike in other neoliberal contemporary cities. While Alejandro felt that he was out of place when he attended the public university, the fact is that La Nacional is highly competitive and considered among the most academically challenging institutions. Consequently, it is often easier for students from private schools to gain admission than students from public schools. The latter often have to rely on technical and vocational training schools.

2. See Aronczyk 2013 for a discussion of the role of culture in the increasingly profitable global business of creating national identities; and Yudice 2004 for the specific case of Latin America.

3. These issues became salient during the second international conference on the future of places held in Buenos Aires, September 1–3, 2014, when dominant definitions of public space, as defined by architects, designers, and urban planners, revolved around top-down re-creations of zones for leisure and entertainment, rarely considering bottom-up reconfigurations. This view clashed with those advanced by some of the scholars present and by many audience respondents and is also challenged by a growing literature highlighting the privatization of public space and its effects on people's social reproduction, on the diminishing rights of street vendors, and on people's ability to express dissent and engage in social protests in public spaces (Mitchell 2003; Dunn 2014).

4. See, for instance, LeBron 2014; Rosas 2012; Zilberg 2011 for the policing and criminalization of immigrants and youth of color, documenting the greater surveillance these groups are regularly subject to, even in so-called public spaces.

5. *El Tiempo,* announcement posted on its website and Facebook page. Debate elicited from the ensuing responses on October 22, 2014.

# BIBLIOGRAPHY

Abad Faciolince, Héctor. 2008. "Estética y narcotráfico." *Revista de Estudios Hispánicos* 42 (3): 513–18.

Acevedo, Tatiana. 2013. "Oda al centro comercial." *El Espectador,* February 6. www.elespectador.com/opinion/oda-al-centro-comercial-columna-403394.

Acland, Charles R. 2003. *Screen Traffic: Movies, Multiplexes, and Global Culture.* Durham, NC: Duke University Press.

Aliaga-Linares, Lissette, and María José Álvarez-Rivadulla. 2010. "Segregación residencial en Bogotá a través del tiempo y diferentes escalas." Lincoln Institute of Land Policy, Cambridge, MA. www.lincolninst.edu/pubs/dl/1833_1084_Aliaga-Alvarez-SP%20Final.pdf.

Angotti, Tom. 2013. "Urban Latin America Violence, Enclaves, and Struggles for Land." *Latin American Perspectives* 40 (2): 5–20.

Angulo, Roberto, Alejandro Gaviria and Liliana Morales. 2013. "La década ganada: evolución de la clase media y las condiciones de vida en Colombia, 2002–2011." Universidad de los Andes, Facultad de Economía. https://economia.uniandes.edu.co/components/com_booklibrary/ebooks/dcede2013-50.pdf.

Appadurai, Arjun. 1996. *Modernity at Large: Cultural Dimensions of Globalization.* Vol. 1. Minneapolis: University of Minnesota Press.

———. 2000. "Spectral Housing and Urban Cleansing: Notes on Millennial Mumbai." *Public Culture* 12 (3): 627–51.

Ariztía, Tomás. 2009. "Moving Home: The Everyday Making of the Chilean Middle Class." PhD diss., London School of Economics and Political Science.

———. 2012. "Decorating the New House: The Material Culture of Social Mobility." In *Consumer Culture in Latin America,* edited by John Sinclaire and Anna Cristina Pertierra, 93–106. London: Palgrave Macmillan.

Arjona, Ana. 2015. "Guest Voz: Colombia's Rampant Racism Deserves National Spotlight and International Awareness." *Latina Lista,* May 11. http://latinalista.com/columns/guestvoz/guest-voz-colombias-rampant-racism-deserves-a-national-spotlight-and-international-awareness.

Aronczyk, Melissa. 2013. *Branding the Nation: The Global Business of National Identity.* Oxford University Press.

Arteaga, Natalia. 2014. "De los 19 supermercados que compró Exito, le quedarán 15." *El País,* September 17. www.larepublica.co/de-los-19-supermecados-que-compr%C3%B3-%C3%A9xito-le-quedar%C3%A1n-15_168956.

Avilés, William. 2006. *Global Capitalism, Democracy, and Civil-Military Relations in Colombia.* Albany: SUNY Press.

Babb, Florence. 2010. *The Tourism Encounter: Fashioning Latin American Nations and Histories.* Stanford, CA: Stanford University Press.

Baker, Michael. 1997. "REIT-Owned Shopping Centers." *ICSC Research Quarterly* 4 (3): 16–18.

Ballvé, Teo. 2012. "Everyday State Formation: Territory, Decentralization, and the Narco Landgrab in Colombia." *Environment and Planning-Part D* 30 (4): 603–22.

———. 2013. "Grassroots Masquerades: Development, Paramilitaries, and Land Laundering in Colombia." *Geoforum* 50 (December): 62–75.

Barstow, David, and Alejandra Xanic von Bertrab. 2012. "The Bribery Aisle: How Wal-Mart Got Its Way in Mexico." *New York Times,* December 17. www.nytimes.com/2012/12/18/business/walmart-bribes-teotihuacan.html?pagewanted=all&_r=0.

Barth, Gunther. 1982. *City People: The Rise of Modern City Culture in Nineteenth-Century America.* Oxford: Oxford University Press.

Baud, Jan M., and Johanna Louisa Ypeij. 2009. *Cultural Tourism in Latin America: The Politics of Space and Imagery.* Leiden: Brill.

Beckford, George. 1999. *Persistent Poverty: Underdevelopment in Plantation Economies of the Third World.* Kingston, Jamaica: University of the West Indies Press.

Benzecry, Claudio. 2014. "All Together, Now: Producing Fashion at the Global Level." *Society Pages,* May. http://thesocietypages.org/papers/all-together-now/.

Berlant, Lauren. 2011. *Cruel Optimism.* Durham, NC: Duke University Press.

Berney, Rachel. 2011. "Pedagogical Urbanism: Creating Citizen Space in Bogotá, Colombia." *Planning Theory* 10 (1): 16–34.

Best, Lloyd, Kari Polanyi Levitt, and Norman Girvan. 2009. *Essays on the Theory of Plantation Economy: A Historical and Institutional Approach to Caribbean Economic Development.* Kingston, Jamaica: University of the West Indies Press.

Betancourt, Carlos. 2012. "Centros comerciales en Colombia." Medellín, Encuentro de Profesionales de la Industria de los Centros Comerciales de América–EPICCA.

Bird Picó, María. 2006. "The Family Way." *Shopping Centers Today,* April: 77–79.

———. 2007. "Ejecutivos dicen que los malls tipo condominio tienen mala reputación." *SCT Latinoamerica,* September: 18.

———. 2011. "Siguen adelante los malls de Medellín." *Shopping Centers Today,* August.

———. 2013. "Big Money: Private Equity Funds Are Speeding the Growth of Latin America's Retailers." *Shopping Centers Today,* May: 232–38.

————. 2014a. "Expectativa pública, propiedad privada." *Shopping Centers Iberoamerica,* October: 25–28.

————. 2014b. "Grandes oportunidades en pequeños lugares." *Shopping Centers Today Iberoamerica,* primer trimestre, 15–18.

Bodamer, David. 2008. "Lessons from the List." *Retail Traffic* 37 (4): 4.

Bonnett, Piedad. 2013. "Los nuevos templos." *El Espectador,* February 2. www .elespectador.com/opinion/los-nuevos-templos-columna-402565.

Botero, Guillermo. 2012. "Centros comerciales: Destino obligatorio en un plan turístico." *Centros Comerciales,* May: 4.

Bourdieu, Pierre. 1984. *Distinction: A Social Critique of the Judgement of Taste.* Translated by Richard Nice. Cambridge, MA: Harvard University Press.

Bowden, Marilyn. 2014. "Global Shoppers Fuel Miami Malls." *Miami Today,* November 12. www.miamitodaynews.com/2014/11/12/global-shoppers-fuel-miami-malls/.

Brash, Julian. 2011. *Bloomberg's New York: Class and Governance in the Luxury City.* Athens: University of Georgia Press.

Briggs, Adam. 2013. "Capitalism's Favourite Child: The Production of Fashion." In *Fashion Cultures Revisited,* edited by Pamela Church Gibson and Stella Bruzzi, 186–99. London: Routledge.

Cahn, Peter S. 2008. "Consuming Class: Multilevel Marketers in Neoliberal Mexico." *Cultural Anthropology* 23 (3): 429–52.

Caldeira, Teresa P. R. 2000. *City of Walls: Crime, Segregation, and Citizenship in São Paulo.* Berkeley: University of California Press.

Callieri, Christian. 2013. "Global Retail Development Index: Top Destinations for Global Retailers." RECon Latin America, Chile, March 19.

Campbell, Ross W. 1974. "Stages of Shopping Center Development in Major Latin American Metropolitan Markets." *Land Economics* 50 (1): 66–70.

Carbone, June, and Naomi Cahn. 2014. *Marriage Markets: How Inequality Is Remaking the American Family.* Oxford: Oxford University Press.

Carbonell Higuera, Carlos Martín. 2011. "El reordenamiento del espacio urbano en el sector de San Victorino y Santa Inés (Bogotá) en relación con las dinámicas de informalidad y marginalidad (1948–2010)." *Territorios* 24: 131–64.

————. 2013. "El sector de San Victorino en los procesos de reconfiguración urbana de Bogotá (1598–1998)." *Cuadernos de Vivienda y Urbanismo* 3 (6): 220–45.

Castañeda, Jorge G. 2007. "Adios to Poverty, Hola to Consumption: Latin America's New Look." *The Economist,* August 16.

————. 2011. "What Latin America Can Teach Us." NYTimes.com. Accessed January 11. www.nytimes.com/2011/12/11/opinion/sunday/on-the-middle-class-lessons-from-latin-america.html?nytmobile=0.

Castellani, Francesca, and Gwenn Parent. 2011. *Being "Middle-Class" in Latin America.* OECD Development Centre Working Papers. Paris: Organization for Economic Co-operation and Development.

Castellanos, M. Bianet. 2010. *A Return to Servitude: Maya Migration and the Tourist Trade in Cancun.* Minneapolis: University of Minnesota Press.

Catchpole, Karen. 2014. "Colombiamoda, Latin America's Fashion Week—Medellín, Colombia." *Trans-Americas Journey* (September). http://trans-americas.com/blog/2014/09/colombiamoda-latin-america-fashion-week-sort-medellin-colombia/.

Cepeda, Maria Elena. 2010. *Musical ImagiNation: U.S.-Colombian Identity and the Latin Music Boom.* New York: New York University Press.

Chin, Elizabeth. 2001. *Purchasing Power: Black Kids and American Consumer Culture.* Minneapolis: University of Minnesota Press.

Ciccolella, P. 1999. "Globalización y dualización en la región metropolitana de Buenos Aires: Grandes inversiones y restructuración socioterritorial en los años noventa." *EURE* (Santiago) 25 (76): 5–27.

Cifuentes Quin, Camilo Andrés, and Nicolas Tixier. 2012. "An Inside Look at Bogotá's Urban Renewal from Broad Urban Stories to Everyday Tales." Sixth Conference of the International Forum on Urbanism, Barcelona, Spain, January, 1–11.

Cline, Elizabeth L. 2013. *Overdressed: The Shockingly High Cost of Cheap Fashion.* Reprint. New York: Portfolio Trade.

Cohen, Lizabeth. 2003. *A Consumers' Republic: The Politics of Mass Consumption in Postwar America.* New York: Vintage Books.

Collet, Gilda, and Heliane Comin. 2010. "The Shopping Centers Shaping the Brazilian City." In *Contemporary Urbanism in Brazil: Beyond Brasília,* ed. Vicente del Rio and William Siembieda, 104–19. Gainesville: University Press of Florida.

Collins, Jane L. 2003. *Threads: Gender, Labor, and Power in the Global Apparel Industry.* Chicago: University of Chicago Press.

Conroy, Marianne. 1998. "Discount Dreams: Factory Outlet Malls, Consumption, and the Performance of Middle-Class Identity." *Social Text,* no. 54 (April): 63–83.

Correa, Jorge. 2013. "Si usted se gana $2.000.000 es rico para el Banco Mundial." *El Tiempo,* May 5. www.eltiempo.com/archivo/documento/CMS-12779552.

Crawford, Margaret. 1992. "The World in a Shopping Mall." In *Variations on a Theme Park: The New American City and the End of Public Space,* edited by Michael Sorkin, 3–30. New York: Hill and Wang.

———. 2014. "Public Space: From the 'Feel Good' City to the Just City." Paper presented at Streets as Public Spaces and Drivers of Prosperity Conference, organized by the Future of Places, Buenos Aires, September.

Cross, John Christopher. 1998. *Informal Politics: Street Vendors and the State in Mexico City.* Stanford, CA: Stanford University Press.

Cutait, Michel. 2013. "Understanding Brazilian Shopping-Center Market Stakeholders." *Retail Property Insights* 20 (1): 19–22.

Departamento Administrativo Nacional de Estadísticas (DANE). 2007. *Hogares por tenencia de la vivienda y carro particular, 1997–2013: Encuesta nacional de calidad de vida 2007.* Serie Observatorios. Bogotá: Departamento Administrativo Nacional de Estadística.

———. 2013. Encuesta Nacional de Calidad de Vida 2013 (ECV). www.dane.gov.co/files/investigaciones/condiciones_vida/calidad_vida/Boletin_Prensa_ECV_2013.pdf.

Dávila, Arlene. 2004. *Barrio Dreams*. Berkeley: University of California Press.

———. 2012. *Latinos, Inc.: The Marketing and Making of a People*. Berkeley: University of California Press.

———. 2012. *Culture Works: Space, Value, and Mobility across the Neoliberal Americas*. New York: New York University Press.

Dávila-Santiago, Rubén. 2005. *El Mall: Del mundo al paraíso*. San Juan: Ediciones Callejón.

DeHart, Monica. 2010. *Ethnic Entrepreneurs: Identity and Development Politics in Latin America*. Stanford, CA: Stanford University Press.

De Mattos, C. 1999. "Santiago de Chile, globalización y expansión metropolitana: Lo que existía sigue existiendo." *EURE* (Santiago) 25 (76): 29–56.

De Simone, Liliana. 2013. "La ciudad del consumo: Reflexiones en torno a la mercantilización urbana y el desarrollo de la infraestructura de retail en Santiago Chile, 1982–2013." *Metropolis* 15 (2): 30–43.

———. 2015. *Metamall: Espacio urbano y consumo en la ciudad neoliberal chilena*. RIL Editores—Instituto de Estudios Urbanos y Territoriales.

Dickinson, Marla, and Rogerio Jelmayer. 2015. "'Ghost Malls' Haunt Brazil." *Wall Street Journal*, May 5. www.wsj.com/articles/ghost-malls-haunt-brazil-1430818675.

Draper, Susana. 2012. *Afterlives of Confinement: Spatial Transitions in Postdictatorship Latin America*. Pittsburgh, PA: University of Pittsburgh Press.

Dulitzky, Ariel. 2005. "A Region in Denial: Racial Discrimination and Racism in Latin America." In *Neither Enemies nor Friends: Latinos, Blacks, Afro-Latinos*, edited by Suzanne Oboler and Anani Dzidzienyo, 39–60. New York: Palgrave.

Dunn, Kathleen. 2014. "Street Vendors in and against the Global City: VAMOS Unidos." In *New Labor in New York: Precarious Workers and the Future of the Labor Movement*, edited by Ruth Milkman and Ett Ott, 134–49. Ithaca, NY: ILR Press.

Economía. 2013. El drama de los textileros. *Semana*, January 26. www.semana.com /economia/articulo/el-drama-textileros/330717–3.

Edmonds, Alexander. 2010. *Pretty Modern: Beauty, Sex, and Plastic Surgery in Brazil*. Durham, NC: Duke University Press.

EFE. 2013. "El 68% de la población laboral activa en Colombia es informal." *El Espectador*, April 30. www.elespectador.com/noticias/economia/el-68-de-poblacion-laboral-activa-colombia-informal-articulo-419329.

Elle España. 2014. "Cómo una diseñadora española se apropió, por no decir robó, las mochilas Wayúu." *Pulzo*, March 28. www.pulzo.com/estilo/como-una-disenadora-espanola-se-apropio-por-no-decir-robo-las-mochilas-wayuu-108256.

Ellin, Nan. 2001. "Thresholds of Fear: Embracing the Urban Shadow." *Urban Studies* 38 (5–6): 869–83.

Escobar, Arturo. 2008. *Territories of Difference: Place, Movements, Life, Redes*. Durham, NC: Duke University Press.

———. 2011. *Encountering Development: The Making and Unmaking of the Third World*. With a new preface by the author. Princeton, NJ: Princeton University Press.

El Espectador. 2013a. "Petro: 'No se van a meter prostíbulos en Andino o en Centro Comercial Santafé.'" *El Espectador,* May 16. www.elespectador.com/noticias /bogota/petro-no-se-van-meter-prostibulos-andino-o-centro-comer-articulo-422384.

———. 2013b. "130 mil predios de estratos 1, 2 y 3 sí deberán pagar valorización." *El Espectador,* June. 20 www.elespectador.com/noticias/bogota/130-mil-predios-de-estratos-1-2-y-3-si-deberan-pagar-va-articulo-429109.

———. 2013c. "Los 25 detalles del caso Fabio Salamanca." *El Espectador,* August 26. www.elespectador.com/noticias/investigacion/los-25-detalles-del-caso-fabio-salamanca-articulo-442459.

———. 2013d. "Polémica por 'Manual de Buen Vestir' en Fondo Nacional de Garantías." *El Espectador,* September 18. www.elespectador.com/noticias /nacional/polemica-manual-de-buen-vestir-fondo-nacional-de-garant-articulo-447027.

Ewen, Stuart, and Elizabeth Ewen. 1992. *Channels of Desire: Mass Images and the Shaping of American Consciousness.* 2nd ed. Minneapolis: University of Minnesota Press.

Farrell, James J. 2010. *One Nation under Goods: Malls and the Seductions of American Shopping.* Washington, DC: Smithsonian Books.

Feagin, Joe R. 1983. *The Urban Real Estate Game: Playing Monopoly with Real Money.* Englewood Cliffs, NJ: Prentice-Hall.

Fernandes, Sujatha. 2010. *Who Can Stop the Drums? Urban Social Movements in Chávez's Venezuela.* Durham, NC: Duke University Press.

Fernández-Kelly, Patricia, and Jon Shefner. 2006. *Out of the Shadows: Political Action and the Informal Economy in Latin America.* University Park: Pennsylvania State University Press.

Finanzas Personales. 2013. "Clase media en Colombia: Frágil, pero en crecimiento." *Finanzas Personales,* August. www.finanzaspersonales.com.co/trabajo-y-educacion/articulo/clase-media-colombia-fragil-pero-crecimiento/48836.

Fiske, John. 2010. "Shopping for Pleasure." In *Reading the Popular,* 10–33. New York: Routledge.

Forero-Peña, Alcira. 2015. "Of Beauty and 'Beauties': Female identities and Body Image in Colombia." In *Body Image and Identity in Contemporary Societies,* edited by Ekaterina Sukhanova and Hans-Otto Thomashoff, 104–14. New York: Routledge.

Franco, Rolando, Arturo León, and Raúl Atria. 2007. *Estratificación y movilidad social en América Latina: Transformaciones estructurales de un cuarto de siglo.* Santiago: UN Comisión Económica para América Latina y el Caribe, CEPAL.

Freeman, Carla. 2000. *High Tech and High Heels in the Global Economy: Women, Work, and Pink-Collar Identities in the Caribbean.* Durham, NC: Duke University Press.

———. 2014. *Entrepreneurial Selves: Neoliberal Respectability and the Making of a Caribbean Middle Class.* Durham, NC: Duke University Press.

Fresneda, Ana María. 2013. "Nuevos proyectos abrirán sus puertas con novedosos diseños." *El Tiempo,* July 27.

Friedman, Vanessa. 2015. "Fashion's Racial Divide." *New York Times,* February 12. www.nytimes.com/2015/02/12/fashion/fashions-racial-divide.html?hp&action= click&pgtype=Homepage&module=mini-moth&region=top-stories-below&WT .nav=top-stories-below&_r=0.

Foucault, Michel. 1984. "Of Other Spaces, Heterotopia." *Architecture /Mouvement/ Continuité* 5 (October): 46–49.

Galvis, Juan P. 2011. "Managing the Living City: Public Space and Development in Bogotá." PhD diss., University of Washington.

Ganti, Tejaswini. 2012. *Producing Bollywood: Inside the Contemporary Hindi Film Industry.* Durham, NC: Duke University Press.

García, Carlos. 2014. "Colombianos, los más endeudados de Latinoamérica." *El Tiempo,* November 10. www.eltiempo.com/economia/finanzas-personales /creditos-y-deudas-de-los-colombianos/14811756.

García Canclini, Néstor. 2001. *Consumers and Citizens: Globalization and Multicultural Conflicts.* Translated by George Yudice. Minneapolis: University of Minnesota Press.

———. 2005. *Hybrid Cultures: Strategies for Entering and Leaving Modernity.* Minneapolis: University of Minnesota Press.

Garrido, Marisol. 2007. "Language Attitude in Colombian Spanish: Cachacos vs. Costeños." *Lenguaje y Literatura* 2 (2). http://ojs.gc.cuny.edu/index.php/11journal /article/view/246/257.

Gibson-Graham, J.K. 2006. *The End of Capitalism (As We Knew It): A Feminist Critique of Political Economy.* Minneapolis: University of Minnesota Press.

Gilbert, David. 2013. "A New World Order? Fashion and Its Capitals in the Twenty-First Century." In *Fashion Cultures Revisited: Theories, Explorations and Analysis,* edited by Stella Bruzi and Pamela Church Gibson, 11–30. New York: Routledge.

Gilbert, Dennis L. 2007. *Mexico's Middle Class in the Neoliberal Era.* Tucson: University of Arizona Press.

Gill, Leslie. 2004. *The School of the Americas: Military Training and Political Violence in the Americas.* Durham, NC: Duke University Press.

Gilliom, John, and Torin Monahan. 2012. *SuperVision: An Introduction to the Surveillance Society.* Chicago: University of Chicago Press.

Gómez, Ángela María Robledo, and Patricia Rodríguez Santana. 2008. *Emergencia del sujeto excluido: Aproximación genealógica a la no-ciudad en Bogotá.* Bogotá: Pontificia Universidad Javeriana.

Gómez, Constanza. 2013. "Almacenes Éxito será nuevo socio de las tiendas de barrio." *Portafolio,* July. www.portafolio.co/negocios/almacenes-exito-socio-las-tiendas-barrio.

———. 2014. "Centro Mayor, el más visitado de Bogotá en el 2013." *Portafolio,* April 1. www.portafolio.co/negocios/centro-comerciales-mas-visitados-bogota-el-2013.

Gomez Kopp, Milena. 2013. "La Guaca? The Internationalization of Colombia's Housing Market." In *Transbordering Latin Americas: Liminal Places, Cultures and Powers,* ed. Clara Irazábal, 217–40. New York: Routledge.

Goss, Jon. 1993. "The 'Magic of the Mall': An Analysis of Form, Function, and Meaning in the Contemporary Retail Built Environment." *Annals of the Association of American Geographers* 83 (1): 18–47.

Gradin, Greg. 2007. *Empire's Workshop: Latin America, the United States, and the Rise of the New Imperialism.* New York: Holt Paperbacks.

Gregory, Steven. 2006. *The Devil Behind the Mirror: Globalization and Politics in the Dominican Republic.* Berkeley: University of California Press.

Grupo de Inteligencia de Mercado del ICSC para América Latina. 2015. *Reporte 2015 de la industria de centros comerciales en América Latina.* New York: ICSC.

Gurian, Elaine Heumann. 2006. "Threshold Fear: Architecture Program Planning." In *Civilizing the Museum, the Collected Works of Elaine Heumann Gurian,* 115–26. London: Routledge.

Harvey, David. 2004. "The 'New' Imperialism: Accumulation by Dispossession." *Socialist Register* 40: 63–87.

Hincapié, Juan David. 2013. "Vivir con precios del primer mundo y salarios del tercero." *Finanzas Personales,* August. www.finanzaspersonales.com.co/columnistas/articulo/vivir-precios-del-primer-mundo-salarios-del-tercero/51409.

Ho, Karen. 2009. *Liquidated: An Ethnography of Wall Street.* Durham, NC: Duke University Press.

ICSC New York. 2014. "Shopping Centers: America's First and Foremost Marketplace." October 2.

Inmobiliare. 2013. "Planigrupo, 2012 a Year of Consolidation and the Challenges for 2013." *Inmobiliare.* http://inmobiliare.com/planigrupo-2012-a-year-of-consolidation-and-the-challenges-for-2013/.

Irazabal, Clara. 2008. *Ordinary Places/Extraordinary Events: Citizenship, Democracy and Public Space in Latin America.* New York: Routledge.

———. 2009. "Revisiting Urban Planning in Latin America and the Caribbean." Regional Study Prepared for Revisiting Urban Planning Global Report on Human Settlements. www.unhabitat.org/grhs/2009.

Johnston, Hank, and Paul Almeida. 2006. *Latin American Social Movements: Globalization, Democratization, and Transnational Networks.* New York: Rowman & Littlefield.

Jones, Gareth A., and Maria Moreno-Carranco. 2007. "Megaprojects: Beneath the Pavement, Excess." *City: Analysis of Urban Trends, Culture, Theory, Policy, Action* 11 (2): 144–64.

Kliest, Nicole. 2014. "Why You Should Know about Colombia's Fashion Week." *WhoWhatWear,* July 28. www.whowhatwear.com/colombiamoda-fashion-week.

Kolson-Hurley, Amanda. 2015. "Shopping Malls Aren't Actually Dying." *Citilab, the Atlantic,* March 25. www.citylab.com/design/2015/03/shopping-malls-arent-actually-dying/387925/.

Kozameh, Sara, and Rebecca Ray. 2012. "Surviving the Global Recession: Poverty and Inequality in Latin America." *NACLA Report on the Americas* 45 (2): 22–26.

Lash, Scott, and Celia Lury. 2007. *Global Culture Industry: The Mediation of Things.* Cambridge: Polity Press.

Lattman, Peter, and Simon Romero. 2013. "Brazil, Fortune and Fate Turn on Billionaire." *New York Times,* July 23. www.nytimes.com/2013/06/24/business /global/brazil-fortune-and-fate-turn-on-billionaire.html.

LeBrón, Marisol. 2014. "Violent Arrest: Punitive Governance and Neocolonial Crisis in Contemporary Puerto Rico." PhD diss., New York University.

Lefebvre, Henri. 1992. *The Production of Space.* New York: Blackwell.

Lewellen, Ted. 2006. "The Anthropology of Development and Globalization: From Classical Political Economy to Contemporary Neoliberalism." *American Anthropologist* 108 (1): 240–41.

Lewin, Juan Esteban. 2011. "Una nueva victoria de los vecinos de Unicentro: La destitución de la curadora cuarta." *La Silla Vacía,* April 12. http://lasillavacia .com/historia/una-nueva-victoria-de-los-vecinos-de-unicentro-la-destitucion-de-la-curadora-cuarta-23254.

Liechty, Mark. 2002. *Suitably Modern: Making Middle-Class Culture in a New Consumer Society.* Princeton, NJ: Princeton University Press.

Lomnitz, Claudio. 2001. *Deep Mexico, Silent Mexico: An Anthropology of Nationalism.* Minneapolis: University of Minnesota Press.

Londoño, Johana. 2012. "Aesthetic Belonging: The Latinization of Cities, Urban Design, and the Limits of the Barrio." PhD diss., New York University.

López, A. Ricardo. 2012a. "Conscripts of Democracy: The Formation of a Professional Middle Class in Bogotá during the 1950s and Early 1960s." In *The Making of the Middle Class: Toward a Transnational History,* edited by A. Ricardo López and Barbara Weinstein,161–95. Durham, NC: Duke University Press.

López, A. Ricardo, and Barbara Weinstein, eds. 2012. *The Making of the Middle Class: Toward a Transnational History.* Durham, NC: Duke University Press.

Low, Setha. 2000. *On the Plaza: The Politics of Public Space and Culture.* Austin: University of Texas Press.

———. 2004. *Behind the Gates: Life, Security, and the Pursuit of Happiness in Fortress America.* New York: Routledge.

Low, Setha M., and Denise Lawrence-Zúñiga, eds. 2003. *The Anthropology of Space and Place: Locating Culture.* Malden, MA: Wiley-Blackwell.

Low, Setha, Dana Taplin, and Suzanne Scheld. 2005. *Rethinking Urban Parks: Public Space and Cultural Diversity.* Austin: University of Texas Press.

Lulle, Thierry, and Catherine Paquette. 2007. "Los grandes centros comerciales y la planificación urbana: Un análisis comparativo de dos metrópolis latinoamericanas." *Estudios Demográficos y Urbanos* 22 (2): 337–61.

Lury, Celia. 2004. *Brands: The Logos of the Global Economy.* London: Routledge.

Manchego Morales, Martha. 2012. Se duplica la clase media en Colombia. *Portafolio,* July 29. www.portafolio.co/negocios/se-duplica-la-clase-media-colombia.

Martin, Randy. 2002. *Financialization of Daily Life.* Philadelphia: Temple University Press.

Martín-Barbero, Jesus. 1993. *Communication, Culture and Hegemony: From the Media to Mediations.* London: Sage.

McCracken, Grant David. 1990. *Culture and Consumption: New Approaches to the Symbolic Character of Consumer Goods and Activities*. Bloomington: Indiana University Press.

McCrossen, Alexis, ed. 2009. *Land of Necessity: Consumer Culture in the United States–Mexico Borderlands*. Durham, NC: Duke University Press.

McGuirck, Justin. 2014. *Radical Cities: Across Latin America, in Search of New Architecture*. New York: Verso Books.

McKittrick, Katherine. 2013. "Plantation Futures." *Small Axe* 17 (342): 1–15.

McLinden, Steve. 2013. "Leasing Mall a Global Village." *RECon News ICSC,* May 20, 42.

Medeiros, Carmen. 2005. "The Right to 'Know How to Understand': Coloniality and Contesting Visions of Development and Citizenship in the Times of Neo-Liberal Civility." PhD diss., Graduate Center of the City University of New York.

Méndez L., María Luisa. 2008. "Middle-Class Identities in a Neoliberal Age: Tensions between Contested Authenticities." *Sociological Review* 56 (2): 220–37.

Milanesio, Natalia. 2013. *Workers Go Shopping in Argentina: The Rise of Popular Consumer Culture*. Albuquerque: University of New Mexico Press.

Miller, Daniel. 1995. *Acknowledging Consumption: A Review of New Studies*. London: Routledge.

———. 1998. *A Theory of Shopping*. Ithaca: Cornell University Press.

———. 2010. *Stuff*. Cambridge: Polity Press.

———. 2012. *Consumption and Its Consequences*. Cambridge: John Wiley & Sons.

Miller, Jacob C. 2013. "The Spatial Dialectics of Modernity and Retail Affect at Abasto Shopping, Buenos Aires, Argentina." *Urban Geography* 34 (6): 843–63.

Miller, Toby. 2007. "Global Hollywood 2010." *International Journal of Communication* 1 (1): 1–4.

Ministerio de la Educación Superior. 2012. *Resultados de las condiciones laborales de los graduados de educación superior 2001–2012 y los certificados de educación para el trabajo y el desarrollo humano, 2010–2012*. Documento técnico. Bogotá: Observatorio Laboral para la Educación.

Mintz, Sidney Wilfred. 1986. *Sweetness and Power: The Place of Sugar in Modern History*. New York: Penguin Books.

Mitchell, Don. 2003. *The Right to the City: Social Justice and the Fight for Public Space*. New York: Guilford Press.

Mitchell, Timothy. 2002. *Rule of Experts: Egypt, Techno-Politics, Modernity*. Berkeley: University of California Press.

Moffett, Matt. 2011. "A Rags-to-Riches Career Highlights Latin Resurgence." *Wall Street Journal,* November 11. www.wsj.com/articles/SB10001424052970204422404576595211776435404.

Molotch, Harvey. 2014. *Against Security: How We Go Wrong at Airports, Subways, and Other Sites of Ambiguous Danger*. Princeton, NJ: Princeton University Press.

Mondragón, Sandra. 2014. *Universidad y ciudad: Desarrollo de las universidades en Bogotá, 1950–1990*. Colección Punto Aparte. Bogotá: Facultad de Artes. Universidad Nacional de Colombia.

Morales, Martha. 2012. "Se duplica la clase media en Colombia." *Portafolio,* July 29. www.portafolio.co/detalle_archivo/DR-56777.

Moreno, Julio. 2003. *Yankee Don't Go Home! Mexican Nationalism, American Business Culture, and the Shaping of Modern Mexico, 1920–1950.* Chapel Hill: University of North Carolina Press.

Mosse, George L. 1997. *Nationalism and Sexuality: Respectability and Abnormal Sexuality in Modern Europe.* New York: Fertig.

Muller, Jan Marco. 1997. "La plaza privatizada: Los centros comerciales y recreacionales y su adaptación al espacio urbano latinoamericano. El caso de Santafé de Bogotá, Colombia." Simposio presented at 49 Congreso Internacional de Americanistas (ICA), Quito, Ecuador.

Murphy, Edward. 2008. "What's New in Neoliberalism? A Review of Recent Scholarship on Chile." *Journal of Latin American and Caribbean Anthropology* 13 (2): 499–510.

Noticias Caracol. 2014. "Justicia pareciera que se clasificara por estratos: Víctimas de Salamanca." *Noticias Caracol* (Colombia), February 26. www.noticiascaracol .com/nacion/justicia-pareciera-que-se-clasificara-por-estratos-victimas-de-salamanca.

Observatorio de Culturas. 2011. "Resultados encuesta bienal de culturas." Secretaría de Cultura, Recreación y Deporte, Bogotá. www.culturarecreacionydeporte.gov .co/observatorio/documentos/encuesta/encuesta11/d_resultados.html.

Observatorio Económico de Moda. 2015. Datos del comercio exterior Colombiano del sistema de moda, con datos de DANE (Departamento Administrativo Nacional de Estadísticas). Bogotá.

O'Dougherty, Maureen. 2002. *Consumption Intensified: The Politics of Middle-Class Daily Life in Brazil.* Durham, NC: Duke University Press.

———. 2006. "Public Relations, Private Security: Managing Youth and Race at the Mall of America." *Society and Space* 24 (1): 131–54.

Offner, Amy. 2012. "Public Housing and Private Property: Colombia and the United States, 1950–1980." *Progressive Planning Magazine,* no. 193 (Fall): 26–29.

Ong, Aihwa. 2006. *Neoliberalism as Exception: Mutations in Citizenship and Sovereignty.* Durham, NC: Duke University Press.

Ortiz-Gomez, Andres, and Roger Zetter. 2013. "Market Enablement and the Configuration of Urban Structure in Colombia." In *Market Economy and Urban Change: Impacts in the Developing World,* edited by Mohamed Hamza and Roger Zetter, 185–205. New York: Routledge.

Ortiz-Negrón, Laura L. 2004. *Shopping en Puerto Rico: Prácticas, significados y subjetividades de consumo.* BookBaby ebook.

Ospina, Lucas. 2012. "La tenaz suramericana (Apología al grafiti)." *Esferapública,* September 16. http://esferapublica.org/nfblog/la-tenaz-suramericana-apologia-al-grafiti/.

Parker, David S., and Louise E. Walker. 2012. *Latin America's Middle Class: Unsettled Debates and New Histories.* New York: Rowman & Littlefield.

Peck, Jamie. 2005. "Struggling with the Creative Class." *International Journal of Urban and Regional Research* 29 (4): 740–70.

Peebles, Gustav. 2010. "The Anthropology of Credit and Debt." *Annual Review of Anthropology* 39 (1): 225–40.

Pham, Minh-Ha T. 2014. "Fashion's Cultural-Appropiation Debate: Pointless." *Atlantic,* May 15. www.theatlantic.com/entertainment/archive/2014/05 /cultural-appropriation-in-fashion-stop-talking-about-it/370826/.

*Portafolio.* 2013. "Investigación por dumping a calzado y marroquinería china." Portafolio.com.co, August. www.portafolio.co/negocios/investigacion-dumping- calzado-y-marroquineria-china.

———. 2014a. "Bogotá, con los arriendos que más crecen para tiendas." *Portafolio,* December 2. www.portafolio.co/negocios/bogota-arriendos-tiendas.

———. 2014b. "¿Cuánto valen los mismos productos en estratos diferentes?" *Portafolio,* November 14. www.portafolio.co/finanzas-personales/lo-que-cuesta-hacer- mercado-distintos-estratos.

———. 2014c. "Vienen US$4.000 millones para centros comerciales." *Portafolio,* November 27. www.portafolio.co/negocios/crecimiento-centros-comerciales- colombia.

Portes, Alejandro, and Kelly Hoffman. 2003. "Latin American Class Structures: Their Composition and Change during the Neoliberal Era." *Latin American Research Review* 38 (1): 41–82.

Quevedo, Norbey. 2013. Los 25 detalles del caso Fabio Salamanca. *El Espectador.* August 26. http://www.elespectador.com/noticias/investigacion/los-25-detalles- del-caso-fabio-salamanca-articulo-442459.

Quijano, Aníbal. 2000. "Coloniality of Power and Eurocentrism in Latin America." *International Sociology* 15 (2): 215–32.

RADDAR. 2012a. "Dinámica de la propiedad y del crédito, 1993–2011." Microeco- nomic Outlook Database. Proprietary Study by RADDAR, Inc., Bogotá.

———. 2012b. "Lugar de compra autodeclarado de última Compra." *Consumer Track Views.*

ConsumerTrack Database. Proprietary Study by RADDAR, Inc., Bogotá.

Rathbone, John Paul. 2013. "Colombia: A Rediscovered Country." *Financial Times,* June 3. www.ft.com/intl/cms/s/0/1a1fbe60–9dfde2–9ccc-00144feabdc0 .html#axzz3PCel7I90.

Redacción Bogotá. 2013. "Vecinos de Cedritos queman recibos en protesta por val- orización." *Diario AND,* January 26. http://diarioadn.co/bogota/mi-ciudad /protesta-en-cedritos-por-los-cobros-de-valorizaci%C3%B3n-1.43371.

———. 2014. "Bogotá se valorizó 309 por ciento en seis años." *El Tiempo,* February 3. www.eltiempo.com/archivo/documento/CMS-13445416.

Redacción El Tiempo. 2015. "Ciudades intermedias, claves en expansion del sector." Especial Centros Comerciales, *El Tiempo,* March 24.

La República. 2013. "Por tarjeta de crédito, cada colombiano debe $2,4 millones." *La República,* November 23. www.larepublica.co/finanzas/por-tarjeta-de-cr%C3% A9dito-cada-colombiano-debe-24-millones_84791.

Retail Traffic. 2010. "The Top Ten." *Retail Traffic,* June.

Reuters. 2015. "Colombiamoda Featured Bright Colors and Hot Looks." *Toronto Sun,* August 3. www.torontosun.com/2015/07/31/colombiamoda-fashion-featured-bright-colours-and-hot-looks.

Reyes Posada, Alejandro. 1990. "La Violencia y la expansión territorial del narcotráfico." In *Economía y política del narcotráfico,* edited by Juan Tokatlian and Bruce Michael Bagley, 117–40. Bogotá: Ediciones Uniandes.

———. 1997. "Compra de tierras por narcotraficantes." In *Drogas ilícitas en Colombia: Su impacto económico, político y social,* edited by Francisco E. Thoumi, 280–346. Bogotá: Ariel, PNUD, and DNE.

Reyna, Maria Soledad, ed. 2008. *Pedro Gómez, 40 años: Un mejor modo de vivir.* Bogotá: Letra Arte Editores.

Rico, Laura. 2008. "La nueva torre de Unicentro: Una pelea con los vecinos y con el distrito." *La Silla Vacía,* August 14. http://lasillavacia.com/historia/17364.

Rincón, Omar. 2009. "Narco.estética y narco.cultura en Narco.colombia." *Nueva Sociedad,* no. 222: 147–63.

———. 2013. "Todos llevamos un narco adentro: Un ensayo sobre la narco/cultura /telenovela como modo de entrada a la modernidad." *Matrizes* 7 (2): 1–33.

Rincón, Omar, and Maria Paula Martínez. 2013. "Colombianidades Export Market." In *Contemporary Latin@ Media: On Production, Circulation, and Politics,* edited by Arlene Dávila and Yeidy Rivero, 169–85. New York: New York University Press.

Rivas, Cecilia M. 2014. *Salvadoran Imaginaries: Mediated Identities and Cultures of Consumption.* New Brunswick, NJ: Rutgers University Press.

Robinson, William I. 2008. *Latin America and Global Capitalism: A Critical Globalization Perspective.* Baltimore, MD: Johns Hopkins University Press.

Rodríguez-Barrera, Juan Ignacio. 2010. "Retail Development Surges in Mexico." *Retail Property Insight* 17 (3):7.

———. 2015. "Breve panorama de la oferta de centros comerciales en Latinoamerica." *Inmobiliare* 15 (88): 102–6.

Rodríguez Garavito, César. 2015. "Dos caras del racismo." *El Espectador,* July 30. www.elespectador.com/opinion/dos-caras-del-racismo.

Rofel, Lisa. 2007. *Desiring China: Experiments in Neoliberalism, Sexuality, and Public Culture.* Durham, NC: Duke University Press.

Rolón, Carlos Fernando. 2013. "Zara transforma la moda colombiana." *F Market,* November 13. https://thefmarket.wordpress.com/2013/11/15/zara-transforma-la-moda-colombiana/.

Rosa, Jonathan. 2010. "Looking Like a Language, Sounding Like a Race: Making Latina/o Panethnicity and Managing American Anxieties." PhD diss., University of Chicago. ProQuest/UMI (AAT3419689).

Rosas, Gilberto. 2012. *Barrio Libre: Criminalizing States and Delinquent Refusals of the New Frontier.* Durham, NC: Duke University Press.

Ross, Miriam. 2010. *South American Cinematic Culture: Policy, Production, Distribution and Exhibition.* Cambridge: Scholars Publishing.

Roy, Ananya. 2005. "Urban Informality: Toward an Epistemology of Planning." *Journal of the American Planning Association* 71 (2): 147–58.

Roy, Ananya, and Aihwa Ong. 2011. *Worlding Cities: Asian Experiments and the Art of Being Global.* London: Wiley.

Ruiz Granados, Cinthya. 2014. "Entre $3,000 y $563.000 aumentara el impuesto predial de Bogotá este año." *La República,* January 30.

Salcedo, Rodrigo and Lilliana de Simone. 2012. *Los Malls en Chile: 30 años.* Santiago: Camara Chilena de Centros Comerciales.

Samper Pizano, Daniel. 2013. "Si usted fuera campesino . . ." *El Tiempo,* August 25. www.eltiempo.com/archivo/documento/CMS-13011986.

Sánchez Voelkl, Pilar. 2011. "La construcción del gerente: Masculinidades en élites corporativas en Colombia y Ecuador." Quito, Ecuador: FLACSO. http://repositorio .flacsoandes.edu.ec/handle/10469/3080.

Sarlo, Beatriz. 1994. *Escenas de la vida posmoderna: Intelectuales, arte y videocultura en la Argentina.* Buenos Aires: Ariel.

Sassen, Saskia. 1999. *Globalization and Its Discontents.* New York: New Press.

Schipani, Andrew. 2013. "Security for Export: The New Colombia." *Financial Times,* June 4.

Schwartz, Nelson D. 2015. "The Economics (and Nostalgia) of Dead Malls." *New York Times,* January 3. www.nytimes.com/2015/01/04/business/the-economics-and-nostalgia-of-dead-malls.html.

Seabrooke, Leonard. 2014. "Epistemic Arbitrage: Transnational Professional Knowledge in Action." *Journal of Professions and Organization* 1 (1): 49–64.

Secretaría de Planeación. 2013. *Última actualización de estratificación en Bogotá asignó estrato a más de 35,000 viviendas.* Boletín no. 060. Bogotá: Secretaría de Planeación.

Seigel, Micol. 2005. "Beyond Compare: Comparative Method after the Transnational Turn." *Radical History Review* 2005 (91): 62–90.

Selby, Martin. 2004. *Understanding Urban Tourism: Image, Culture and Experience.* London: I. B. Tauris.

Shankar, Shalini. 2015. *Advertising Diversity: Ad Agencies and the Creation of Asian American Consumers.* Durham, NC: Duke University Press.

La Silla Vacía. 2014. "El Clasismo VIP." *La Silla Vacía,* November 10. http://lasillavacia .com/queridodiario/confi-top-49072.

Silva, Armando. 2003. *Bogotá imaginada.* Bogotá: Convenio Andŕes Bello.

Skov, Lise. 2011. "Dreams of Small Nations in a Polycentric Fashion World." *Fashion Theory: Journal of Dress, Body & Culture* 15 (2): 137–56.

Smith, Neil. 1996. *The New Urban Frontier: Gentrification and the Revanchist City.* New York: Routledge.

Stecker, Andrew, and Kevin Connor. 2011. "Fishing for Taxpayer Cash: Bas Pro's Record of Big-League Subsidies, Failed Promises and the Consequences for Cities across America." *Public Accountability Initiative.* http://public-accountability .org/2010/06/fishing-for-taxpayer-cash/.

Stillerman, Joel. 2015. *The Sociology of Consumption: A Global Approach*. Malden, MA: Polity Press.

Stillerman, Joel, Jennifer Parker, and Rodrigo Salcedo. 2013. "Glocalizing Malls in the Global South: Shopping Centers, Cities and Consumers in Chile, Turkey, and India." Paper presented at annual meeting of the American Sociological Association, New York.

Stillerman, Joel, and Rodrigo Salcedo. 2012. "Transposing the Urban to the Mall Routes, Relationships, and Resistance in Two Santiago, Chile, Shopping Centers." *Journal of Contemporary Ethnography* 41 (3): 309–36.

Stoler, Ann. 2002. *Carnal Knowledge and Imperial Power: Race and Intimacy in Colonial Rule*. Berkeley: University of California Press.

Suárez, Juana. 2010. *Sitios de contienda: Producción cultural colombiana y el discurso de la violencia*. Colección Nexos y Diferencias. Madrid: Iberoamericana Vervuert.

———. 2012. *Critical Essays on Colombian Cinema and Culture: Cinembargo Colombia*. New York: Palgrave Macmillan.

Taussig, Michael. 2009. *What Color Is the Sacred*. Chicago: University of Chicago Press.

———. 2012. *Beauty and the Beast*. Chicago: University of Chicago Press.

Telles, Edward E. 2006. *Race in Another America: The Significance of Skin Color in Brazil*. New Brunswick, NJ: Princeton University Press.

The Economist. 2012. "Peace, Land and Bread." November 24. www.economist.com/news/americas/21567087-hard-bargaining-starts-peace-land-and-bread.

El Tiempo. 1976. "Hoy Bogotá es mas ciudad, se inauguró Unicentro." *El Tiempo*, April 28.

———. 1996. "Un nuevo centro para el comercio en el occidente." *El Tiempo*, November 15. www.eltiempo.com/archivo/documento/MAM-591859.

———. 2008. "Casa Estrella ahora será Falabella." *El Tiempo*, November 14. www.eltiempo.com/archivo/documento/MAM-3188553.

———. 2011. "Golpe a dos 'zares' de los sanandresitos de Bogotá—Archivo." *El Tiempo*, March 17. www.eltiempo.com/archivo/documento/CMS-9028246.

———. 2012. "Centro Comercial Titán Plaza provoca trancón en la Avenida Boyacá." *El Tiempo*, August 17. www.eltiempo.com/archivo/documento-2013/CMS-12136625.

———. 2013a. "Plantón en Cedritos por cobro de valorización incluyó quema de recibos." *El Tiempo*, January 25. www.eltiempo.com/archivo/documento/CMS-12549143.

———. 2013b. "Suba y Bosa protestan por valorización." *El Tiempo*, February 3. www.eltiempo.com/archivo/documento/CMS-12574934.

———. 2013c. "Éxito pasó de ser competidor a socio de las tiendas de barrio—Archivo." *El Tiempo*, July 9. www.eltiempo.com/archivo/documento/CMS-12922304.

———. 2014a. "Qué es ser rico en Colombia." *El Tiempo*, January. www.eltiempo.com/Multimedia/infografia/ricosencolombia/index.html.

———. 2014b. "Bogotá se valorizó 309 por ciento en seis años." *El Tiempo,* February 2. www.eltiempo.com/archivo/documento/CMS-13445416.

———. 2014c. "La lucha cotidiana de los afros desplazados en Bogotá." *El Tiempo,* May 16. www.eltiempo.com/bogota/situacion-de-los-afrocolombianos-en-bogota/13999300.

———. 2014d. "Tiendas de barrio tienen el 53 por ciento del comercio minorista." *El Tiempo,* October 13. www.eltiempo.com/economia/sectores /aumentan-compras-en-tiendas-de-barrio/14681117.

Thrift, Nigel. 2007. *Non-Representational Theory: Space, Politics, Affect.* London: Routledge.

Tible, Jean. 2013. "¿Una nueva clase bedia en Brasil? El Lulismo como fenómeno político-social." *Nueva Sociedad,* no. 243: 4–17.

Tu, Thuy Linh Nguyen. 2010. *The Beautiful Generation: Asian Americans and the Cultural Economy of Fashion.* Durham, NC: Duke University Press.

Tubridy, Michael. 1998. "Mall Openings, 1987–2000: How and Why They've Changed." *ICSC Research Quarterly* 5 (2): 1–4.

———. 2006. "Defining Trends in Shopping Center History." *ICSC Research Review* 13 (1): 10–14.

Underhill, Paco. 2000. *Why We Buy: The Science of Shopping.* New York: Random House Audio.

———. 2004. *Call of the Mall: The Author of "Why We Buy" on the Geography of Shopping.* Reprint ed. New York: Simon & Schuster.

Unidad de Información y Análisis Financiero (UIAF). 2013. "Compilación de tipologías de lavado de activos y financiación del terrorismo." Bogotá. file:/// Users/adavila/Downloads/Tipologias%20de%20lavado%20de%20activos%20 y%20financiacion%20del%20terrorismo%202004%20-%202013.pdf.

Urciuoli, Bonnie. 2009. "Talking/Not Talking about Race: The Enregisterments of Culture in Higher Education Discourses." *Journal of Linguistic Anthropology* 19(1): 21–39.

Uribe-Mallarino, Consuelo. 2008. "Estratificación social en Bogotá: De la política pública a la dinámica de la segregación social." *Universitas Humanística,* no. 65: 139–71.

Urrea Geraldo, Fernando, Carlos Augusto Viáfara López, and Mara Viveros Vigoya. 2014. "From Whitened Miscenegation to Tri-ethnic Multiculturalism." In *Pigmentocracies: Ethnicity, Race and Color in Latin America,* edited by Edward Telles, 81–125. Chapel Hill: University of North Carolina Press.

Valencia, Cristian. 2008. "Los quijotes de la modernidad." In *Unicentro: El lugar donde se encuentra todo,* 57–72. Bogotá: Consuelo Mendoza Ediciones.

Valenzuela-Aguilera, Alfonso. 2013. "Power, Territory and the Social Control of Space in Latin Ameirca." *Latin American Perspectives* 189 (40): 21–34.

Veblen, Thorstein. 1994. *The Theory of the Leisure Class.* New York: Dover.

Wade, Peter. 1995. *Blackness and Race Mixture: The Dynamics of Racial Identity in Colombia.* Baltimore, MD: Johns Hopkins University Press.

Wallace, Arturo. 2014. "Estrato 1, estrato 6: Como los colombianos hablan de sí mismos, divididos en clases sociales." *BBC Mundo,* September 24. www.bbc.com/mundo/noticias/2014/09/140919_colombia_fooc_estratos_aw

Wallace, Claire, and Rossalina Latcheva. 2006. "Economic Transformation Outside the Law: Corruption, Trust in Public Institutions and the Informal Economy in Transition Countries of Central and Eastern Europe." *Europe-Asia Studies* 58 (1): 81–102.

Williams Castro, Fatimah. 2013. "Afro-Colombians and the Cosmopolitan City: New Negotiations of Race and Space in Bogotá, Colombia." *Latin American Perspectives,* no. 40: 105–17.

Way, John. 2012. *The Mayan in the Mall: Globalization, Development, and the Making of Modern Guatemala.* Durham, NC: Duke University Press.

Williams, Rosalind H. 1991. *Dream Worlds: Mass Consumption in Late-Nineteenth-Century France.* Berkeley: University of California Press.

Wilson, Ara. 2004. *The Intimate Economies of Bangkok: Tomboys, Tycoons, and Avon Ladies in the Global City.* Berkeley: University of California Press.

Woods, Ngaire. 2006. *The Globalizers: The IMF, the World Bank, and Their Borrowers.* Cornell Studies in Money. Ithaca, NY: Cornell University Press.

Wright, Erik Olin, ed. 2005. *Approaches to Class Analysis.* New York: Cambridge University Press.

Yúdice, George. 2004. *The Expediency of Culture: Uses of Culture in the Global Era.* Durham, NC: Duke University Press.

Zelizer, Viviana A. 2007. *The Purchase of Intimacy.* Princeton, NJ: Princeton University Press.

Zilberg, Elana. 2011. *Space of Detention: The Making of a Transnational Gang Crisis between Los Angeles and San Salvador.* Durham, NC: Duke University Press.

Zukin, Sharon. 2004. "Consumers and Consumption." *Annual Review of Sociology* 30: 173–97.

———. 2005. *Point of Purchase: How Shopping Changed American Culture.* New York: Routledge.

# INDEX

115, 129; dating and marriage in relation to, 122–23, 124; emerging classes, 3, 4; fashion and, 124–33; fears of class mingling, 77; intraclass mingling, 106, 112, 122; language and class differentiation, 119–22, 124; malls stratified by, 9, 71, 99–112; naming practices and, 123, 183n6; new rich associated with illegal activities, 117; in New York investment firms, 67; performance and, 160; processes of class differentiation, 15; race and, 123–24; *rolezinho* flash mobs and, 94; shopping behavior and, 137–38; social imaginaries of, 1; as social project of culture making, 11; strata system of Colombia and, 94–95; temporality in use of shopping malls and, 175n3; upper-class disdain for malls, 74–75; valuation of land and, 78; weekend leisure at malls and, 74. *See also* middle classes; ñero style; new middle classes; *traqueto* culture; upward mobility; workers/working class

class differentiation, 15, 105, 109, 119, 183n1; exclusivity and customization associated with, 144; policing of boundaries related to consumption, 98; status and, 5, 11, 56, 95, 116, 121

classism, 16, 110, 112, 152, 162, 164, 185n4; of bogotano culture, 15; consumption and, 158; cultural hierarchies, 115; against displaced populations, 116–17; fear of crime/disorder and, 100; market research and, 65; opposition to housing for poor and, 79; of shopping mall managers, 165–66

Cohen, Alfredo, 39–40, 46

Colombia, 9–10, 16, 30, 176n5; "Anglo-Saxonness" of, 35–36; climate regions of, 152; coming-of-age of, 135; common property model in, 60; credit and debt in, 90–91; cross-regional investment in shopping malls, 41–42; economy tied to United States, 80–81; elite families of, 97–98; free trade agreements ratified by, 82, 180n7; history of conflict and civil war in, 13, 35, 36, 69; informal economy in, 86; justice system's bias

favoring elites, 131; *mestizaje* ideology in, 123; middle classes in, 93; multiplex movie theaters in, 85; national retailers and brands, 81; number of shopping malls constructed in, 4, 12, 39, 108–9, 175n1, 177n16; Plan Colombia and War on Drugs, 13, 37; REIT business model in, 63; shopping mall professionals, 53; shopping malls as tourist icons, 34–35; urbanization in, 39, 93, 178n14; as U.S. ally, 13, 36. *See also* strata system

Colombiamoda (annual fashion festival), 149, 184–85n3

Conconcreto (construction company), 41

Constructora Sambil, 39, 46

consumer culture, 8, 10, 133

consumers, 1, 2, 25, 134, 147; changing communities of, 28; "coming of age," 9; consumer confidence, 20; informal economy and, 86; intelligence gathering on consumer behavior, 17; "middle-class," 3; "new consumers," 6; social pressure to look like, 137, 139, 140, 141, 143–44

consumption, 1, 3, 72, 171, 172; anxieties related to, 114, 132–33; "authentic" class status and, 112; class and, 6; improper and excessive, 131; increases in cost of consumer products, 78–79; local production and, 15; middle classes and, 6–16; ostentatious display of wealth and, 117; "overconsumption," 14; policing of status boundaries, 98; questionable upwardly mobile identities and, 133; social maneuvering through, 114; strata system of Colombia and, 94; taste and, 126

Cooper, Milton, 19

corruption, 60–62; as *mordidas* ["bites"] (bribes), 60, 61, 67; as "soft costs," 60–61. *See also* money laundering

*La Costeña y el Cachaco* (TV soap opera), 127

costeño/a culture, 119, 126, 127, 128, 164. *See also* Afro-Colombians

country clubs, 98, 126

clothes imported from China in, 151;
fake brands at, 154

Santa Fe shopping center (Bogotá), 73,
183n2

Santos, Juan Manuel, 76, 180n5

San Victorino district (Bogotá), 81, 88, 132,
140, 181nn13–14, 185n7; casual
atmosphere of, 144; location in center
of historic district, 99; *madrugón* (early
bird sale) in, 87, 156

School of the Americas, 51–52, 179n8

Sears, 46

security, 16, 17, 61; Afro-Colombians hired
as guards, 104; in high-income
residential neighborhoods, 73;
hypersecurity, 5; mall security guards,
79, 103, 104, 142, 164; north–south
class divide of Bogotá and, 100;
"performance" of, 100, 102. *See also*
surveillance

self-styling, 8, 16, 115, 136, 151, 159; *buena
presencia* presented through, 127;
contrived informality, 130; identities
defined through, 135; social media and,
157

Sephora, 40

"settling institutions," 3, 10, 176n12. *See also*
plantation model

sexism, 162, 166

sexuality, 7–8, 114, 116, 120; access to malls
and, 114; homophobia and, 152, 162–64;
language and, 120; LGBT "kissathons"
protest, 16, 162; transnational
heterosexuality in malls, 7, 122, 162

shopping, as activity, 17, 38; casual versus
scrutinized modes of, 144–45;
Christmas splurges versus year-round
shopping, 107; as hard work, 154–55;
social pressure to look like a consumer,
137, 139, 140, 141; and "authenticity," 73,
130, 151; window-shopping, 140–41

shopping mall industry, 14, 177n12; of
Bogotá, 5, 12; definitions of expertise and,
52, 55, 64–66, 179n11; financialization of,
18–28, 60; "footprint" acquisition as
central practice, 17; globalization of, 68;
global shopping centers associations and,
45; internationalization of, 44; Latin

American industry as outcome of U.S.
industry, 64; political economy of, 1, 23;
"pre-modern" family/network relations
and, 67; professionalization of, 15, 22, 68;
standardization of, 47, 48; in United
States, 6

shopping malls: accessibility to popular
classes, 10, 15, 114; aspirational identity
and, 88, 183n2; "authenticity" and, 130;
built on former detention and terror
sites, 10–11, 177n14; cities come to
resemble, 173; Class A, 19; class-
stratified, 9, 71, 172; as "clubs for the
poor," 74; commercial property prices
in, 69, 73; as contested public spaces,
161–73; cross-regional investment in,
41–42; dead malls (death of the mall), 3,
23, 27, 42, 176n6; as destinations, 24; as
educational and styling tools, 159;
enclaves and, 8; as experiences, 24; fast
fashion (*pronta moda*) and, 135; food as
primary reason for visiting, 108; as
"footprints," 3, 17, 18, 22, 24; as full-
service spaces, 4; funding for
construction of, 40, 59; ICSC official
formats for, 56; informal markets and,
153; as key urban landmarks, 1; leisure
and, 3, 12, 101; megaplex movie theaters
in, 41; modernity and, 2; music in, 102;
north–south class divide of Bogotá and,
99–112, 164; number and frequency of
visitors, 109, 182–83n8; ownership
concepts and, 59, 60, 69; politicization
of, 16; postmodern culture and, 2, 175n3;
precarity and, 11, 91, 172; protests
against, 32; reliance on imported goods,
15; repurposing of, 27–28; retail workers
in, 110–11, 119; sales and promotions in,
17, 107, 152–53, 163; as "settlement
institutions," 3; spatial transformations
and, 1, 175n2; standardization of, 47, 48,
89; urban planning and, 76, 168; urban
reclamation and, 71; as worlding
mechanisms, 17, 28, 34; zoning laws
and, 27, 28, 29

Simon Property Group, 19, 21, 22, 70

SISBEN (government-subsidized health
service), 98